GREAT OUTDOOR ADVENTURES OF HAWAII

Rick Carroll

Foghorn Press

Copyright ©1991 by Foghorn Press.

Great Outdoor Adventures
of Hawaii

All rights reserved. This book may not be reproduced in full or in part without the written permission of the publisher, except for use by a reviewer in the context of a review. Inquiries and excerpt requests should be addressed to: Foghorn Press, P.O. Box 77845, San Francisco, California 94107. Telephone: (415) 241-9550.

Library of Congress Catalog-in-Publication Data

Carroll, Rick.
Great Outdoor Adventures of Hawaii, by Rick Carroll.
p. cm.
Includes index
ISBN 0-935701-08-7 $14.95
1. Outdoor recreation—Hawaii
2. Hawaii—Description and travel
I. Title.
GV191.42.H3C37   1991
790'.09969—dc20
91-27604
CIP

GREAT OUTDOOR ADVENTURES OF HAWAII

Rick Carroll

Foghorn Press Inc.

Book Credits

Editor..Ann Marie Brown
Book Design...I. Magnus
Cover Design.......................................Gilda Gonzales
Cover Photo.................Douglas Peebles Photography
Maps...Luke Thrasher
Proofreading...................................Tim Moriarty

Photo Credits

1st page	*volcano*	Douglas Peebles Photography
2nd page	*hang-glider*	Sunstar
4th page	*horseback riders*	Werner Stoy/Camera Hawaii
	yellow outrigger canoe	Sunstar
5th page	*Mauna Kea in snow*	
	Douglas Peebles Photography	
	windsurfer	Sunstar
	protea flower	Douglas Peebles Photography
6th page	*surfer on wave*	
	Mike Waggoner/Douglas Peebles Photography	
	bicyclist on Mauna Kea	Sunstar/Pacific Stock
	snorkeler with fish	Ed Robinson/Pacific Stock
7th page	*2 kayaks on Napali coast*	
	Douglas Peebles Photography	
	couple under waterfall	
	Douglas Peebles Photography	
8th page	*island off Oahu*	Douglas Peebles Photography

Petroglyphs

The images found at the start of each chapter are rubbings of Hawaiian petroglyphs (rock carvings).

Dear Readers:

We've done our best to make this the most accurate and complete guide to outdoor adventures in Hawaii possible. However, the face of adventure is always changing, so if you have a suggestion, revision or addition for this book, please send it to us at FOGHORN PRESS, P.O. Box 77845, San Francisco, CA 94107. Thank you.

*No alien land in all the world
has any deep, strong charm for me
but that one;
no other land could so longingly
and so beseechingly haunt me,
sleeping and waking,
through half a lifetime, as that one has done.
Other things leave me,
but it abides; other things change,
but it remains the same.
For me its balmy airs are always blowing,
its summer seas flashing in the sun;
the pulsing of its surfbeat is in my ears;
I can see its garlanded crags,
its leaping cascades,
its plumy palms drowsing by the shore,
its remote summits
floating like islands above the cloud rack;
I can feel the spirit of its woodland solitudes;
I can hear the plash of its brooks;
in my nostrils still lives the breath of flowers
that perished twenty years ago.*

    Mark Twain

TABLE OF CONTENTS

i
Preface

2
IS IT OKAY TO DRINK THE WATER?
And Answers to 23 Other First-Timers' Questions

23
OAHU
THE GREAT URBAN ADVENTURE

Dawn Patrol at Waikiki · Climb a Volcano in Thirty Minutes · Two Almost Secret Oahu Beaches · Three Peak Oahu Adventures · The World's Best Surfing Wave · Surfing Waikiki · Best Snorkel Spot on Oahu · World Championship Kayak Race · Hawaiian Ocean Fest · Hang Gliding Oahu · Cat Fishing in Nuuanu · Hawaii's Most Adventurous Golf Course · Two Great Oahu Waterfalls · Chasing After Rainbows · Architectural Tour of Honolulu · Exploring Chinatown · Two Oahu Peace Memorials · Three Great Places to Go When it Rains in Honolulu · Three Lesser Adventures · Four Great Outdoor Places to Shop · In Search of the Perfect Aloha Shirt · Adventures After Dark in Waikiki · Great Adventures in Dining · Three Great Honolulu Seafood Restaurants · Best Places to Stay

Great Outdoor Adventures of Hawaii

85
MAUI
THE WOWIE ISLAND

Haleakala, The House of the Sun · Sunrise on Haleakala · Bicycling Up (or Down) Haleakala · On the Hana Road · Stargazing in Kaanapali · Of Whales and Maui · Snork Molokini · Fly Hookipa Beach · Walking Tour of Old Lahaina

113
HAWAII
BIG ADVENTURES IN PARADISE

Gazing at the Volcano · In Search of Great Blues · Dive with Sharks · Best Place to See the Humuhumunukunukuapua'a · Going to the Summit · Ski Hawaii · Horseback Riding Way, Way Out West · The Ultraman: The World's Greatest Endurance Adventure · A Garden of Eden Hike Anyone Can Do · Waipi'o Valley · See Mo'okini Luakini · Pu'uhonua O Honaunau · On the Puako Trail · Big Island's Best Restaurants · Great Places to Stay on the Big Island's Kohala Coast

155
KAUAI
THE MYSTIQUE ENDURES

Koke'e: Hawaii's Yosemite · Na Pali by Sea · Best Place to Catch Rainbow Trout · Shooting Captain Cook's Goats · Up the Huleia by Kayak · National Tropical Botanical Garden · On the Beach at Sunset with Smoky · Two Great Places to Birdwatch · Four Rainy Day Places · Visit the First Fantasy Resort · The Legendary Tahiti Nui Mai Tai · Kauai's Best Restaurants · Places to Stay on Kauai

185
MOLOKAI
TRUE ADVENTURES IN OLD HAWAII

Hike the Wild Kamakou Preserve · Molokai Mule Ride · Hike to Halawa Valley Falls · Molokai Ranch Wildlife Safari Park · Big Wind Kite Factory · Molokai's Best Restaurant · Best Places to Stay on Molokai

Table of Contents

199
LANAI
PINEAPPLES, PICKUPS, AND PETIT FOURS
Hiking the Munro Trail · Stalking the Axis Deer · Four-Wheeling Lanai · Diving Cathedrals · Best Places to Stay on Lanai

211
NIIHAU
"FORBIDDEN" ADVENTURES
Fly to Forbidden Island · Snorkeling Niihau · Shelling on Niihau · Niihau Shell Leis

219
KAHOOLAWE
THE "TARGET" ISLAND

GREAT HAWAIIAN ADVENTURES

225
All-Time Top Ten Great Hawaii Adventures

228
The Secrets of Hawaii

232
Three Best Chopper Rides

236
Three Best Trail Rides

238
Best Nude Beaches

241
Three Best Windsurf Spots

243
Three Best Roads to Cruise With the Top Down

248
Three Great Waterfalls

250
Best Sea Cruises

253
Kayaking the Islands

255
Three Great Adventure Resorts

260
Best Water Features

264
Best Places to See Hula

267
Three Great Hollywood Adventures in Hawaii

269
Five Things Kama'ainas Never Do

273
Weddings in Hawaii

APPENDIX

277
Who's Who - Great Adventurers of Hawaii

295
Best Books - An Adventurer's Bibliography

299
Best Numbers - A Directory of Important Numbers

Great Outdoor Adventures of Hawaii

by Rick Carroll

Adventure happens when what you plan doesn't happen. You set out to see or do one thing and discover something else you never imagined. It happens all the time, if you let it. You are probably standing in a bookstore, dreaming of white sandy beaches, blue lagoons and palm trees, wishing you were on a tropical island, somewhere. That used to be me, yearning for the sun-blessed tropics, until I quit my big city job and bought a one-way ticket to real-life adventure in the Pacific.

Now, I'm on the beach in Hawaii planning my next adventure—I'm bound for the South Seas on a tramp freighter—and you are still standing there, wishing you were here.

You can be if you buy this book and start planning your adventure, whether it's for two weeks or the rest of your life. You never know what will happen. You just never know. That's the greatest adventure of all.

Adventure is where you find it, some say, but I think adventure finds you if you are open to it and ready to meet the challenge of anything out of the ordinary. That, I think, is the essence of great adventure.

While this book is a practical, how-to-do-it manual based on actual experiences in Hawaii, it is only a guide to possibilities. The real adventure is up to you.

Unlike most Hawaii guidebooks, which are dream books written by someone who visits once a year for two weeks, this book gets into the reality of the place from the inside out.

I live in Hawaii and daily seek out the best possible things to see and do so you don't waste your time and money. This book shows you a Hawaii you never imagined.

Take it with you, stuff it in your suitcase or backpack, tear the pages out, make field notes. Let me know what you discover because you can live all your life here and still miss some things.

After two decades in the Pacific, mostly in Hawaii, I have seen the islands by helicopter, small planes and jets, from surfboards, kayaks, sailboats and cruise ships, in four-wheel drive vehicles, on motorcycles, bicycles and on foot. I have been on, above and all around every main island, including Niihau and Kahoolawe, but I still haven't seen and done it all. Sorry, Don Ho, maybe next year.

My goal is to start you down the path to great adventures in Hawaii. If you discover something new, let me know. Write to me at Great Outdoor Adventures of Hawaii, 777 Kapiolani Boulevard, Suite 2315, Honolulu, Hawaii 96813. Better yet, FAX me at (808) 263-8317.

Life is too short to miss a great adventure.

Rick Carroll
Honolulu, Hawaii

ACKNOWLEDGEMENTS

Unattributed quotes appear throughout this book, and I am delighted to thank in print all those who captured the island experience with the right words:

"If you wear it, the handbill hustlers in Waikiki leave you alone..."
Lee Quarnstrom

"....to enrich and delight...."
Princess Bernice Pauahi Bishop

"Da kine was huhu...."
Jay McWilliams

"...embrace the gift of each day."
A. M. Rosenthal

"...like campfires of a great army far away."
Isabella Bird

"...huge sluttish pleasures of Hawaii's Nipponized beachfront hotels."
Paul Theroux

"like traveling up the intestinal tract of an extinct large fossilized creature of undetermined species...."
Victoria Nelson

"...a perpetual world's fair..."
Francine du Plessix Gray

"...ski to the sea."
Chris Langan

"Grand Canyon of the Pacific"
Mark Twain

"...endangered bird capital of the world."
Paul Erlich

Portions of the author's work in this book have appeared in articles elsewhere, namely: "Trouble at Home: Geothermal Development Imperils Hawaii's Rain Forest," (San Francisco Chronicle); "Whither Honolulu Architecture?" (Manoa Valley Times); "The Perfect Aloha Shirt," "Search for the One True, Original Mai-Tai," "Visit to Forbidden Island of Niihau," (Honolulu Advertiser); "Sailing Hawaii's Volcano Coast," (Miami Herald); "Windsurfing on Kailua Bay," (Santa Cruz Sentinel); "World's Richest Man Builds Waikiki Beach Hotel," (The Bangkok Post); "Hawaii's Golf Course for Gods," (Arab Daily News); "Travels with Sinoto," (Aloha The Magazine of Hawaii and the Pacific).

"To adventure, the shadow of every red-blooded man.
To the Game.
To every lost trail, lost cause and lost comrade.
To Gentlemen Adventurers."

Official toast of The Adventurer's Club of Honolulu,
founded April 9, 1954.

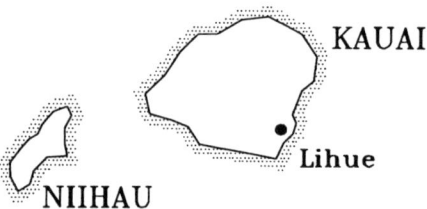
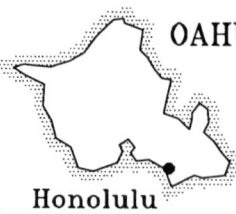
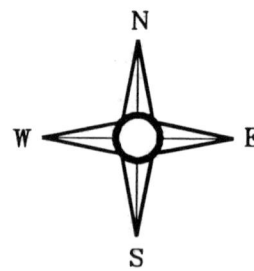

v   Great Outdoor Adventures of Hawaii

The Hawaiian Islands

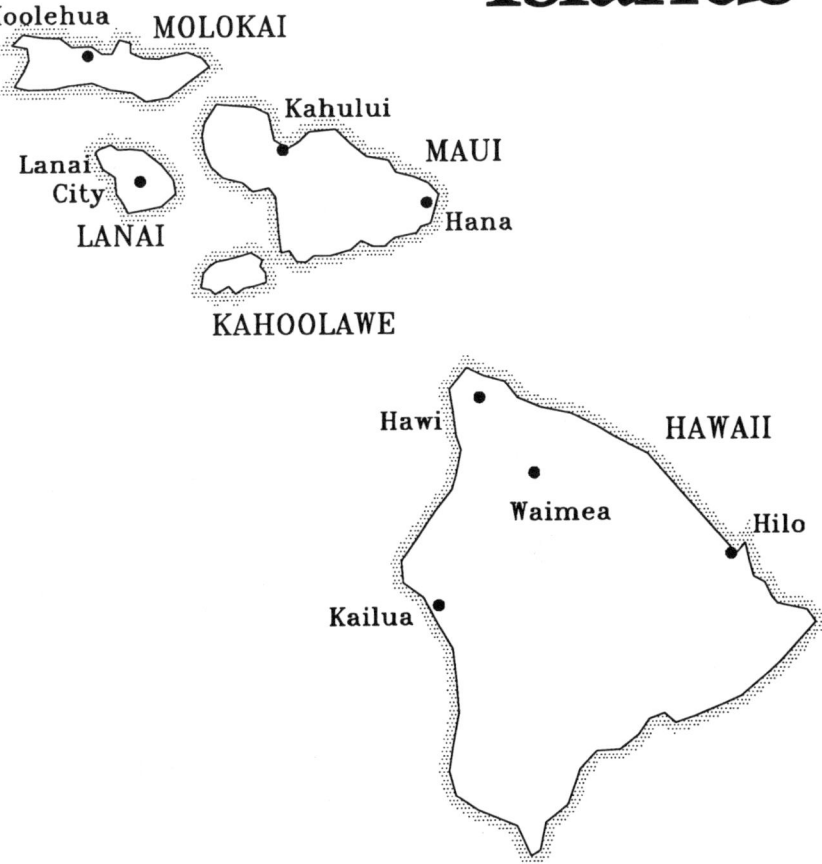

Following page: *A helicopter ride over Kilauea on the Big Island takes you as close as you can get to the volcano.*

Next two pages: *For the adventurous, sail the wind for a bird's-eye view of the islands*

Left page:

Top; Learning to paddle an outrigger canoe

Below; Horseback riding at Waimea on the Big Island

This page:

Clockwise from right;
The snow-covered summit of Mauna Kea

Windsurfing legend Robby Naish with daughter Nani

A single protea among a lush garden on Kauai

This page:
Clockwise from top; Solitary mountain biker rides down snowy Mauna Kea

Snorkeling with parrotfish & surgeon fish

Derrick Ho tackles winter waves at Pipe

Right page:
Top; Kayaking the Napali coast, Kauai

Below; Sharing a quiet moment under a waterfall

Following page:
Chinaman's Hat on the windward side of Oahu

Is It Okay to Drink the Water?
AND ANSWERS TO 23 OTHER FIRST-TIMERS' QUESTIONS

Is It Okay to Drink the Water?

AND ANSWERS TO 23 OTHER FIRST-TIMERS' QUESTIONS

※

MOST of you are probably *coast haoles* who fly over to surf North Shore, fish for mahimahi or climb Mt. Olomana whenever you get a three day weekend. Some of you are *malahinis* (newcomers) and need to know some basic information. Like where it is, how far it is, what time it is there, what the weather's like, when's the best time to go, and important facts like where to stay and great places to eat.

The water's fine, you don't need a passport, or a visa or immunization shots. You can bring fruit in but you can't take it out. American greenbacks are the currency, but we accept yen.

The natives are friendly, if you can find one. Everyone speaks English here. No topless maidens will meet you in canoes with flower leis. Nobody thinks you look funny wearing a lei. There are no diamonds on Diamond Head.

The volcano goes off whenever it feels like it. Rainbows appear whenever you are between the sun and a rain cloud.

Waikiki is $15 by taxi from the airport. We tip here. The pink hotel is the Royal; the white one is the Moana.

Nobody lives in the Royal Palace. The last king died in 1891 and the last queen died in 1917. The average wait to see Pearl Harbor is 90 minutes. Yes, Japanese tourists go there, but most are too young to remember the actual event.

Molokai is an island, not something to eat; that's a loco moco, not to be confused with a local moke. The Tongans are the big guys in skirts, so no make fun. That's pidgin for don't poke fun. Pidgin is that funny language everyone speaks that you don't understand at first. *Byumby,* you talk *li'dat.*

Inter-island planes leave about every 20 minutes. Everything costs more because Hawaii is in the middle of the Pacific. No, you won't see Tom Selleck. Sharks are friendly. James Michener wrote *Hawaii* but he lives in Florida. Nobody thinks "I Got Lei-d In Hawaii" T-shirts are funny, anymore.

Where Is Hawaii?

Hawaii is near the center of the Pacific Ocean about 2,390 miles southwest of California, or five hours by jet from the West Coast. You can be there in the time it takes to eat lunch, watch a movie and check out a few of your favorite adventures in this book.

The seven inhabited islands—Hawaii, Maui, Oahu, Kauai, Molokai, Lanai and Niihau—lie southeast to northwest across the Tropic of Cancer between 154° 40' and 178° 25' west latitude and 18°54' to 28°15' north latitude. That puts them in the North Pacific, not, as most people believe, in the South Seas.

Hawaii is just inside the tropical zone and while it shares the same latitude with Mexico City, Havana, Hong Kong, Calcutta, Mecca and the Sahara Desert, its climate is well suited for outdoor adventure every day with plenty of sunshine, balmy tradewinds and temperatures in the low 80s. Perfect, in other words.

... In Relation to Botswana?

Honolulu is 2,498 miles from Denver, 3,850 miles from Japan, 4,829 miles from Washington, D.C., 4,900 miles from China and 5,280 miles from the Philippines. It is 1,700 miles north of the Equator. Its antipodes—those places diametrically opposed on the globe—are Botswana and Southwest Africa.

Peaks of Submerged Mountains

There are 132 islands in the Hawaiian chain, from tiny Kure Atoll in the Northwest Hawaiian Islands to the 4,038-square mile Big Island of Hawaii, the biggest island in the tropical Pacific and the southernmost point in the U.S.

The islands are peaks of a submerged mountain chain that sits in the North Pacific (check your atlas), 2,400 miles off the California coast, with most of them just a click enough below the Tropic of Cancer to be truly tropical.

Main Attractions

The main group of islands includes Oahu, Hawaii, Maui, Kauai, Lanai, Molokai and uninhabited Kahoolawe.

Each one is different and everyone has a favorite. I like each one for different reasons. Oahu's where it all happens and Molokai is where people from Honolulu go to get away from it all. It just proves everything is relative. You might save a lot of hassle and head for Molokai now.

The weather is different on each island. Kauai is cooler and wetter; the Big Island is warmer and drier, generally speaking; Oahu gets hot and sticky in the summer because of all the concrete and high-rises, and Maui is just about right most of the time.

Basic Stuff You Need To Know

Even though you've flown five or more hours, you are still in the good old USA. Check out the flag. Stars and stripes.

The other one is the Hawaii state flag. It looks like Great Britain's Union Jack because the islands were first claimed by the British. Hawaii is the last and 50th state, admitted to the union on August 21, 1959, as The Aloha State.

The State Seal

King Kamehameha II and the Goddess of Liberty appear on the official state seal. The Goddess of Liberty holds the Hawaii state flag. A phoenix appears at the bottom in a garden of taro, banana and maidenhair fern. The shield is inscribed with the state motto ("The life of the land is perpetuated in righteousness") and dated 1959, the year Hawaii became a state.

State Bird is A Goose

The humpback whale is the official state marine mammal. The yellow hibiscus is the official state flower. The Nene goose is the state bird. The *humuhumunukunukuapua'a* is the state fish. You will see them all. But you'll be lucky to see the 'O'o honeycreeper, one of Hawaii's rare birds, last seen in the rainforest 20 years ago.

What Time is It in Hawaii?

When it's noon in San Francisco, it's 10 a.m. in Honolulu. Hawaii is two hours earlier than the West Coast and five hours earlier than the East Coast. When it's noon in New York, it's 7 a.m. in Honolulu.

Hawaii is in its own time zone. It's called Hawaii Standard Time or HST. Hawaii does not observe daylight savings time like the U.S. mainland does between April and October. With nearly 12 hours of sunshine daily almost year-round, there's no need. Hawaii's longest and shortest days—in June and December—are 13 hours and 26 minutes and 10 hours and 50 minutes, respectively. When the mainland changes its clocks, there is a three-hour difference to the West Coast and six to the East Coast.

When is the Best Time To Go?

Anytime you can. There are so-called high and low seasons, but Hawaii is a popular world destination year-round. Peak tourist traffic from the U.S. mainland occurs between Christmas and April, and July and August. Plan your visit before or after those months and you'll enjoy Hawaii more.

It rains a lot in February and March and sometimes the temperature gets down below 70 degrees. August and September are usually hot and humid, with temperatures in the high 80s to low 90s.

Before I moved to Hawaii, I usually spent the month of October in Hanalei on Kauai because the weather is pluperfect (low humidity, light tradewinds, no rain) for swimming, hiking, bicycling, snorkeling and sailing. Crowds are gone, so I had lagoons, waterfalls and beaches almost always to myself. October is still the best month in my book.

Only Two Seasons

There are two seasons—wet and dry, sort of like winter and summer on the mainland. The temperature for all islands is seldom below 72 or over 90 degrees. The normal daily mean temperature is 77—it's the best in the United States.

What Should I Wear?

"The appearance of ... the chattering and almost naked savages, whose heads and feet and much of their sunburnt skins were bare, was appalling. Some of our number, with gushing tears, turned away from the spectacle. Others, with firmer nerve, continued their gaze, but were ready to exclaim, 'Can these be human beings?'"

The Rev. Hiram Bingham, 1820

Forget Boston missionaries and their weird ideas about tropical clothing. Just wear a smile and a swimsuit and you'll fit in everywhere along the coast.

Inland, you may want to wear more—shorts, a T-shirt and flip-flops. Blue jeans, polo shirts and tennis shoes are usually too hot, but a good idea if you're going hiking.

Campers, you've got a whole new wardrobe to consider, including a poncho, sweatshirt (when tropical nights get below 70) and maybe even a sweater.

Most of the time in the islands, it's BB (basic beach). I wear swim trunks (I've got about two dozen) or shorts (same count) and one of my favorite T-shirts. I go barefoot almost all the time unless I've got to run into Honolulu for lunch, or see my lawyer, or attend a funeral, but even such otherwise maudlin occasions call for "aloha attire" — bright tropical print shirts worn untucked over white pants and sandals. It's island-style.

Aloha shirts, the brighter the better, were perfected in Hawaii in 1931, by Ellery Chun, a Yale graduate who came back to Honolulu and made a fortune. And, yes, women still wear those awful Mother Hubbard missionary sacks called *muumuus* which make women look like what it sounds like.

Pack light, just one carry-on, skip Baggage Claim, be the first one on your plane at the beach. Most people bring too much or stuff that's too warm or inappropriate. Like neckties. Or those rectangular rock-hard cosmetic cases. Leave it behind.

At the beach, almost anything goes—from Rio thongs at Waikiki to number 30 sunscreen and a smile on Hawaii's more secluded beaches.

❂ *Akamai Tip:* Unlike Europe, French Polynesia and California, topless bathing is banned at Waikiki; most Saturday sailors skinny-dip five miles off Waikiki or find a secluded beach.

A Panama straw hat looks good and is right in the tropics (buy one here, leave it when you go), but a visor is often cooler. Don't forget your sunglasses and sunscreen. The Hawaiian sun is hotter than you think.

A Few Words About Haole Feet

In Hawaii we go barefoot a lot. Most of the time. Sandals are too hot. Tennis shoes are like walking around with your feet stuck in a sauna. Those Japanese rubber slippers known as *zoris* really don't work outside the shower for anyone with *haole feet.* That's what Hawaiians call big, lazy soft feet that live in argyles and Italian loafers and only come out at night.

Most adventure-seeking women leave their high heels at home but I have noticed some hard-core fashion slaves refuse to go bare-legged and actually wear panty hose in the tropics. Incredible.

The problem with going barefoot all the time is that your feet spread. Honest. They are so glad you kicked the shoe habit they expand to their natural size. I gained a half-size my first year. That's what people here call "luau feet."

The best shoe for Hawaii, I think, is a good boat shoe, one of those all-leather, all-weather, waterproof Timberland jobs that can take the hot sun, salt water, lava stone scuffs and red dirt and still look fairly decent when you go to the Ritz-Carlton for dinner. Only don't wear socks.

The Hawaiian Lei Explained

A friend of mine, who comes to Hawaii several times a year, claims he's figured out the best lei to wear—a single twist of ti leaf.

"If you wear it," he said, "the handbill hustlers in Waikiki leave you alone. They think you live here." His observation—that leis are "read" by people here—is keen.

The flower lei not only extends aloha and represents Hawaiian hospitality, it stands for many things. There are, in fact, leis for certain days and occasions.

"There is no such thing as an all-purpose lei," says Lois Taylor, the *Honolulu Star Bulletin* garden columnist. And there definitely is a hierarchy of appropriate flowers.

A politician, she points out, would never get elected wearing five strands of pikake. A college graduate deserves more than a single strand of plumeria. A bride would never wear a red carnation lei.

"But put the carnations on the politician, the pikake on the bride, the plumeria on the arriving tourist, maile on the graduate—and *lokahi*, or harmony, is restored."

Leis have been a Hawaiian custom for many years. Ancient Hawaiians wore leis for personal and religious celebrations, and used shells, seeds, plants, bird feathers and flowers for adornment.

Today leis are used to say hello and goodbye and always aloha. A lei can mean many things: welcome, happy birthday, or I love you. They are worn at luaus, dedications, political functions, weddings and graduations.

"A lei expresses almost any emotion—love, sorrow, happiness, a greeting, a goodbye," says Barbara Meheula, floral designer for the Mauna Kea Beach Hotel. "A lei makes an occasion significant. It brings peace to the heart."

Often, when you visit a lei stand, the flower maker will ask you what it is for, so you may pick the right lei.

"You don't give *lei ilima* to an arriving tourist but you would give them to your parents for an anniversary," says Marie McDonald, author of *Ka Lei,* the best book on Hawaii's leis. "*Lei ilima* recognizes someone of high rank, someone who has accomplished something great."

The lei even has its own day. May Day was officially proclaimed Lei Day in Hawaii on May 1, 1928, when poet Don Blanding thought Hawaii's lei aloha tradition should be celebrated statewide. On that day, lei makers compete to create the most expressive flower garlands and everyone wears a lei.

Leis also ride the tide of popularity. The plumeria is the current favorite but the ti leaf lei is becoming popular, especially twisted with pikake or lantern ilima. A lei is designed for one occasion and valued for its brief existence. Each Hawaiian island has its own flower lei. They are: Oahu, Ilima; Molokai, Kukui; Kauai, Mokihana; Big Island, Lehua; Maui, Lokelani; Lanai, Kaunaoa; Niihau, Pupu shell; Kahoolawe, Hina Hina.

Although the lei did not originate in Hawaii (the floral garlands popular in Hawaii came from Polynesia and had their origin in Asia), it has become the floral symbol of the islands.

Hawaiian Words You Need to Know

You probably already know some Hawaiian words, like *aloha* (hello, goodbye and love), and *mahalo* (thanks), and *wahine* (woman) and *kane* (man). A *malihini* is a newcomer, a *kama'aina* is someone who lives here, usually for a long time. *Pau* means finished or over. And *pau hana* means the day's work is done, time for *pupus*—hors d'oeuvres, to you. *Wiki wiki* means hurry up, which you don't ever want to do.

Another useful word is *akamai,* which means island smart, which is what you want to be.

The language only has 12 letters; seven consonants (H, K, L, M, N, P and W) and five vowels (A, E, I, O, U). Words are usually formed with more vowels than consonants which makes the words roll off the tongue like undulating waves.

Hawaiian words might look impossible to say because they don't look like anything Anglo-Saxon, but it's easy—just pronounce every vowel.

How to Talk 'li'dat

You are fresh off the plane, ringed by a flower lei, heading for Baggage Claim and you overhear a conversation between two local girls.

"Da kine wuz huhu cuz he we'n stay ovah deah li'dat! Wot she wen' t'ink? Da buggah nevah like go with' her!"

"Fo real? Humbug da guy!"

Welcome to the colorful world of pidgin, the local style of speaking in the islands.

It's a patois invented by the Chinese to do business; in fact, pidgin is short for bidness, Chinese-style. Only Hawaii has made it a daily part of linguistics, a quick expressive often picaresque speech. It's *da kine talk, 'li dat. 'Eh fo' real, brah.* (It's true, pal.)

Basic Pidgin Vocabulary

'owzit! : contraction for "How's it?", a common greeting.

wen : verb, "I wen go to da beach."

da kine : means good kind, the type most popular.

try wait : instead of "wait a minute."

laters : short for "See you later," or "goodbye."

shaka, brah : a form of agreement, accompanied by a single shake of the hand with thumb and little finger extended.

moah bettah : a comparative phrase, meaning best, i.e., "Da kine guide book moah bettah."

ono : tasty or delicious, usually applied to food, i.e., "Dis Maui potato chip ono."

chance 'em : contemporary, local, means take a chance, go for it.

stink eye : mild form of disapproval, a dirty look, i.e., "Wen dat wahine bump my car door, I geev her one stink eye."

Get the Best Map

When I'm not traveling, I look at maps. I always look for unusual details that may lead to a new adventure. Without a map in Hawaii you might as well sit on the beach. The islands are quite easy to find your way around, but if you get lost and have to ask directions, they likely will go like this:

"Go down the road to the big coconut tree, go makai two blocks, turn right at the saimin shop..."

Get a map. The best maps of Hawaii, bar none, are published by University of Hawaii Press. They are full color topos, a bargain at $2.95.

Each map includes a detailed network of island roads, large-scale inset maps of towns, points of interest and historical importance, both natural and cultural; hiking trails, parks and beaches, waterfalls, peaks and ridges (with altitudes); and many other amazing details.

Best of all, they are printed on heavy, pre-creased paper that even I can refold to the original 5 x 10- inch format.

My favorite detail appears on the map of Hawaii, the Big Island, which, on the southwest rift of the Ka'u Desert, near the Ke'amoku Lava Flow (see G-5, about in the middle), identifies "Footprints in Ash 1790." It is the only clue to a 200-year-old mystery. I have always wondered who left his or her footprints in the hot lava and why.

If your bookstore does not have the official University of Hawaii maps of the islands, you may order one by writing to Marketing Department, University of Hawaii Press, 2840 Kolowalu Street, Honolulu, Hawaii 96822. Specify which island you want. They also will send you a free catalog of great books about Hawaii and the Pacific, if you ask.

How to Tell Your Mauka from Makai

There is no north and south on an island, it's leeward or windward, like on a ship. In Hawaii, it's also mauka and makai. It means to the mountain or to the sea.

On Oahu, we also say Diamond Head and Ewa for south and north. Diamond Head is the volcano and Ewa is the once great plain of pineapples now sprouting three-bedroom two-bath tract houses.

Ask a Honolulu police officer for directions and he may say: "It's on the Diamond Head mauka corner," which would be southeast to you. Officers also carry compasses, so they can show you, in case you still don't get it.

Adventures in Paradise

> *"There is something magical about all islands—because they are cut off, distant, isolated, circumscribed by the sea. An island is adrift from the world and out of touch—untainted—which is why only an island can be Paradise."*
>
> Paul Theroux

Some people come only to get a tan and sip Mai-Tais. They kick back at Waikiki, rub on number 15 sunscreen and stare out to sea. Once in a while, they wade into the warm Pacific, splash a bit, then resume the prone position on the hot sand. While it is *their* vacation, these idle bodies in search of a summer tan seem to be missing all the fun. The true adventures in Paradise are beyond the beach.

There is nothing wrong with sitting on the beach at Waikiki—it's the best for people-watching—but there's a lot more going on in the islands than number 15 sunscreen.

Some say it's the people, others the climate, but I think Hawaii's greatest attraction is its great outdoors: erupting volcanos, emerald rainforests, coral sand beaches, waterfalls, lagoons and perfect waves, an infinite variety of cloud-wreathed peaks, valleys and ridges and those perfect Pacific sunsets. You can't find a better setting for great adventures than Hawaii.

There are more real adventures in Hawaii than anyone can experience in a lifetime—and you've only got two weeks—so we better get down to it.

There's something for everyone and nearly all the adventures are unique to Hawaii—like watching the world's most active volcano go off.

If you miss something, you can always come back. A lot of people do and some never leave; there's even a word for it: "imparadised."

On the Road to Adventure

The first adventure in Hawaii may not be so great if you don't know what to expect after your plane touches down. Here are the best ways to get where you're going with the least amount of hassle.

Taxis and Limos

Chances are your taxi driver won't speak English, probably Cambodian, Vietnamese or Korean and he will only know the usual way to Waikiki, but it's only a silent 30 minute relationship that costs $15 bucks or so, plus tip.

There is only one *haole* taxi driver in Honolulu that I know of, so you're going to deal with the East-West twain the minute you get your bags. Relax. Here's the best way to catch a taxi at Honolulu International: Be casual, make eye contact with the guy at the curb wearing a yellow "Taxi" vest and carrying a cellular phone. Then smile—go ahead don't be shy—and say "owzit?" It won't hurt to keep smiling. When he responds (usually by smiling or wiggling his eyebrows) say, "Taxi, please." Don't be in a big mainland hurry. Remember, 1,400 international flights arrive daily and you are just another fish in the pond. The "Taxi" man will summon one curbside in a Honolulu minute, which isn't like a New York minute, so be patient. Tip him a buck and don't forget to say "mahalo" with a big smile, like you mean it. It makes all the difference, so mean it! Everyone else you just left behind will still be trying to figure out your secret.

Even better, call a limousine. The best kept secret about Honolulu limos is that they cost the same as the usual boring taxi. So why not travel in style?

Call my friend John Lee on his car phone (955-2509) and, if he's not busy, he'll pick you up in a silver stretch Cadillac limousine with television, bar and sunroof.

Tear my picture out of this book and give it to John as proof you are *akamai*. If he likes the cut of your jib, he'll probably give you a 10 percent discount. It all depends on his mood—

and when you call. The best time is between 9 a.m. and 4 p.m. daily, except Sunday. That's when John goes to the beach. Don't call me, I'm at the beach then, too.

Shuttle Service

A 24-hour shuttle service between Honolulu International Airport and Waikiki is provided by Airport Motor Coach. It costs $6 from the airport to the tourist quarter and $5 to return. Don't ask why. Half-price for ages six to 12. Under six free. Only two pieces of luggage and a carry-on are permitted. Look for the gray van with black and red trim. Call (808) 926-4747 for reservations.

Rental Cars

If you don't plan to leave Waikiki, you don't need a car. If you are in search of great adventures, you can't live without one. Nearly every major car rental agency (and some you never heard of) has a desk at Honolulu International Airport, although rental cars are cheaper in Waikiki—about the only thing that is. Best time to rent a car: when you make airline or hotel reservations. Ask for a fly/drive deal to save bucks.

Or, if you want to blow some bucks, rent a red Ferrari Testarossa 328 from Ferrari Rentals, 1958 Kalakaua Avenue, Waikiki (808) 942-8725. If you have to ask how much it costs, you probably can't afford it.

❂ *Akamai Tip:* Unless you rent a Ferrari, all rental cars look alike, especially when you park next to other rental cars. Instant Avis fleet. Leave some personal item—a sea shell, a flower lei or even this book—on the dashboard or front seat and you can easily find your car wherever you park.

TheBus

You can have great adventures on Oahu without renting a car if you know how to ride TheBus (that's how it's spelled). The only problem with TheBus is that you can't board with suitcases. I don't know why, some dumb law, so don't try to catch TheBus if you have TheBags. After you are in place, it's the cheapest, most reliable transportation on Oahu. The municipal transit system has 470 air-conditioned buses, more than 60 routes and 4,000 bus stops. It goes almost everywhere, almost around the clock, from 5:00 a.m. to about midnight, seven days a week. More than 250,000 people ride TheBus daily.

For only 60 cents, exact change, please, you can ride around Oahu on an all-day adventure. It's the best travel bargain in the islands.

The most popular route is the Number 8 line which shuttles between Waikiki and Ala Moana Shopping Center, one of two main stops in Honolulu. The other is Hotel Street transit mall. You can ride the bus to almost every adventure in Oahu, including Diamond Head crater, Hanauma Bay, the North Shore, Lanikai Beach, Chinatown and most trail heads for urban hikes in Honolulu. Wherever possible, I will tell you which bus to catch to great adventures on Oahu.

◎ *Akamai Tip:* Timetables are available at TheBus office at 811 Middle Street and all Satellite City Halls. For exact information on all bus routes, call TheBus office at 848-5555 between 5:30 a.m. and 10:00 p.m.

Waikiki Trolley

It's a new tourist ride that's so popular, people who live here ride it. Sure, it looks silly—a motorized San Francisco cable car complete with ring-a-ding bell—but it's open air, makes a regular circuit from downtown Honolulu to Waikiki and it's fun. The 34-passenger trolley runs every 30 minutes from 8:30 a.m. to 4 p.m. between the Royal Hawaiian Shopping Center in Waikiki and Chinatown. You can get on and off wherever you like to eat lunch, shop or take a closer look at a point of interest. All day fare $10 adults, $5 children under 11. Telephone: (808) 526-0112.

Inter-Island Planes

Two major inter-island air carriers provide seven-day-a-week service from Honolulu to the outer islands.

They are Aloha Airlines and Hawaiian Airlines, each home-based in Honolulu at the new inter-island terminal, just mauka of the international terminal.

Both have jet service, which is ridiculous when the islands are only about 15 minutes apart at 600 miles an hour.

I like Aloha Airlines because it offers the most flights between islands and is mostly on time. There's another reason I like Aloha: They fly prop-planes which are fuel-efficient and more adventurous. The smaller the plane the greater the adventure.

◎ *Akamai Tip* : If you're going above Hawaii in a small plane or helicopter always catch the first flight after sunrise. The air is still and the sky is usually cloud-free. You'll see more and enjoy the flight.

Aloha Airlines: Reservations and Flight Information, (808) 836-1111. Baggage Service Lost & Found, (808) 836-4196.

OAHU

THE GREAT URBAN ADVENTURE

Oahu

FI	fishing - Nuuanu Reservoir - page 48
HG	hang gliding - Mokapu'u Ridge/Kaneohe - page 47
HI	hike - Koko Head Park - page 30
HI	hike - Diamond Head - page 34
HI	hike - Kaiwa Ridge, Lanikai - page 34
HI	hike - Mt. Kaala, Waialua - page 33
HI	hike - Sacred Falls, Hauula - page 50
KA	kayaking - Mokulua Islands, Kailua Bay - page 226, 253
SB	secret beach - Malaekahana - page 32
SB	secret beach - Lanikai - page 32
SN	snorkeling - Hanauma Bay - page 40
SU	surfing - Waikiki - page 38

24 *Great Outdoor Adventures of Hawaii*

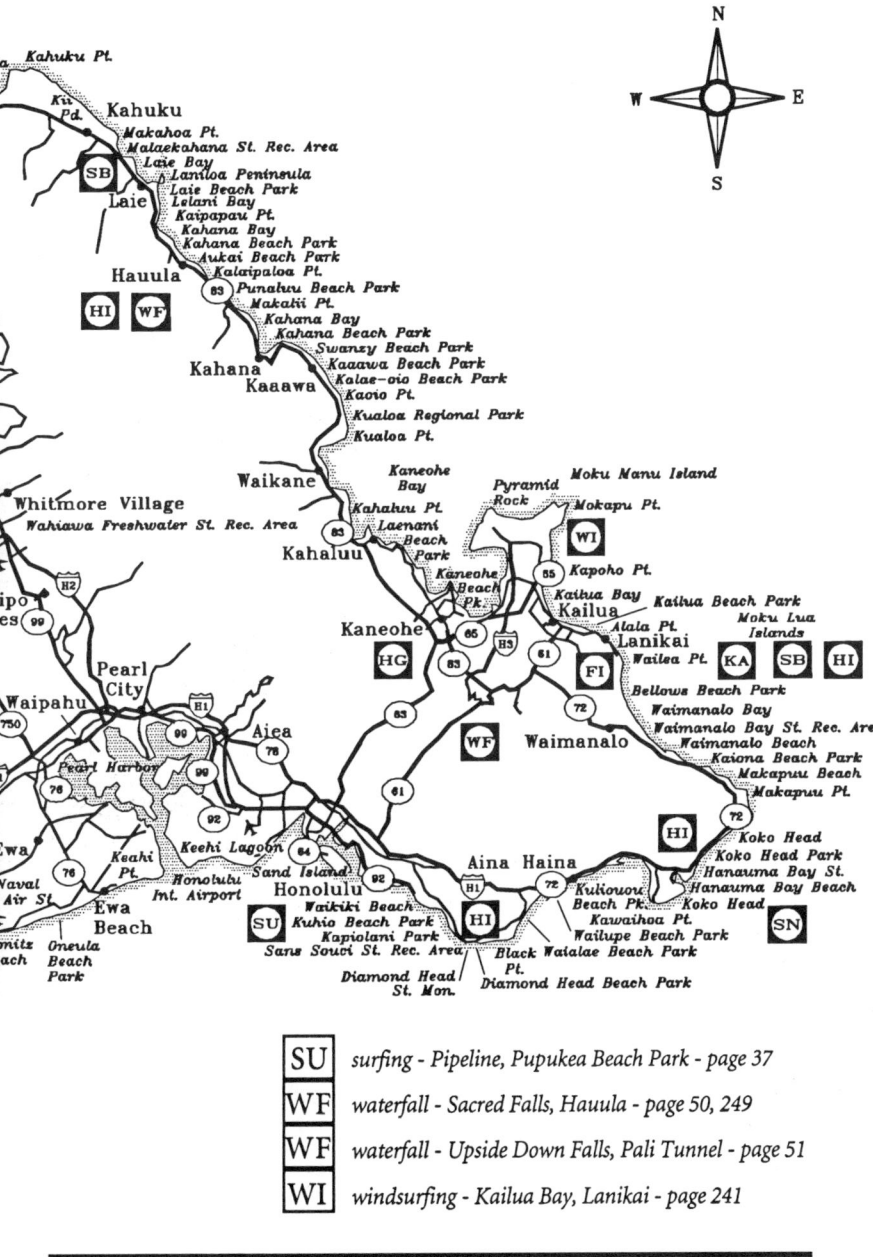

|SU| surfing - Pipeline, Pupukea Beach Park - page 37
|WF| waterfall - Sacred Falls, Hauula - page 50, 249
|WF| waterfall - Upside Down Falls, Pali Tunnel - page 51
|WI| windsurfing - Kailua Bay, Lanikai - page 241

OAHU

THE GREAT URBAN ADVENTURE

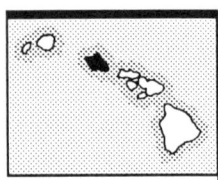

Oahu
(oh-aw-hoo)

Nickname
the Gathering Place

Flower
Ilima

Color
Orange

Capital
Honolulu

Area
594 square miles

Population
830,700

Highest Point
Kaala Peak
4,020 feet

AT first glimpse, as your 747 banks over the tropical coast, Oahu looks like Manhattan except you've never seen water that color before, or waves so perfect. Even the airport smells good, like tropical flowers.

Welcome to Oahu, the perfect tropical island in paradise. Don't take my word for it. I know a rich man who can live anywhere in the world, who collects islands like you and I collect books, and he chooses to live on Oahu, and in of all places, Waikiki.

The reason is simple: everything anyone needs except maybe the Bolshoi Ballet is on Oahu. It's got the best beaches, big city excitement, small town friendliness and more adventures than you can imagine.

You can hike to waterfalls, soar on glider wings over the north shore, see the moon rise between twin islands in a blue lagoon, or explore a tropical rain forest full of singing tree frogs.

It isn't just adventures like those that make Oahu the most fun. It's the possibilities. You can catch a wave on an outrigger canoe. Ride a stretch limo to the nearly all-night discos. Gaze at Hockney, Charlot and Warhol at the Contemporary Museum of Art. Order a raw quail egg to top off your sushi. Eye the girls (and the guys) in teeny weeny bikinis at Waikiki. Window-shop at Chanel, Hermes, Cartier, Georgio Armani, Christian Dior and Louis Vuitton. Or sing along in Japanese karaoke bars. Shop Chinatown for jade and pearls. Ride a humongous Banzai Pipeline wave. (Or watch someone else risk their neck.)

And get into Hawaiiana. Learn to hula. See the last grass shack at the Bishop Museum. Snorkel Hanauma Bay.

Learn the words to "Aloha Oe." Try two-finger poi. Oh, go ahead, it won't hurt you!

The once drowsy little seaport of Honolulu, founded by a king, has come of age under a long silent volcano as the first city of the Pacific. The auto-oriented city stretches along misnamed interstate Highway One for 26 miles between two California-like suburbs and runs up and over the five hills and into the valleys of the Koolau mountains and down to the sea.

City dwellers live mostly in 800-square-foot condos amid palms and plumeria and go about life with a style at once insular and cosmopolitan.

Everyone from all over the world seems to be represented here, and the music of many tongues is underscored by two official languages—English and Hawaiian—and the unofficial local patois known as pidgin. The juxtaposition of ethnic groups and the inevitable mix makes Honolulu the first true

Amerasian city—which usually throws first-time visitors who think all the different Asian people are Japanese visitors.

Founded by the pagan King Kamehameha, "reformed" by Boston missionaries and once dominated by the "Big Five" sugar and land cartels, Honolulu is awakening to a new vision as the Pacific center of commerce and fun, reshaping its waterfront, opening new art museums and galleries, attracting new restaurants—all the while attempting to preserve its Polynesian heritage.

There are more than 6,000 restaurants in Hawaii, and they serve a lot more than fish and poi these days. European chefs and trendy ex-California restauranteurs serve fresh fish, tropical fruits and vegetables in an island-style cuisine that blends the best of Asian and Pacific traditions.

And then, there's that beach. You just got back? Pretty crowded, yeh? The famous beach, once surfed by kings, is a thin crescent covered by suntan oil-slick, solar-baked people of various size, shape and color, ranging from bone white to flame red. The sand is imported from Australia, but that doesn't bother the millions of sunbathers who assume the prone position, splash in curly waves, lounge in grand seaside hotels, dine in fancy restaurants, then dance the night away in clubs that close 90 minutes before dawn before collapsing in their rooms to prepare to repeat the bake/rinse/spin cycle.

Don't like your room? Change it. There are hotels of every variety from $50-a-night bed and breakfasts to $2,500-a-night luxury suites. I'll give you the rundown on the best places to stay, whether you're on a budget or you just won the state lottery.

Of all 36 major attractions on Oahu, the National Memorial Cemetery of the Pacific draws the biggest crowd (5.1 million), followed by the *U.S.S. Arizona* Memorial (1.8 million), the Polynesian Cultural Center (870,000), Honolulu Zoo (801,418), and Sea Life Park (684,530).

With 11.2 million people on Waikiki Beach every year, including most of the 7 million annual visitors; and Oahu's 838,500 residents going about normal lives, it really is a wonder, as famous New York travel writer Horace Sutton once said, that Oahu doesn't sink.

The nicest thing about Oahu is that you can drive a short distance and find yourself in a rainforest, by a waterfall, at a secluded beach or on a desert island.

Come, great adventurer, follow me...

Dawn Patrol at Waikiki

Sunrise surfers call it "dawn patrol." It's a unique and often singular Oahu adventure which is rare for Waikiki.

The right time is when the moon is setting in the west, just before the sun pops over Diamond Head. While night owls sleep, paddle your surfboard out from **Waikiki Beach**, where Hawaii's kings showed their stuff on surfboards from sunrise to sunset.

Jump in the water, paddle slowly—don't worry, there are no sharks, and besides, the 78-degree water is only four feet deep. Enjoy the offshore vista of Waikiki's cityscape. Watch for bright tropical fish when the blue water begins to reflect

Five Places to Get a Decent Cup of Coffee

Where coffee grows on trees, you'd expect a great cup of coffee. Except in Hawaii. Even though it's America's only coffee-growing state, Hawaii has yet to serve a decent cup of coffee. It exports its best beans to Japan where coffee costs $5 a cup.

Resort hotels serve swill. Restaurants offer something hot and brown that tastes like crankcase oil. I import my own fresh roasted beans from Graffeo in San Francisco's North Beach and grind my own daily. It's the only way.

Most people drink tea in the islands; it's the Japanese and Chinese influence. If you want a good cup of coffee on Oahu, here's where to go:

Croissanterie
222 Merchant Street
(808) 533-3443

On Saturday mornings officers of the cruise ships come to Hawaii's best coffee bar for a cup of espresso, which tells you something an orange glow as day begins and Oahu starts to come to life.

You will experience a keen sense of smell—of salt and coconut oil, of fresh-roasted coffee onshore and the faint scent of distant plumeria. Catch the day's first waves with Oahu's dawn patrol or—if you don't surf—just paddle out for a Hawaii adventure you will never forget.

Rent your board the night before at the surfboard stand on Kuhio Beach, at the Diamond Head end of the Sheraton Moana Surfrider Hotel. Take it to your room, ask room service for a "dawn patrol" wake up. If they don't know what you mean, you're staying in the wrong place. Go quietly before dawn.

Climb a Volcano in 30 minutes

I call Koko Head the 30-minute wonder hike because it only takes that long to experience Oahu's wonderful south shore views.

This is Oahu's easiest summit hike, a short and sweaty one-miler that is a guaranteed eye-pleaser. The 642-foot tuff cone offers unusual views of Diamond Head, the Koolau mountains, the 6,000-acre Hawaii Kai subdivision built by industrialist Henry J. Kaiser, Hanauma Bay and, on a clear day, the island of Molokai 25.8 miles across the sea.

Go at sunrise or sunset for the best godrays, coronas and chiaroscuro light effects. From February to May, you may even see whales in the Kaiwi Channel between Oahu and Molokai.

According to legend, Pele, the goddess of volcanoes, attempted to make a home for herself on Oahu in Koko Head Crater, which now is home to a botanical garden of cactus and bridle trails.

Drive 12 miles from Honolulu southeast on H-1, which becomes Route 72, then right on Hanauma Bay Road to the parking lot. Walk up the bay road to the highway to thing since sailors always know a good cup of coffee.

Lions Coffee Roasters
831 Queen Street
(808) 521-3479
Honolulu's caffeine freaks follow their noses to Hawaii's premiere coffee roaster which serves freshly brewed coffee day-long in a no-frills outdoor bar.

Kailua & Cream
108 Hekili Street, Kailua
(808) 262-9727
It's the only coffee house on windward Oahu, and serves 47 different roasts from around the world.

The Coffee Works
at
The Ward Warehouse
(808) 545-1133
Sidewalk coffee bar in the shopping mall between Waikiki and downtown Honolulu which offers the best selection of gourmet coffees.

reach the trailhead. A gate blocks cars but you may go around and hike to the summit.

In summer months take the Beach Bus to Hanauma Bay, the rest of the year take Bus Number 57 (Kailua/Waimanalo) to Lunalillo Home Road and walk uphill.

Two Almost Secret Oahu Beaches

Not yet a postcard, **Malaekahana Bay** seldom appears in guide books and shows up in mouse type on Oahu's map. Yet, this almost mile-long white sand crescent beach less than two hours from Waikiki lives up to everyone's image of the perfect Hawaii beach. Rich Honolulu folks still own (and rent out) summer cabins here but the beach is now a state park. On any weekday you may be the only one on Malaekahana beach, but should some net fisherman —or kindred soul— intrude upon your delicious privacy, swim out to Goat Island (or wade across at low tide) and you can play Robinson Crusoe on your own desert island. The islet is a sanctuary for sea birds and turtles, so no chase 'em. You can also camp at Malaekahana Bay, but the permit process is long and arduous. Be sure to check out this beach, though, one of Oahu's best kept secrets.

Drive over the Pali Highway, turn left on Kamehameha Highway past Kaawa, Punaluu, Hauula, Laie and just before Kahuku, a brown wooden sign points to the Laie-end of the park. About a 90 minute drive from Waikiki.

Secluded and seldom visited even by Honolulu residents, **Lanikai Beach** is immediately recognizable by two islands that pierce the aquamarine lagoon, its soft white coral sand and the fact that it's virtually empty except on weekends. Residents may act as if this beach is private but no beaches in Hawaii are, so stroll with alacrity down one of the seven beach accesses off Mokulua Drive and discover what the "real" Hawaii is all about. This reef-protected beach with small, gentle, lapping waves is ideal for families and surf toddlers. The islands a half-mile offshore are bird sanctuaries but you may sail or kayak to them to gain a sense of the whole. The larger one on the left is easiest to reach; it has a sandy beach, tide pools, a wave-lashed seaward cove frequented by sharks and a unique panoramic view of Oahu's windward coast.

Take H-1 to the Pali Highway (State Highway 61). Go to Kailua on the Pali Highway which becomes Kailua Road. Drive straight through Kailua town to the T-intersection at Kalaheo Drive, turn right and stay on Kalaheo until Alala Street, turn left and go uphill with the lagoon on your left, past a stone pillar that says Lanikai. Drive down A'Alapapa Drive which loops through the small beach community and returns as Mokulua Drive. Park on Mokulua and walk down the public accesses to Lanikai Beach.

Three Peak Oahu Adventures

Three hikes offer peak adventures on Oahu. Only one, Diamond Head, the most popular, is recommended for families.

The other two, a moderate hike up Kaiwa Ridge on the Windward side and the scary ascent of Mount Kaala on the North Shore, are seldom attempted even by people who live in Hawaii.

All three offer a different and unforgettable look at Oahu. The last should be attempted only by hardy, fearless, experienced hikers. I have not reached all three summits, but, in this case, two out of three ain't bad.

Others may climb Everest or Fuji, but in Honolulu do what many hikers do—climb **Diamond Head**. The hike to the summit of the 760-foot high volcanic crater takes about 45 minutes. The reward is a breathtaking 360-degree view of Oahu with Waikiki, Honolulu and the Pacific Ocean at your feet. The most popular hike in Hawaii, this one is for everyone, especially kids.

Enter at Monsarrat and 18th Avenues on the crater's mauka side. Or take Bus Number 58 from Ala Moana Shopping Center.

The first great secret of the Windward coast of Oahu is that the sun rises out of the ocean between two pyramid-shaped islands that sit on the edge of a green lagoon. You've probably seen the islands in travelogues, on travel magazine covers, postcards and in television commercials, especially in Japan.

The second great secret is that you can climb **Kaiwa Ridge** to an old World War II coastal defense bunker and enjoy this natural phenomenon. Or you may want to plan your ascent to watch the full moon climb out of the Pacific on a summer night.

The ridge takes its name from the black, fork-tailed frigate bird, which Hawaiians call Iwa. The great seabirds are often seen soaring above the ridge's skyline, which is gull-winged like the bird.

The two islets offshore are the Mokulua, which are the natural habitat of red-footed boobies and weekend catamaran sailors and kayakers.

The trail is steep and precipitous but the hike is brief—about 40 minutes—and the panoramic view includes not only the Mokulua islets but also the island of Molokai, and often at dawn, Maui and the summit of the Big Island, 150 miles distant. If you go for moonrise, make sure you bring a flashlight. Expect young lovers at the top.

From Honolulu, drive over the Pali Highway to Kailua. Go straight through Kailua on Kailua Road until the T–intersection. Turn right on Kalaheo Road and stay on it 2.5 miles until Alala Road. Turn left and go up a rise to a stone pillar that marks the entrance to Lanikai, an exclusive beach neighborhood. Drive down A'alapapa Drive one block, turn right on Kaelepulu Street. The trailhead begins between the last house and the gated entry to Bluestone, a condo development overlooking the Mid-Pacific Country Club golf course. Begin climbing the ridge. Take Bus Number 57 from Ala Moana Shopping Center, transfer to the Lanikai Shuttle.

Few have scaled the peak of **Mount Kaala**, the distant, 4,025-foot summit of Oahu's Waianae Range, but those who do never forget the experience.

The reward of this rugged, 13.6 mile hike (roundtrip) is enormous: a keen challenge, a rare look at native plants like ohia lehua *(Metosideros polymorpha)*, hapuu *(Cibotium chamissoi)*, and Hawaiian tree ferns; and a breathtaking adventure that culminates in an unparalleled island view.

The view takes in Kaena Point, all of the North Shore, the Makaha Valley to Nanakuli and even Kaneohe on the Windward coast.

◆ *Warning:* The Mount Kaala hike is dangerous, rated by all as Oahu's most difficult. The 6.8 mile **Dupont Trail** to the 4,025-foot summit of the 2.5 million year old mountain range corkscrews through swampy bogs and over brittle razorback ridges with, in the last mile, sheer drops of 2,000 feet into a valley.

Many turn back before attempting the last mile and you should too if you are afraid of heights. Many inexperienced hikers have been injured; one is known to have fallen to his death. This is the one I didn't make—how did you guess?

It's best to go with a hiking club or volunteer ecologists who help the State Division of Forestry maintain the natural preserve by rooting out non-native blackberries, which along with bitter-tasting Hawaiian raspberries *(Rubus hawaiiensi)* are the sole, trailside sustenance.

If you go, you must get permission from the State Division of Forestry and sign a waiver of liability from the Waialua Sugar Company.

Drive 30 miles from Honolulu. Take the H-1 freeway to the H-2 exit. Continue on Route 99, then bear left at Route 803. At the traffic circle, take Route 930 west to Waialua and just past Waialua High School, turn left on the cane road. Drive 1.5 miles up the road and park by the second gate.

The World's Best Surfing Wave

You've probably seen it on *Hawaii Five-O*. Or, maybe, you've stood awestruck on Oahu's North Shore as the **Pipeline** comes curling out of the Pacific like a classic *tsunami* in a Japanese horror film.

Your really have to see and hear and feel the Pipeline in person to believe it; anything else is a reasonable facsimile.

Bryan Di Salvatore of *The New Yorker* called it "the world's most dramatic surfing wave." And even that's an understatement.

Unless you're a world-class surfer, or foolhardy, grab a front row seat on the beach on the other side of Kalalua Point and catch this wave through binoculars, especially during Hawaii's so-called winter when the Pipeline starts to pump.

Only mad dogs, pro surfers and Warren Bolster, Hawaii's top surf photographer, go out in Oahu's winter surf. For most it's enough just to stand on shore and watch as four-story waves crash in foam at your feet. Watch your step, because some winters the huge waves, estimated at up to 50 feet, lash ashore and flood Kamehameha Highway.

Hawaii's top surfers risk their necks to ride the winter surf—and nearly all survive—but it's far better to be a fearless spectator at the Pipeline than to *chance 'em, brah.*

From Waikiki, take the H-1 freeway ewa to the North Shore, veering off at H-2, which becomes Kamehameha Highway. Go until you hit a British-style circus, as in Picadilly, only *sans* blokes, statues and pigeons. Turn right and head for the funky little surf town of Haleiwa, and drive by Waimea Bay to the big waves on your left, just past Pupukea Beach County Park.

Surfing Waikiki

> "I tried surf-bathing once...but made a failure of it. I got the board placed right, and at the right moment, too; but missed the connection myself. The board struck the shore in three-quarters of a second, without any cargo, and I struck the bottom about the same time, with a couple of barrels of water in me."
>
> Mark Twain

In summer when the south swell comes up from Tahiti and the trade winds blow offshore, that's the very best time to surf Waikiki. The perfect waves surfed by millions from around the world once were the private playground of Hawaiian chiefs who staged *he'e nalu* (wave sliding) contests and bet on who could ride the longest and farthest.

Now, anyone can catch a wave year-round at Waikiki, the most popular of Oahu's 594 surfing sites.

If you didn't bring your own board, you can find a wide selection to rent by the hour or by the day at the Kuhio Beach surfboard stand where beachboys stand ready to give lessons.

Waikiki's best surf lane for beginners is **Canoes**, just off the Royal Hawaiian Hotel.

Choosing the right board is the key. A beginner should choose a board that provides good flotation and is proportional to body weight. If you are between 130 and 180 pounds, get a 10–foot board. Rails should be rounded and the nose should have a good scoop.

Paddle out, wait in line, pick a wave, face the board straight in toward shore and start paddling until the power of the wave catches the board, go from prone position to standing in one fluid motion, find your balance on the board and you are off.

I tried surfing Waikiki one summer when I was 17 and had the same initial success as Mark Twain. In a way, it's like learning how to ride a bicycle. Keep at it until it comes naturally. Then, try to stop.

❂ *Akamai Tip:* World surfing champion Fred Hemmings offers beginners these helpful pointers:

If you start to pearl (the nose dips under water), move back on the board to avoid wiping out (losing the board).

If you wipe out, fall away from the surfboard into the face of the wave.

Fall flat and roll under the wave. Stay under until the wave passes.

Come up with arms over your head so you don't get conked by your board. Retrieve it quickly to reduce hazards for others.

Once you've got it all down, Bobby Achoy will take a classic photo of you surfing Waikiki with Diamond Head in the background (about $7.00) as proof you've mastered the "sport of kings."

Go about 7:30 a.m. any day of the week to the orange Kuhio Beach surfboard stand, at the Diamond Head side of the Sheraton Moana Surfrider Hotel. Say you want to learn how to surf. Practice on the beach first, then go for it.

Best Snorkel Spot on Oahu

I know, it's too crowded and the fish eat out of your hand, but for smooth, clear, warm water, abundance of fish (more than 150 tropical varieties), scenic beauty, open ocean protection and easy access, there is no place like **Hanauma Bay**. And that's the problem: it's being loved to death.

Get here late (after 10 a.m.) and you'll see more than fish; you may even get finned in the face by a common *Americanus bloatus*.

Two reefs, inner and outer, offer adventure for novice and expert. Snorkelers hug the calm and shallow (10-feet) inner bay which is like swimming in an open-air aquarium at feeding time. Experienced SCUBA divers shoot "the slot" (a passage through the reef) to gain Witch's Brew, a turbulent cove; then brave strong currents in 70-foot depths at the bay mouth to see coral gardens, turtles and, oh yes, sharks.

Beware the Molokai Express, a strong current that sweeps the bay's mouth.

The best thing about Hanauma Bay is that everyone can join in the adventure. Just wade in waist-deep and look down.

You will see more than 50 of the 400 species of reef and inshore fish common in Hawaiian waters which regularly appear in Hanauma Bay, including Orangespine Unicornfish, Orange Butterflyfish, Blue-Eye Damselfish, Spotted Puffer, Banana Trumpetfish, Moorish Idol, Convict Tang, Rainbow Wrasse and, if you are really lucky, the fancy Hawaiian Turkeyfish.

Take H-1 East until the freeway becomes Kalanianaole Highway (State Highway 72). Stay on Kalanianaole Highway past shopping centers and subdivisions to the stoplight at Lunalillo Home Road. An overhead sign on a pedestrian walk points the way to Hanauma Bay. Go straight as the road climbs. Look for the Hanauma Bay sign on the right, turn in and proceed to the parking lot.

World Championship Kayak Race

Each year since 1976, Olympic paddlers and world champions set off in solo kayaks from Molokai to Oahu across the 32-mile **Kaiwi Channel**, one of the most challenging and treacherous in the islands.

The world championship of ocean kayak racing attracts hundreds of male and female paddlers from around the globe, including winners of long distance races in Australia and New Zealand.

The race, organized by Kanak I'Kaika, Hawaii's oldest organized kayak racing association, is sanctioned by the American Canoe Association.

Now in its sixteenth year, the world championship kayak race begins at 9 a.m. in the water at Papohaku Roadstead, in front of Colony's Kaluakoi Hotel & Golf Club, on the west end of Molokai.

Hours later, kayakers cross the finish line inside the waterway at Hawaii Kai on Oahu.

Oscar Chalupsky of South Africa holds the men's record of three hours, 27 minutes and 31 seconds. Lorey Bode of Hawaii is the women's record holder with a time of four hours, 44 minutes and 17 seconds.

The best vantage point to see the race, except on a chase boat across the channel, is the finish line on the ocean promenade at Koko Marina Shopping Center in Hawaii Kai. To get there, take the H-1 freeway toward Diamond Head to Kalanianaole Highway, turn left at Lunalilo Home Road, enter at the 76 Union gas station, park and walk to the docks facing Koko Isle.

To enter the world championship, write race director David Marchant, 3830 Tantalus Drive, Honolulu, Hawaii 96822.

Hawaiian Ocean Fest

No city on earth takes its pleasure from the ocean quite like Honolulu, the sports and entertainment capital of the Pacific. At any moment every day, somebody somewhere in the islands is swimming, snorkeling, kayaking, canoeing, sailboarding, paddle-boarding or surfing. If not, they are making plans to get wet and have fun.

Each year since 1990, generally in the third week of August, **Hawaiian Ocean Fest** puts it all together for everyone, visitor and resident alike, in an action-packed, week-long festival of ocean sports.

It's a kind of tropical Olympics for world class athletes, professional lifeguards and local amateurs and a great outdoor adventure for all, which includes a beach party and sea cruise with the victors. Contestants come from around the world to compete in a variety of water-related events from outrigger canoe racing off Waikiki to wave-jumping on sailboards under Diamond Head's brow.

Created and sponsored by the Waikiki Oahu Visitors Association (WOVA), Hawaiian Ocean Fest not only celebrates ocean sports in the islands, but also recognizes great international athletes.

Now that it's an annual tradition, thousands of spectators head for Honolulu each summer to catch the action at two of the world's top "action" beaches—**Waikiki** and **Makapu'u**.

Here's a summary of the events:

*Hawaiian International
Ocean Challenge*
Makapu'u Beach and Waikiki Beach

Big hardbodies crash into the surf in paper thin kayaks. They paddleboard around dangerous island points in white-capped waves, take on the open ocean in outrigger canoes, then run hard and long around an extinct volcano in tropical heat. It's man against ocean and nation against nation in the ultimate ocean challenge, which *Men's Fitness* magazine called "Lifeguard Hell."

The world's top lifeguards vie for athletic supremacy, personal and national pride—and a $15,000 purse—at Hawaii's Waikiki and Makapu'u beaches.

From Australia, New Zealand, Great Britain, Southern California and Hawaii, five six-man teams challenge each other and the ocean over two days in five events designed to test skill and stamina.

The five events are:

Paddle Board Race: 3.4 mile race in Makapu'u surf

Surf Rescue Swim: 300-yard swim with "live" victim

Kayak Race: 4.3 mile race around Rabbit Island

Outrigger Canoe Race: 1,200-yard outrigger canoe race

Ocean Medley Relay: 2,000-yard run, swim, kayak, paddleboard race

Diamond Head Wahine Classic
Diamond Head

Power and grace. You can see it all here, under the volcano of Diamond Head, home of the world's first and only all-woman windsurfing event—the **Diamond Head Wahine Classic.** Here, where the sport began in the islands, the world's best women (*wahine*) boardsailors challenge the big Pacific's summer swell.

Two dozen of the world's top women windsurfers compete over two days for $10,000 in cash prizes in two events—slalom races and wave jumping—all of which may be seen on ESPN, the all-sports television network.

The Diamond Head Wahine Classic is recognized by the Professional Boardsailers Association International of London and Maui. And women of the world.

Waikiki King's Race
Kapiolani Park, Waikiki

Inspired by Hawaii's proud past, the **Waikiki King's Race** is the first of its kind in the world. It challenges today's athletes in four sports the king, himself, practiced: running, canoeing, swimming and paddling.

Strictly for world-class athletes, the Waikiki King's Race tests entrants in four disciplines, under hot sun over a grueling course from the still waters of the Ala Wai Canal to the Pacific's pounding surf.

This royal event is an international invitation for world class men and women athletes who must have the endurance and ability to excel in four sports.

Contestants run 1.75 miles through Kapiolani Park, paddle the 2.8-mile Ala Wai Canal, swim a mile from Duke Kahanamoku Beach to Waikiki Beach, then return to the surf on paddleboards for a one–mile sprint back to Duke's Beach. The four-sport race creates a natural handicapping system for triathletes and ocean athletes who will trade the lead several times in this exciting event.

Strong runners and swimmers may take the lead in one part of the race, only to lose it to ocean athletes who excel at paddling and kayaking.

The ocean swim may be a coin toss, but then it's an all-out paddleboard sprint through Waikiki's famed surf-breaks to the finish line.

And the winner is ... any one of the great athletes from Europe, America and the Pacific who will compete for the

$5,000 purse in the first annual Waikiki King's Race. King Kalaukaua would have loved it.

Hawaiian Roughwater
Makapu'u Beach

At one of Hawaii's most beautiful beaches, 100 world-class Speedo-clad men and women swimmers will plunge into the blue Pacific and turn it to froth.

It's the **Hawaiian Roughwater**, a 1.3 mile open international competition through high surf and strong currents between two islands off Oahu's scenic south coast to an offshore buoy and back.

This 30-minute race with a $2,500 purse begins at Makapu'u Beach with a 15-yard run to the surf and ends with a 25-yard run to the finish line. In between, there are riptides, undertows and sometimes sharks.

There they go, windmills in the waves, thrashing along Oahu's jagged 1,000-foot south shore cliffs, bound for glory and the finish line of the Hawaiian Roughwater.

Any athlete may obtain an application blank to enter the Hawaiian Ocean Fest by writing Dave Nicholas at Event Marketing Inc., 735 Bishop Street, Suite 325, Honolulu, Hawaii 96813.

Spectators may write for information about the week-long event, usually held each year in the third week of August.

Hang Gliding Oahu

Fliers drive up Oahu's 1,200-foot **Mokapu'u Ridge**, fasten their wings, and soar away at 60 miles per hour on three-hour flights down the 30-mile Koolau mountain range. The range is known as the "Green Wall," one of the best spots on earth for soaring.

While Mokapu'u is only for experts, beginners can try their wings without fear now that the world's longest "fail-safe" trainer, called a Hang Glider Simulator, is open on Oahu at John Morgan's Kualoa Ranch and Activity Club.

They hook your wing to a three-eighth-inch cable and let you experience lift as you soar a quarter mile. You experience hanglider flight in absolute safety.

You can be afraid of heights and still do it, claims Mike Adams, who has been flying since 1974, despite a fear of heights. "It's a different sensation," he says. "When I'm on the edge it's one thing, but when I'm flying it's a different sensation.

"The best time to fly," Adams says, is "when the wind is too high for kayaking and too gentle for windsurfing."

Contact Mike Benson at Tradewinds Hang Gliding at (808) 396-8557, or Kualoa Ranch and Activity Club at (808) 926-6069 or Sport Aviation Hawaii, 46-389 Nahewai Street, Kaneohe, Hawaii 96744, (808) 235-6307.

Cat Fishing in Nuuanu

Catfish came to Hawaii in 1958, one year before statehood, and quickly established themselves as the catch of the day in certain places at special times.

The channel catfish *(Ictalurus punctatus)* is found only on the islands of Oahu and Kauai in reservoirs where it feeds on small fish, crustaceans, clams and snails.

It generally is under 10 pounds, but the state record is 43 pounds 13 ounces and some unofficial catches have exceeded 50 pounds. The world record is 58 pounds in South Carolina.

It spawns in late spring, laying its eggs in jelly-like masses in holes and crevices. The male guards the eggs and hatching occurs after about a week.

Crankbaits or large spinnerbaits are the most effective lures; a catfish weighing 51 pounds (unofficially) was taken from the Wahiawa Reservoir on a spoon. Other baits include tilapia, crayfish, aku belly, liver and various stinkbaits.

The best place to fish for catfish is **Nuuanu Freshwater Fish Refuge**, a 25-acre reservoir on Oahu.

At almost 1,000 feet, the **Nuuanu Reservoir** sits in a rainforest in the Koolau mountain range that divides Oahu's windward and leeward sides.

Easily accessible by car, the reservoir is located between Honolulu and Kailua off the Pali Highway. Take the Pali Highway to Kailua, turn off at the sign pointing to Nuuanu Pali road, drive through the rainforest about two miles until you reach the reservoir on your left.

The reservoir is stocked with channel catfish and other species including the smaller, two-pound Chinese catfish (Clarias fuscus) and tilapia (Tilapia mossambica). The reservoir is open to weekend public fishing three seasons a year, beginning in May, August and November.

Bag limit for channel catfish is two, and any channel catfish 16 inches or larger must be kept by the angler.

✪ *Akamai Tip:* A Freshwater Game Fishing License and Entry Fishing Card are required. A license is $3.75 for Hawaii residents, $7.50 for non-residents. They are available at most fishing supply shops.

Prospective anglers at Nuuanu Reservoir must submit an application to the Division of Aquatic Resources several weeks in advance of an opening. A lottery is held to determine fishing times.

Hawaii's Most Adventurous Golf Course

Imagine a golf course in a rain forest where you chip over rainbows and putt under volcanic peaks, where ancient kings lived and wild parrots still flit through royal palms. The dream course is a reality at the foot of Oahu's steepled Koolau mountains, a 30-minute drive from Waikiki Beach. The first hole of the 36-hole **Royal Hawaiian Country Club** course looks like the opening scene of "Raiders of the Lost Ark."

"There are golf courses by the sea, in the desert and in the forest," award-winning designer Perry O. Dye told me, "but there has never been one like this." He spent more than $25 million over five years to create the low-impact "target" course in the Scottish tradition of links golf. The concept requires players to hit accurate shots to designated areas and uses a minimum of manufactured green, tee and fairway surfaces, letting the natural terrain—sometimes fiendishly augmented—create the "rough." If you stray, you pay. It poses unique challenges for well-heeled players who pay $300,000 a year in membership fees just for the challenge. Worth a visit even if you don't know a putter from a driver.

Drive over the Pali Highway (State Highway 61) toward Kailua but don't go all the way. Turn right at Maunawili Road and turn left immediately. Follow the road into the Maunawili Valley to the clubhouse. If you see cattle grazing in the Kaiwainui marsh (a big green, open space) you missed the turn-off.

Two Great Oahu Waterfalls

There are hundreds of waterfalls on Oahu. I once counted 31 one rainy afternoon while crossing the Koolau mountains on the Pali Highway. Many waterfalls are in remote, difficult to reach locations, which is why resorts now replicate them near the swimming pool. With a little effort and some hiking, you can see the real thing.

Up a narrow valley cut by slippery Kaluanua Stream, past wild guavas and mountain apples, **Sacred Falls** is a 4.4-mile round-trip hike enjoyed by thousands who make a day outing in this cool, green canyon.

The 87-foot falls splash into a cold swimming pool which ancient Hawaiians reputedly believed was bottomless and led to another world inhabited by a demon. To go safely many believers and the superstitious still make a small offering of a stone wrapped in a ti leaf which you will see along the trail.

You won't be the only one here, especially on weekends, but this is one waterfall that is gained by a gentle hike even kids can make without too much complaint.

From Honolulu, drive over the Pali Highway (Route 61), then go left on Highway 83 to Hauula. Turn left at the sign on the left marked "Sacred Falls State Park." Distance: 28 miles.

One of the most unusual falls in the world, **Upside Down Falls** "falls" up—but only when the wind blows the rain backwards. You can see it from your car, if you are lucky. It was made famous years ago by "Ripley's Believe It or Not."

Often visible, especially on rainy, windy days near the crest of the Pali Highway, it's easy to miss. I have seen it only a few times but I am not always looking for it either. When you see it, you will know, because you've never seen anything like it. It is more exciting than the "puka in the mauka" (hole in the mountain) near Anahola on Kauai.

A natural phenomenon, the Upside Down Falls is caused when water roars over a cliff and meets strong updrafts caused by the proximity of the nearby volcanic peaks. Updrafts meet the waterfall and blow it up, hence the "upside down" name, although technically it should be the other way around, right?

Drive up the Pali Highway (Highway 61) when it rains good and hard and start looking for it on the left side while Kailua-bound about a mile before the Pali Tunnel. Be careful craning

Ten Fun Things to Do with Keikis

In Hawaiian, *keiki* means kid, as in children, and there's plenty of great outdoor adventures in Hawaii for youngsters. Here are ten they'll like for sure:

Visit the Honolulu Zoo.

Go to the Waikiki Aquarium.

Fly a kite in Kapiolani Park.

Visit the Aloha Flea Market.

Take a picnic to the beach.

See the world's only "wolphin", a cross between a whale and a dolphin, at Sea Life Park.

Go to the Hawaii Children's Museum of Arts, Culture, Science and Technology.

Visit Waimea Falls.

Eat shave ice at Haleiwa.

Ride the Atlantis submarine.

your neck out the window. It may be wise to pull off to the side of the road if you want a good, long look.

✪ *Akamai Tip:* Observing Hawaii's waterfalls is a rewarding outdoor adventure, especially if you take the plunge in a crystal pool at the end of a hot sweaty hike. Before you go, here are a few tips to enhance your experience:

Stay on the Trail: Avoid risk by staying on the trail. It also minimizes damage to flora. Sniff but don't pick the flowers.

Forget White Tennies: Trails to waterfalls are usually slick, and red volcanic mud leaves an indelible stain on your tennies. Leave them at home. Use boat shoes, hiking boots or do like I do—go barefoot.

Bring Your Own Water: Wild pigs and feral goats tromp through the wilderness and often spoil the streams. Bring your own water, always.

Keep Eye on Clouds: If it starts to rain, the falls will start pumping. Be prepared to get out of harm's way, or you may be washed out to sea. Always head for high ground as streams begin to fill. Flash floods do happen.

Chasing After Rainbows

Rainbows are more plentiful in Hawaii than anywhere else in the world. That's because Hawaii has the right combination of rain and sunshine year–round, a weather pattern that occurs only during summer months elsewhere.

Rainbows appear in the moisture laden sky whenever the sun is directly opposite.

In the 17th century, Sir Isaac Newton demonstrated that as white light enters and leaves a raindrop, it breaks out into red, orange, yellow, green, and blue. Each of the primary colors is reflected back from the rear of the raindrop at its own optimal angle of refraction, between 40 and 42 degrees. The bigger the raindrops, the more brilliant the rainbow.

Rainbows are such a part of everyday life in Hawaii that they have become symbols. You see them on

A Rainbow by Any Other Name is Anuenue

Hawaiians have as many different words for rainbows as Eskimos have for snow. Here are 10 variations on the theme:

anuenue
  rainbow
anuenue kau po
  lunar rainbow
po makole
  night of a lunar rainbow
leiokamahina
  rainbow ring around the moon
pio ke anuenue
  rainbow's arc
ua alaea
  reddish rainbow
hakahakaea
  greenish rainbow
lehopulu
  low-lying, earth-clinging rainbow
kahili
  standing, rainbow shaft
ala muku
  rainbow fragment
luahona
  rainbow around the sun or moon

sails, University of Hawaii football helmets, the Hilton Hawaiian Village's Rainbow Tower and even on shave ice. You can even see them at night.

In an article on Hawaii for *The New Yorker*, I wrote that something was as "rare as a night rainbow," not realizing that such a phenomenon could occur. One full moon night on Maui, while driving to Makena Beach from Lahaina, I could hardly believe my eyes. There, against the West Maui mountains, appeared a night rainbow in muted colors. It is what the Hawaiians call *anuenue kau po*, or lunar rainbow. I have never seen another since.

When it rains in Nuuanu Valley in the late afternoon as the sun sets, the conditions are ideal for rainbows.

Take the H-1 to the Pali Highway after 4 p.m. any afternoon you see a passing shower. Drive toward the Pali Lookout and you likely will be rewarded by a rainbow, often two.

Architectural Tour of Honolulu

"Do people still live in grass shacks?" My seat mate on the 747 out of San Francisco wanted to know. She looked like an otherwise sophisticated New Yorker, so I wasn't sure if she was putting me on. She wasn't. "Well," I said, "not all of us."

The last little grass shack in Hawaii, found in Kauai's Kalalau Valley nearly 100 years ago, stands now inside the **Bishop Museum**. That architectural relic is the sole survivor of an era when anyone could design and build their own home using river stones for the floor, *kamani* and *naio* wood for the studs and rafters, and palm fronds, *pili* grass and sennit for the thatch roof.

Early Hawaiian houses were perfectly suited to the tropical climate; they were open and airy, with double-hipped roofs to shed the torrential downpour and wide lanais so people could go outside when it rained without getting soaked.

When the missionaries came in 1820, they imported little wooden saltbox houses with tiny windows that cheated the tradewinds and made life in the tropics unbearable, which probably contributed to their irascibility. Some of those houses still stand at **The Mission Houses Museum**, 553 S. King Street, near the coral block Kawaiahao Church in downtown Honolulu.

More than 100 years later, architects like C.W. Dickey and George "Pete" Wimberly revived the tropical style of architecture, which lives on in several enduring examples that may be seen in Honolulu.

All of Hawaii's architecture is imported from somewhere else: Polynesian Grass Shack, Proper Missionary Pre-Fab, Faux European Monarchy, Tin Roof Sugar Plantation, California Taco Bell Revival, Waikiki Greedy and, in the last few years, Fantasy Resort and Marble Monolith.

What generally is accepted as "Hawaii-style" architecture was introduced by Dickey (1871-1942), who borrowed from California's Spanish Mission Revival to create his most enduring example—the **U.S. Immigration Station**. Wimberly, known as the father of tropical resort architecture, kept the tradition alive in hundreds of projects throughout the Pacific, including the **Royal Hawaiian Hotel**, the new **Ritz-Carlton** on the Big Island and the **Hotel Bora Bora**.

Five Tropical Style Designs

Grass Shack
Bishop Museum
1525 Bernice Street
The traditional Hawaiian house made of pili grass. Inside the Hawaiian Hall at the Bishop Museum. Restored by William T. Brigham, first director of the Bishop Museum.

Hawaii State Capitol
415 S. Beretania Street
Evokes air, land and sea in a volcano-shaped structure. Designed by architect John Carl Warnecke of San Francisco, California.

Moana Hotel
2365 Kalakaua Avenue
Airy Victorian beach resort in beaux–arts style. Designed by architect Oliver Traphagen of Honolulu.

Hilton Hawaiian Village
2005 Kalia Road
A graceful island-style mega-resort on a 20-acre beach site. Designed by architectural firm of Wimberly Allison Tong & Goo of Honolulu.

Other noted architects have created enduring landmarks in Hawaii, like I. M. Pei's **East-West Center**, John Carl Warnecke's **State Capitol**, Alfred Preis' *U.S.S. Arizona* **Memorial**, Minoru Yamasaki's **Queen Emma Garden Apartments**, Vladimir Ossipoff's **Outrigger Canoe Club**, Carey M. Smoot's Lanikai Beach home of Paul Mitchell and Ellerbe Becket's **Hawaii Prince Hotel**.

On the outer islands, two sterling examples of tropical architecture are Skidmore, Owings & Merrill's **Mauna Kea Beach Hotel** on the Big Island and Wimberly Allison Tong & Goo's Dickey-inspired **Hyatt Regency Kauai** at Poipu Beach, Kauai.

Waikiki, designed by dollar signs, has little redeeming architectural value outside of the **Royal Hawaiian** and Oliver Traphagen's Victorian **Moana Hotel**, built in 1901 and wonderfully restored to its original splendor.

Exploring Chinatown

Under moon gates with golden dragons, Oahu's **Chinatown** presents a lively pageant of people, sights, sounds, smells and tastes from all over Asia and the Pacific.

Go anytime, day or night, to explore the 15-block district that thrives under a misnomer amid lei stands and ginseng shops.

It may have been founded by Chinese immigrants 130 years ago, but it's since been infiltrated by Japanese, Koreans, Laotians and Pacific Islanders, as well as Vietnamese and Filipinos. Today, the historic district is the most Asian of all America's Chinatowns, a chop sui place where only five percent of the population is Chinese.

You can still haggle for freshwater pearls and raw silk, sample fresh baked almond cookies, peek inside a *char siu bow* factory, get a lasting souvenir at the **China Sea Tattoo Parlor** and purchase 14 herbs at the **Tak Wah Tong Chinese Herb Shop** that Alan Lau claims is the Chinese cure for a common cold. And while

Outrigger Canoe Club
2909 Kalakaua Avenue
A beach club that blurs indoor/outdoor edges of reality. Designed by architect Vladimir Ossipoff of Honolulu.

Hawaii Prince Hotel
100 Holomoana Street
Chic big-city hotel with tropical flair. Designed by architectural firm of Ellerbe Becket of Santa Monica, California.

Wo Fat's, the oldest chop sui house, founded in 1882, still draws a crowd, the days may be numbered for the **Cebu Pool Hall** where aging Filipinos bet daylong on bank shots.

Every Saturday morning Chinatown teems with shoppers for fresh island opakapaka (blue snapper), young coconuts and, of course, roast duck. I like to shop the Oahu Market, 145 N. King Street, for fresh fish and odd Asian vegetables (you may want to overlook the freshly butchered hog's heads and tripe) sold in 17 separate stalls under one tin roof.

The mouth-watering scents that waft over Chinatown emanate from Maunakea Marketplace, an open market with Hawaii's largest congregation of Asian/Pacific food stalls. You may find Hong Kong-style noodles, steamed manapua (Chinese pastry filled with sweetened pork), Korean ribs, Thai ginger fish, flaky French croissants baked by Vietnamese, Filipino-style chicken adobo and Hakka-style Chinese seafood.

I like Chinatown best after dark, when the neon adds a mysterious glow. Alley cats come creeping and a distant dirty trumpet echoes down Hotel Street, where the Club Hubba Hubba girls show their stuff and hookers begin to prowl in a pale imitation of the "good old days" here.

The famed World War II red light district of James Jones' *From Here to Eternity* is vanishing as urban renewal brings new art galleries, shops and restaurants. But even though it's changing and few call it home, Chinatown still is just Chinatown.

The best guided tour of Chinatown is offered at 9:30 a.m. every Friday by the Hawaii Heritage Center. The two and a half hour walking tour of the 15-block historical district begins at Ramsay Chinatown Gallery, 1128 Smith Street. Cost is $4 a person. Call the Hawaii Heritage Center at (808) 521-2749 for reservations.

Two Oahu Peace Memorials

The sunken battleship still oozes oil a half century later, as if weeping for the 1,100 dead sailors trapped inside. Thirty-five thousand white gravestones march across the crater of an old volcano Hawaiians called *Puowaina* or Hill of Sacrifice.

For those men and women, war was the greatest adventure of their life; they are remembered at two memorials, visited by 7.5 million people a year.

We are standing in the **Punchbowl, National Cemetery of the Pacific**, a big bowl-shaped volcanic crater that is the final resting place of nearly 35,000 great adventurers. This graveyard, a dead volcano once used by early Polynesians for human sacrifice, is Hawaii's most visited site, attracting more than 4 million people a year. On Memorial Day each grave is decorated by a flower lei.

Here, in Punchbowl, as it's called, repose the casualties of three American wars in Asia and the Pacific. Marble tables in The Courts of the Missing bear names of 29,000 lost in battle. The first burial in 1949 was of an unknown serviceman killed in the Japanese raid on Pearl Harbor. World War II correspondent Ernie Pyle is also buried here, next to Hawaii's first astronaut Ellison Onizuka, killed in the Challenger shuttle disaster.

To pay respects, go between 8 a.m. and 5:30 p.m. daily. Take the H-1 Freeway to the Pali Highway (State Highway 61) and exit at 21-B. A sign on the right points the well-marked route that circles around the outside of the crater to Punchbowl's main gate at 2177 Puowaina Drive. No admission charge. Call (808) 541-1430 for information.

At the *U.S.S. Arizona* **Memorial**, the roll call of those lost at sea begins underwater. The names bubble up out of the gray hull of the *U.S.S. Arizona* from a Sunday a half century ago which Americans of a certain age remember always.

In my father's generation the icons are indelible: Pearl Harbor, December 7, 1941; FDR; "day of infamy;" *U.S.S. Arizona*; "Tora, Tora, Tora;" and dark headlines of "WAR!"

The past comes alive in a documentary film, while you wait to board a solemn shuttle boat for the ten–minute ride to the white memorial, designed by Alfred Preis, that spans the *Arizona's* hull like a sagging cross.

One of the most poignant exhibits at the small, open-air Visitors Center is the display of personal items of Paxton Carter, the payroll clerk aboard the *Arizona*, who perished with his colleagues that Sunday 50 years ago.

In summer, 4,500 people visit daily, so go early when it is cool and less crowded. Catch the Number 20 Airport bus from Waikiki or drive about an hour, depending on traffic, to the *U.S.S. Arizona* Memorial. Take Highway 1 (H-1) ewa (north) past Honolulu International Airport. Exit at the Arizona Memorial offramp onto King Kamehameha Highway (State Highway 99). Follow the well-signed route west for a mile to free parking.

The center is operated by the National Park Service and the United States Navy. It is open from 7:30 a.m. to 3:30 p.m. seven days a week. Tours start at 8 a.m. and the last complete tour starts at 3 p.m. Shuttle boats, operated by the U.S. Navy, take visitors to the memorial about every 15 minutes. Admission is free and you may stay as long as you like. In summertime, expect a four-hour wait to visit the memorial. The average wait is about 90 minutes. A free, 21-minute film on the Pearl Harbor attack is offered at the Visitor Center Theater. A museum, gift shop, snack bar and rest rooms are provided. Closed Thanksgiving, Christmas and New Year's Day. Call (808) 422-0461 for a tape-recorded message or (808) 422-2772 for more information. Handicapped facilities for visitors in wheelchairs.

Three Great Places to Go When It Rains in Honolulu

If the same epic Honolulu downpour that inspired W. Somerset Maugham to write his famous short story, "Rain," conspires to keep you indoors, here are three dry places to explore until the sun comes out again, usually in three days.

Everyone should visit the **Bernice Pauahi Bishop Museum**, or the Bishop, as we call it, at least once. A rainy day is best because you won't feel like you're missing anything outdoors. This lava rock Romanesque structure built in 1889 on a hill overlooking Honolulu is a monument to real-life Hawaiian princess Bernice Pauahi Bishop and the best museum in the Pacific. Everything "to enrich and delight" you about Polynesia and the Pacific is here—more than 20 million acquisitions. The last grass shack in Hawaii is here, along with a 50-foot sperm whale, a sea map that depicts the 1,500-mile Hawaiian

Three Places to Find Out-of-Town Newspapers

If you think the IQ of a place is in direct proportion to its distance from the *New York Times*, here's the scoop on where to find a few out-of-town newspapers in Honolulu, which is not a great newspaper town—but then what is?

Honolulu Book Shops
Ala Moana Center
941-2274
Carries the *New York Times, Wall Street Journal, San Francisco Chronicle, San Francisco Examiner, Los Angeles Times,* and *USA Today.*

Tower Records
611 Keeaumoku Street
941-7774
Carries the *Los Angeles Times, Chicago Tribune,* and *Washington Post.*

Waldenbooks,
The Ward Warehouse
533-2711
Carries the *San Francisco Chronicle, San Francisco Examiner, Los Angeles Times,* and *USA Today.*

chain in three-dimensional bas relief, old calabashes, feather capes worn by kings, nose flutes, war clubs, fishhooks and tintypes of topless hula girls. A 100-seat planetarium offers a look at the Pacific sky at 1:00 p.m. and 3:00 p.m., daily. Shop Pacifica, in the lobby, has the best selection of Hawaii books and crafts.

Drive ewa on H-1. Take the Likelike Highway exit, also known as Exit 20A. Drive two blocks, head for the right hand lane, turn right on Bernice Street, go about a half block to the entrance on your right. Free parking.

Now's a good time to explore the **Moana Hotel**, the oldest wooden structure in the Pacific. Designed by Oliver G. Traphagen and built in 1901, the Beaux Arts-style Moana was bought by the Japanese and slated for demolition until her National Historical Landmark status was invoked; instead the First Lady of Waikiki got a multi-million dollar facelift just in time to celebrate her 100th birthday on March 11, 2001.

The only hotel in the state with a three-story porte cochere, the Moana also features Ionic columns in the lobby, a grand staircase, and a grand salon and veranda complete with a white baby grand piano. The Moana's famous banyan tree, under which Webley Edwards broadcast "Hawaii Calls," heard by millions around the world for 40 years, survives in the courtyard. All rooms, $180 and up, are 19th century period pieces except for bedside computer control centers.

Free tours are conducted at 11 a.m. daily, rain or shine, from the lobby. To get there, walk Diamond Head down Waikiki Beach (or Kalakaua Avenue) until you see the white Victorian hotel at 2365 Kalakaua Avenue. Enter the lobby from Kalakaua Avenue. Call (808) 922-3111 for reservations.

On the waterfront, at Pier 7, near Aloha Tower, is the small but important **Hawaii Maritime Museum**, full of artifacts from Hawaii's long proud maritime past — from ocean-going canoes, early surfboards, and whaling ships to Matson ships, seaplanes and high-tech windsurf boards. The Hokule'a, a double-hulled sailing canoe that re-enacted the Polynesian voyages of discovery, is moored here. **Coasters,** an open-air restaurant right on the pier, serves lunch and cocktails.

From Waikiki, go ewa (north) on Ala Moana to Bishop Street, turn left and look for the Hawaii Maritime Museum on your right, next to the Falls of Clyde, a century-old square-rigged four master.

Open 9:00 a.m. to 8:00 p.m. daily. Admission is $6 for adults, $3 for ages six to 17, under six free. Call 536-6373 for information.

Three Lesser Adventures

There are certain things, I guess you just have to do them because they are there, or so you can say you did it, or because somebody else said it was a great thing to do. I call these things lesser adventures. Anyone can do them. They require absolutely no experience, special equipment or great sense of adventure and usually cost more than you think.

They deserve mention because lots of people enjoy them and sometimes you just feel like doing something low-key and unchallenging.

Take parasailing in Waikiki, for example. Dangling from a parachute while being tugged through the sky over water by a speedboat is one of those things I have never understood. I did it years ago in Mazatlan but I never wrote home about it, you know what I mean? It was something to do instead of drinking Pacifico. Yet, it's one of the most popular "adventures" in Waikiki and one that my old pal Harry Press, a former San Francisco sports writer, highly recommends.

Maybe you have to be a certain age to appreciate the wind in your hair from on high while dangling like a kite tail. I can get into the silence and the scenery, but to me it's the tropical equivalent of being towed behind a car on a sled. At least there you can fall off.

Aloha Parasail (it's the red chute with "ALOHA" spelled out in white letters on the canopy) makes several passes daily over the Waikiki coastline, so you can look at the highrises, sunbathers and surfers. Call 521-2446, if you must experience what they call "the thrill of a lifetime."

Maybe it's just me, but I'd rather be *in* the water with the fish instead of on a boat looking at them through a glass bottom. However, if you, like 80 percent of Hawaii's visitors, are afraid of the ocean, only feel safe at poolside or just are not a confident swimmer, then a **glass bottom boat** is just the ticket. It's better than not seeing Hawaii's tropical fish.

The best place on Oahu for a glass bottom boat ride is usually the calm and shallow Kaneohe Bay on the island's windward side, where bright tropical fish abound in coral reefs. You will see Moorish idols, butterfly fish, parrotfishes, wrasses and surgeonfish as they feed on coral polyps.

The great advantage here is that when you tire of looking at fish under glass, usually after 10 minutes, you are already in one of Hawaii's biggest, most beautiful and little-known bays. Most people sit in awe at the incredible beauty of Kaneohe Bay as clouds sweep over the 2,600-foot high volcanic cliffs of the majestic Koolau range. Of all boat rides on Oahu this one offers the best scenery. And I don't mean fish.

Sail with Captain Bob Dall aboard his 42-foot catamaran *Barefoot One* (it's got the barefoot on the sail). This experienced Kaneohe Bay captain provides glass bottom viewing and more: snorkel and dive equipment, underwater cameras, lunch, drinks, and round-trip transportation from Waikiki. The four-hour adventure cruise goes out Monday through Saturday, costs $65 for adults, and $45 for 17 and under. Call (808) 926-5077 for reservations.

Every night the 26-ship sunset fleet sets out along the Waikiki coast with a thousand landlubbers who don't know port from starboard. The boats are called the **booze cruise**.

If you think you're missing all the fun, go on the *Leahi*, the green-sailed catamaran, a real sailing experience with real nice people.

The 45-foot *Leahi,* a racing catamaran, sails from Waikiki Beach five times a day on one-hour sight-seeing cruises. Adults $12, children 7-14 $6. The 90-minute sunset cruise is best, $22 for adults, $16 for non-drinkers; $2 for children. Call (808) 922-5665 for reservations.

Four Great Outdoor Places to Shop

Sooner or later you've got to do it. It happens to everybody. Someone forgot their swimsuit and you've got to have a shark's tooth on a neck chain for your nephew, of course. You might as well do it outdoors so you can tan as you shop.

All buses lead to **Ala Moana Shopping Center**; it's Honolulu's retail and transit center, a tropical Coney Island. Fifty acres, big as a battleship, this temple of consumerism outdraws Disneyland. People come here from Tahiti to shop at what French author Francine du Plessix Gray called "a perpetual world's fair." Now three stories high, Ala Moana has 200 shops, including the new chi-chi Palm Boulevard boutiques like Emporia Armani, Etro, Chanel, Cartier, Luis Vuitton, Bruno Magli, Escada, Ann Taylor, Celine, Vittadini and others that appeal to up-scale shoppers from Tokyo and Beverly Hills.

Old men still sit by the carp pond on the second floor (between Cartier and Sharper Image), and in the alley between Sears and Longs, but the place fairly bustles in a shopping frenzy year-round.

Java Java, a new outdoor espresso bar, (across from Gucci) is a welcome addition, and **The Makai Market Food Court**, a collection of 20 ethnic fast food shops from all over the Pacific Rim, is a great grazing place for lunch.

Ala Moana Boulevard is across from Ala Moana Beach Park, almost midway between Waikiki and downtown Honolulu. Plenty of free parking.

On the outskirts of Honolulu's rustbucket Aloha Stadium, home of the nationally televised NFL Pro Bowl, thousands shop at the **Aloha Flea Market** for everything from old aloha shirts and Lincoln Continentals to tree-ripe yard mangos and papayas.

This open-air bazaar is reminiscent of Hong Kong's Stanley Market and it's great fun to browse if only to see the staggering array of new and second-hand goods that somehow found their way to the mid-Pacific. Go early to avoid the hot sun, or late to catch the end-of-day bargains. The Aloha Flea Market is open from 6 a.m. to 3 p.m., Wednesday, Saturday and Sunday.

Take the H-1 Freeway ewa to the Aloha Stadium exit; follow signs to the entrance of the stadium parking lot.

Garage sales are another great place to shop, but it's really a misnomer since most people don't have garages in Hawaii. They sure move a lot of goods around the islands every weekend, though. These neighborhood sales are known for great bargains, too, since most people who leave the islands would rather sell their stuff at ten cents on the dollar instead of paying $4,000 to ship it all back to wherever they came from. My neighbor Michael Dalke, who's made some excellent finds, including a Kamaka pineapple ukulele and a 1956 Mercedes Benz four-door convertible, has this theory about Hawaii garage sales. He says the stuff never leaves the islands, that it just keeps moving around the islands counterclockwise from one garage sale to the next, until it gets worn out and ends up in the Kailua Sanitary Land Fill, where it's often rescued, repaired and returned to circulation.

Check the classifieds just before the weekend, or look for homemade signs stapled to telephone poles in any neighborhood. Some of the most interesting stuff may be found in Kahala and Lanikai.

In Search of the Perfect Aloha Shirt

No shrinking violets, aloha shirts should be gaudy, loud, bold, garish. More is better. Mies van der Rohe would never understand.

Aloha shirts thumb their noses at white shirts. Some are as tacky as pink plastic yard flamingoes. Others are instant classics. All are worth something in the eye of the beholder.

Little wash-and-wear Gauguins, they celebrate tropical scenes in neon colors. They tell stories, and sing songs like "yellow bird in banana tree." They are brash, but user-friendly—ergo aloha.

Souvenirs of Hawaii, aloha shirts became a serious fashion trend in the 30s, thanks to Ellery Chun, who came home from Yale in 1931 to rescue his father's failing garment business and created the aloha shirt using old bolts of bright floral material.

In the islands, by the way, they are called aloha shirts but the mainland refers to them as Hawaiian shirts.

Some folks take them seriously and frame them like works of art. Others wear them, always out. Their loyal fans are legion and disparate. They include Harry Truman, Tom Selleck, Jack Nicholson, Bing Crosby, Elvis and Ike. Bill Cosby collects them, so does Stephen Spielberg. Arthur Godfrey and Bob Hope wore them first on television. Tom Selleck made his black one with white and purple orchids as famous as red Ferraris. Originally made of silk and cotton, then rayon, most are made of cotton today. Paradise Found has revived the old standards in silk which sell for $60 and up.

Many vintage silkies are worth $250 and up. It depends upon many factors, including who wore it and when; if it appeared in a Hollywood film, expect sticker shock. Take Montgomery Clift's aloha shirt in *From Here To Eternity*, the one he wore in his death scene. It features a panorama of palm trees, clouds and mountains of Hawaii. Current value—$1,000, according to H. Thomas Steele, author of *The Hawaiian Shirt*, the book.

Always in search of the perfect aloha shirt, my Santa Cruz, California pal, Lee Quarnstrom, regularly shows up in Honolulu wearing a classic. He claims he finds the best for under $5 at retro and second hand shops in California, where many great old ones end up on hangers.

In Honolulu, look for aloha shirts at **Bailey's Antique Clothing Shop**, home of the "$1,000 aloha shirt" at 758 Kapahulu Avenue, 734-7628. Open daily from 10 a.m. to 7 p.m. Or search the **Aloha Flea Market**, Aloha Stadium, 486-1529 for information. Wednesday, Saturday and Sunday from 7:30 a.m. to 3:30 p.m. **Linda's Vintage Isle** is the best shop in Waikiki for aloha shirts. Located at 373 Olohana Street, (808) 942-9517. Open 10 a.m. to 4 p.m. unless the surf is up.

Adventures After Dark in Waikiki

Waikiki stays open until 4 a.m., so there's plenty of adventure for night owls. Here are some entertaining diversions you may want to investigate instead of watching CNN in your room:

The Captain's Room
Hawaii Prince Hotel
100 Holomoana
(808) 956-1111

In the land of ubiquitous ukuleles, the blues and jazz are scarce, but Azure McCall—who can sing like Sarah, Carmen and Ella—keeps the flame alive in the chic, all–black–marble jazz club known as The Captain's Room on the second floor of the new Hawaii Prince Hotel. She appears Wednesday through Saturday night with a hot quartet featuring Tennyson Stephenson on piano, Miles Jackson on rhythm, Paul Madison on sax, and Sonny Froman on drums.

Wave Waikiki
1877 Kalakaua Avenue
(808) 941-0424

Boogie to Grace Jones, Dave Valentin, Fleetwood Zoo, Cinderfella Rockefella, Bronski Beat, Bow Wow Wow, George Thorogood and the Destroyers (although not all at once) in

Jack Law's nightclub, Wave Waikiki. Catch the Wave until 4 a.m.; it's Honolulu's crossroads for pop stars on the road.

Club Rock-Za
Kapiolani Boulevard and Kalakaua Avenue
(808) 949-1134

For a Polynesian city, Honolulu displays strange morals. It makes women keep their tops on at the beach by day but lets them take it all off in dark bars after sunset. Nobody gets down to the real nitty–gritty faster than Club Rock-Za girls, no two alike, as they say, who display some very interesting tan lines but little talent for $1 tip.

Great Adventures in Dining

Until recently, Hawaii has been the junk food capital of the Pacific; tourists want cheeseburgers and everyone else orders Spam with two scoops of rice and macaroni salad. The culinary life of Hawaii, however, is improving whether tourists and locals like it or not.

Hawaii is developing a kind of *nouvelle tropicale* cuisine thanks to chefs like Gary Strehl, Roger Dikon, Roy Yamaguchi, Philippe Padovani and Jean-Marie Josselin. Best of all, scores of small wonderful restaurants are opening throughout the islands, neighborhood bistros and unassuming cafes where real food is prepared well and served with great pride. You've never seen these restaurants featured in *Gourmet* magazine but it won't be long; most are off-beat, off-the-trail and they offer what locals call *ono grinds*—good fresh food at a reasonable price.

The Great Adventures in Dining Guide, a wholly subjective personal survey made anonymously each year at my personal expense with gusto, is proud to recommend the following restaurants, beginning on Oahu:

Roy's
6600 Kalanianaole Highway
(808) 396-7697
Dinner and Sunday brunch.

At Roy's, Chef Roy Yamaguchi has created the best neighborhood restaurant on Oahu in, of all places, the burbs of Hawaii Kai, but it's worth the eight-mile, 30-minute commute for his signature dishes that marry diverse cuisines, chiefly the flavors and techniques of Japan, France and California.

From Honolulu, take H-1 south to Hawaii Kai. The freeway becomes Kalanianaole Highway at the Kahala Shopping Center. Keep going until you reach Hawaii Kai Drive, turn left and then right again into the Hawaii Kai Corporate Plaza.

Chiang Mai Northern Thai Cuisine
2239 S. King Street
(808) 941-1151
Dinner from 5:30 to 10 p.m. nightly.

Celebrities flock to orchid-filled Keo's on Kapahulu to see and be seen while they chopstick through the mee krob, but the best Thai food for the price may be found at Chiang Mai on North King Street. It's a small 12-table restaurant run by a family from Chiang Mai and they present authentic Thai food at a modest price.

From Waikiki, take Ala Wai Boulevard to McCully Street, go eight blocks to S. King Street, turn right, go one block, look for Chiang Mai's sign on the right side of the street.

Keo's Thai Cuisine
625 Kapahulu Avenue
(808) 737-8240

Okay, so you haven't been to Keo's and it's on your "must" list. (Remember, it's really Laotian food.) From Waikiki, go Diamond Head on Kalakaua until Kapahulu Street (the Honolulu Zoo is on the corner). Turn left and go makai on Kapahulu Street about 1.5 miles. Turn right at the Jack In The Box and go right again into the "valet only" parking lot.

It's only a buck or two and you don't have to keep going around the block looking for a nonexistent parking place.

Cafe Asia by Keo
500 Moana Boulevard, Suite 2A
Honolulu
(808) 536-6889

Keo Sananikone does it again! Cafe Asia by Keo, his sixth and newest restaurant in Honolulu, is a crowning achievement, worthy of his by-line and quite possibly the best restaurant in Restaurant Row. It introduces all the best foods of Asia—Thai, Indonesian, Filipino, Laotian, Vietnamese, Malaysian, Singaporean—in one central place, a bright, flower-filled tropical bistro that elevates the ethnic restaurant to a new plateau.

It's on the mauka ewa corner of Restaurant Row, the foodie mall on the ground level of two high-rise office towers across Ala Moana Boulevard from the green tile roof of the U.S. Immigration Office. Valet parking.

Huevos Restaurant
P.O. Box 684 (no street address)
Kahuku
(808) 293-1016

In the middle of nowhere, off the beaten track, in Kahuku, the prawn capital of Oahu, is Huevos, the best breakfast joint on the island. Maria Pacheco, a native of Spain, who's lived in Hawaii 13 years, serves more than 200 big, hearty breakfasts of fresh eggs, Portuguese sausage, and short stacks every day. Everything is made fresh and to order, and the service is real Hawaii-style, so kick back and enjoy.

Three Great Romantic Restaurants on Oahu

Dinner by the sea by candlelight, an excellent wine list and great food served by soft-spoken waiters. Whether you're a honeymooner or just in a romantic mood (and who isn't in Hawaii?), you'll find more than romance on the menu at these seaside bistros:

Hau Tree Lanai
New Otani Kaimana Beach Hotel
2863 Kalakaua Avenue
(808) 923-1555

At the Hau Tree Lanai, under the same banyan tree that Robert Louis Stevenson wrote love poems to the young and beautiful Princess Kaiulani at Sans Souci beach, you may enjoy the "quiet, pure air, clear sea water, good food and heavenly sunsets" that inspired Stevenson to write glowingly of the South Seas. Everything remains wonderfully inspirational today.

Moderate, aloha attire, reservations required.

It's a little hard to find. Take the dirt road makai off Kamehameha Road on Oahu's north shore to the only two-story white plantation house with lavender trim. It's the house with all the cars parked outside and people standing in line at 6 o'clock in the morning.

Los Arcos
19 Hoolai Street, Kailua
(808) 262-8196
Lunch 11:30 a.m. to 2 p.m. Monday, Tuesday, Wednesday and Friday; dinner every night except Thursday from 5:30 p.m.

Sooner or later, it'll happen: you'll crave Mexican food. It's the climate. But a good hot tamale is hard to find in Hawaii. We've got too many chain beaneries run by mainland gringos who learned their stuff at Señor Taco. Nobody in Hawaii knows what real Mexican food is except Hank and Mary Magana who run Los Arcos and prepare authentic regional specialties like Calamares Borrachos (drunken squid) and Pollo con

Rajas, Carne Tampiquena and Huachinago Vera Cruz. Los Arcos even looks like a real Mexican restaurant.

Drive over the Pali Highway (State Highway 61) to Kailua; the highway becomes Kailua Road. Drive one block past the stop light at Hamakua Drive, turn left on Hoolai Street. Los Arcos is on the left.

LaMariana Restaurant & Bar
50 Sand Access Road
(808) 848-2800
Lunch 11 a.m. to 2:30 p.m.; dinner 6 p.m. to 9:30 p.m. seven days a week.

Not exactly a blue blazer, brass button yacht club, LaMariana Restaurant & Bar, a tin and thatch-roof harbor front cafe right out of a South Seas novel, looks like it washed ashore in a tsunami. It's the Honolulu haunt of the chic and salty, including real sea-going sailors who drop anchor at the pier for the

La Mer
Halekulani Hotel
2199 Kalia Road
(808) 923-2311

La Mer is on the second floor of an open-air Hawaiian-style bungalow by the sea at the Halekulani Hotel (made famous by Earl Derr Biggahs, author of *House Without a Key*). You will be enchanted by this elegant, low-key restaurant where tuxedoed waiters serve Hawaii's nouvelle island cuisine.

Expensive, jackets for gentlemen, reservations required.

The Willows
901 Hausten Street
(808) 946-4808

The Willows is a tropical oasis in a pocket of the city. It will surprise you the minute you enter. In a jungle of tropical flora, thatched roof huts sit amid ponds of carp fish. The soft plink of the ukulele fills the night as a Hawaiian trio sings like angels. Local fish and curries are featured in this fantasy setting.

Moderate, aloha attire, reservations required.

best fresh fish in the islands at reasonable prices. *Da kine place, fo' real.*

From Bishop Street (near the Aloha Tower) in downtown Honolulu, go ewa (north) on Ala Moana (State Highway 92) as if you are heading toward Honolulu International Airport. Ala Moana becomes Nimitz Highway. Stay on it about five miles until you see the Sand Island Access Road turnoff. Turn left; drive through an industrial zone past a marine supply shop and a mountain of crushed cars. Turn right at the hand-painted LaMariana sign with the arrow (just past the McKesson Warehouse). Go down a bumpy dirt access road with no name. LaMariana is on your left.

L'Auberge Swiss
117 Hekili St., Kailua
(808) 263-4663

When Freddie Mueller left the Bali Room at the Hilton Hawaiian Village years ago to open his own restaurant, L'Auberge Swiss, it was Waikiki's loss and Kailua's gain. This talented Swiss chef runs his restaurant with personal care as if he invited you to his house for dinner.

Drive over Pali Highway (State Highway 61) to Kailua; the highway becomes Kailua Road. Turn right at the first stop light onto Hamakua Drive. Take the next left which is Hekili Street. The restaurant is on the right, next to Napa Auto Supply. Park in the rear.

Three Great Honolulu Seafood Restaurants

Yes sir, we've got catfish and rainbow trout and locally grown Alaska Salmon and even California abalone and mahimahi and ahi, too. It is almost impossible to get through the day in Hawaii without running into a fish on your plate. We eat it raw, steamed, grilled, sauteed, baked and blackened. Chop it up and serve it with seaweed, green onion and sesame oil. That's called poke and variations on the theme are limited only by imagination.

Fish tastes better in Hawaii because it's caught fresh daily, expertly prepared and served in more than 6,000 restaurants. Honolulu's also got the best sushi bars this side of Tokyo, so there's no excuse not to catch a seafood meal in the islands. Here are three great Honolulu seafood restaurants:

John Dominis
43 Ahui Street
(808) 523-0955

In a fish cannery district, at the edge of Kewalo Basin, John Dominis' waterfront restaurant has a fish-eye view of the Pacific, Diamond Head and Waikiki. The seafood is fresh, well-prepared and way overpriced.

While heading toward the airport on Ala Moana, look for Ahui Street on the left; it's just after the Mercedes Benz dealer. Drive past a boat yard and fish canneries, almost to the end of the street. Look for the restaurant on your left. Valet parking.

Four Great B&Bs on Oahu

Bed and breakfasts are one of the best ways to discover the "real" Hawaii. They also help you beat the high cost of hotels.

More than 100 Oahu bed and breakfasts now book guests from around the world who seek a personal, authentic experience off the well-worn tourist trail.

Some advertise in mainland newspapers, others are known only by word-of-mouth. All are very popular, so if you plan to reserve a Hawaii-style bed & breakfast, call or write early, especially if you're planning a holiday visit.

Accommodations range from a small private room to a 1,200-square foot suite with ocean view. Rates run between $50 to $150 a night, depending on location. Even with Hawaii's 4.16 percent sales tax and 5.25 percent hotel tax, you can save a bundle and stay in the islands longer.

Most bed and breakfasts require a 20 percent non-refundable deposit, with the balance due upon

Prince Court
Hawaii Prince Hotel
100 Holomoana Street
(808) 956-1111

Chef Gary Strehl at the **Prince Court** couldn't find catfish the night Dizzy Gillespie came to town, so he served opakapaka, salmon, ahi, mahimahi and fresh oysters, instead. "You are surrounded by fish," a dazzled Dizzy said. Nobody in Hawaii cooks and serves fish better than Chef Strehl.

While heading into Waikiki, turn right on Holomoana Street, the first street on the right just after the bridge over the Ala Wai. The Prince Court is on the second floor of the Hawaii Prince Hotel. Valet parking.

Pacific Broiler
7192 Kalanianaole Highway
(808) 395-4181

Out on the outskirts of Honolulu in a suburban shopping center sits **Pacific Broiler**, an award-winning contemporary grill on the waterfront that few people, except denizens of Hawaii Kai, know about.

Drive south on H-1 to Hawaii Kai, turn left off Kalanianaole Highway at Koko Marina Shopping Center. The restaurant is on the water about in the middle of the shopping center.

✪ *Akamai Tip:* The best place to catch fish in Honolulu without going fishing is Tamashiro Market. Look for a giant orange crab on the side of a two-story New Orleans style building. Inside you will find more than 100 varieties of fresh local seafood, some still on the hoof, including ahi, aku, mahi, au, ono and opakapaka. Tamashiro Market is in Kalihi, the first neighborhood ewa of Chinatown. It's at 802 North King Street, corner of Palama Street and North King Street. (808) 841-8047.

arrival. None accept credit cards; cash or traveler's checks are preferred.

A typical Hawaii bed and breakfast is a private room and bath at or near the beach or in a garden which offers overnight lodging, usually a three-night minimum, and a Hawaii-style continental breakfast. Some hosts serve Kona coffee and fresh papayas and bananas from their yard.

All hosts have an "insider's" knowledge of Hawaii, its flora and fauna, customs and culture. They can provide valuable information on the best things to see and do. And their island homes are good examples of the tropical style of architecture. Here are a few B&Bs on the windward side of Oahu:

Lanikai Bed and Breakfast
Homer & Mahina Maxey
1277 Mokulua Drive
Kailua, Hawaii 96734
(808) 261-1059

Just a minute away from Oahu's best swimming and windsurfing beach, the Lanikai offers a sunny garden studio apartment with a private entrance and lanai, queen-size bed, private bath and continental breakfast for $55 a night.

Hawaiian Dream Bed and Breakfast
Tom Paseka and
Ric Custer
142 Haokea Drive
Kailua, Hawaii 96734
(808) 263-6395

In a tropical garden at Lanikai Beach, two refugees from Minnesota have created a special paradise which offers complete privacy in two charming units, a one-bedroom and a studio; for $65 and $55 a night, respectively.

Windward Bed and Breakfast
Donald Munro and
L. De Chambs
46-251 Ikiiki Street
Kaneohe, Hawaii 96744
(808) 235-1124

Under swaying coco palms overlooking Kaneohe Bay, the Windward is full of antiques and features a Victorian guest room with double bed and

Best Places to Stay

Halekulani
2199 Kalia Road
Honolulu, Hawaii
(808) 923-2311
$220–$380, suites $525–$3,000.

Nothing even comes close to Halekulani. This marbled oasis at the beach is in a league by itself. The view is inspiring, the oceanfront restaurants are romantic, the service is efficient and the staff, friendly. Everything you expect from Waikiki's only Five Diamond hotel, including price.

Moana Hotel
2365 Kalakaua Avenue
Honolulu, Hawaii
(808) 922-3111
$195–$300, suites from $525.

The oldest beach hotel in the Pacific, the Moana Hotel was built in 1901, and restored to Victorian elegance to regain its position as the "first lady" of Waikiki.

The Hawaii Prince Waikiki
100 Holomoana Street
Honolulu, Hawaii
(808) 956-1111
$180–$320, suites $400 to $2,500.

The Hawaii Prince Waikiki is a chic "big city" hotel with fine dining, a jazz club, an ocean view from every room, and excellent restaurants with Gary Strehl, one of Hawaii's best chefs, in residence.

Waikiki Joy
320 Lewers Street
Honolulu, Hawaii
(808) 921-7272
$115–$250.

Waikiki Joy is the first and, so far, best, Waikiki boutique hotel. It just got better with **Cappuccinos**, an intimate bistro featuring contemporary American cuisine by chef Ernesto Mera of Newport Beach.

Royal Hawaiian
2259 Kalakaua Avenue
Honolulu, Hawaii
(808) 325-3535
$210–$380, suites $380–$2,200.

The faded Pink Lady lives on its laurels.

private bath, swimming pool and library. Continental breakfast and afternoon tea. $55 a night.

House of Blue Ginger
Eve and Dennis Kiehn
47-504A Lulani Street
Kaneohe, Hawaii 96744
(808) 235-1124

On a hill above a harbor on Oahu's north shore, Eve and Dennis Kiehn have created a hideaway that takes its name from the exotic tropical foliage surrounding it. The Tree Top Room with king bed is $50; a Garden Room with twin bed, $45; each with private bath.

Two Oahu agencies now specialize in national and international booking of Hawaii-style bed and breakfasts:

Pacific Hawaii
Bed and Breakfast
19 Kai Nani Place
Kailua, Hawaii 96734
(808) 262-6026

Bed and Breakfast
Honolulu
3242 Kaohinani Drive
Honolulu, Hawaii 96817
(808) 595-6170

Kahala Hilton
5000 Kahala Avenue
Honolulu, Hawaii 96816
(808) 734-2211
$220–$550, suites $620–$2,200.

The Kahala Hilton is a resort unto itself.

New Otani Kaimana Beach Hotel
2863 Kalakaua Avenue
(808) 421-8795
$85–$200, suites $150–$330.

The best deal in Waikiki, the New Otani Kaimana Beach Hotel, is under the brow of Diamond Head, away from the clatter of the fun zone. This small, personal hotel by the sea attracts artists, musicians, writers and frequent visitors to the islands who appreciate the sophisticated location, moderate rates, sexy suites and the intimate Hau Tree Lanai restaurant, a perfectly romantic setting for sunset cocktails and lingering candlelight dinners by the sea.

Maui
The Wowie Island

Maui

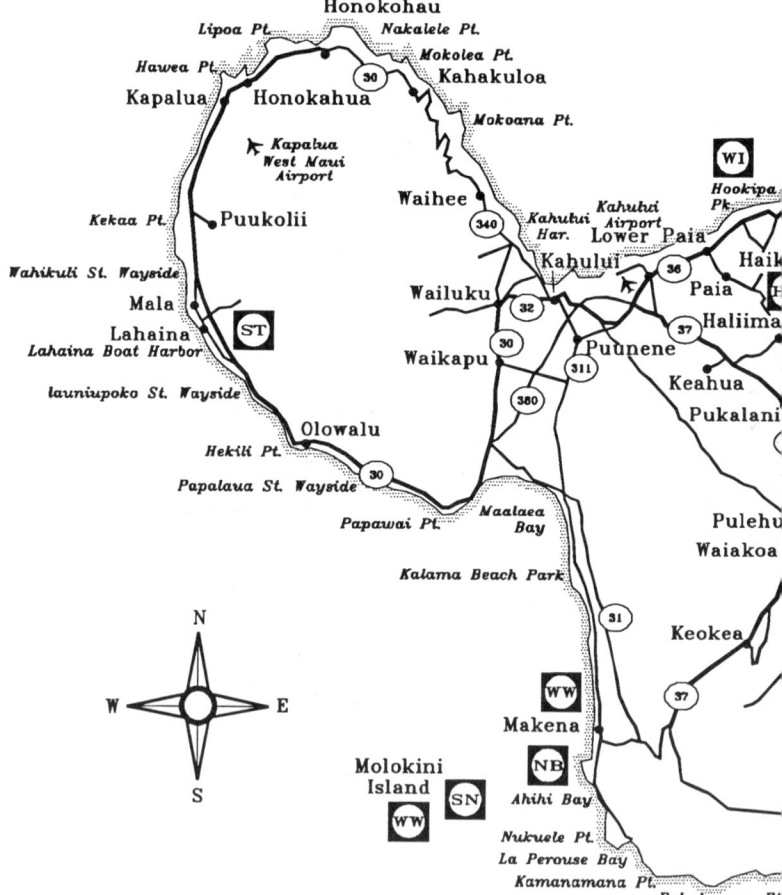

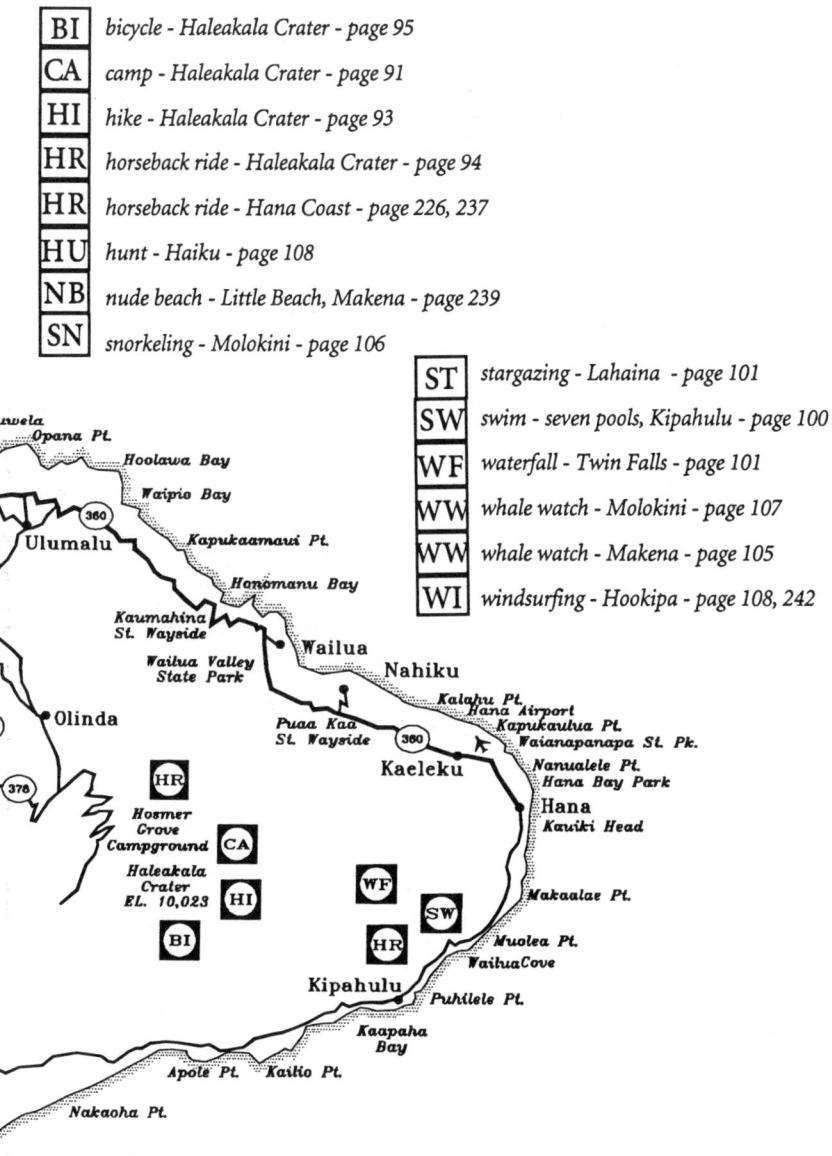

MAUI

THE WOWIE ISLAND

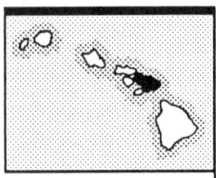

Maui
(mow-ee)

Nickname
the Valley Isle

Flower
Lokelani
cottage rose

Color
Pink

Capitol
Wailuku

Area
728.8 square miles

Population
90,000

Highest Point
Mt. Haleakala
10,023 feet

THERE is something heroic about any island named for the superman of Polynesia and the fact that he's a Pacific legend makes it all the better.

In case you've been snorkeling, Maui, the demi-god, fished up his namesake island from the bottom of the sea. He did this with quite a few other Pacific islands, too.

Only Maui calls attention to its mythical origin with a small town Chamber of Commerce slogan: *"Maui No Ka Oi."* You will hear people say it and see it printed on T-shirts. It means "none better than Maui."

While Oahu attracts the lion's share of Hawaii's seven million annual tourists, Maui likes to think of itself as the best place to be—and it is for Hollywood stars who consider Hana a tropical suburb of Beverly Hills.

Adventures on Maui are unique but one puts Maui ahead of all the other islands. It is not the twisty road to Hana, or even the sight of a whale in full breach. Waterfalls and leaping whales may be found elsewhere in the islands, but when the sun comes up at Haleakala there is nothing to compare. It is one of the world's natural wonders.

Once again, we have Maui to thank, since legend has it that he plucked the sun out of the sky as it passed overhead and placed it in the imposing crater.

You also can hike and camp inside the crater, but most people are content to look at it and take its picture.

The dormant volcano which last erupted in 1790, also serves as the key prop to a great adventure that's a real coast—a bicycle ride down the volcano.

Created by two volcanoes whose lava spill met and formed the big valley that inspires its nickname, the Valley Isle, Maui ranks second in size and popularity. It attracts two million fans a year who flock to see the sunrise, relax at the sun-drenched Kaanapali resorts, golf at championship courses and kick up their heels in Lahaina after dark.

The old whaler's and sailor's town of **Lahaina** is a working port for fishing boats, whale watch boats, sunset skippers and glass bottom boat captains bound for the Olowalu reef on the Kaanapali coast. The former Hawaiian capital of Lahaina is now a Carmel-like art colony of boutiques and bistros like Avalon and Tasca's, to name two of my favorites.

Maui was the first to create a master-planned resort zone and today, the **Kaanapali Beach Resort**, served by its own private Kapalua West Maui airport, offers Maui's best choice of top-ranked beach hotels, including the architecturally stunning

Hyatt Regency Maui with waterfalls, swan-filled lagoons and great halls filled with Asian art.

Golfers tee off at two championship courses, The Royal Kaanapali North and South, often seen on nationally televised tournaments. The Wailea, Kapalua and Makena golf courses also attract similar attention from duffers and spectators.

Once planted with sugar cane, Maui now produces its own wine and beer and an illegal leaf that contributes to the estimated $2 billion state crop of *"pakalolo"*—the Hawaiian word for marijuana, which literally means "stupid smoke," although everyone else calls it "Maui Wowie."

The higher, "up country" elevations also produce Kula onions, sweeter than Vidalias; fields of flowers and open ranchland for cattle and real Hawaiian cowboys, called *paniolos*.

Cowboys and whales, onions and art, old craters and new stars are some of the odd elements that put people in a Maui state of mind.

Just going to Maui is an adventure for most people. Once you've arrived, it's like a hardware store: everything you're looking for and some things you aren't, are all there.

Haleakala, The House of the Sun

Haleakala, The House of the Sun, is big enough to hold the entire island of Manhattan, including the Statue of Liberty. It is where America's astronauts trained for their 1969 moon landing.

The House of the Sun is the world's largest dormant volcano. It is 10,023 feet high, 3,028 feet deep, seven miles long, two miles wide and 21 miles in circumference with a total area of 33 square miles.

It used to be 12,000 feet high but millions of years of erosion have whittled Haleakala down to its present size.

Adventurers daily enter The House of the Sun to hike, camp and horseback ride. It last erupted in 1790 and is called dormant because it could go off at any time, so watch your step. If your karma's good, you'll probably make it.

The crater is home to a variety of strange things; like Hawaiian snow, a lichen that grows on *a'a* lava; the rare silversword plant *(Argyroxiphium sandwicense)*; a bubble cave big enough to sleep in; thornless Hawaiian raspberries *(Rubus hawaiiensis)*; descendants of Capt. Cook's goats; the claw-footed Hawaiian goose; a rare, dark-rumped sea bird that barks like a dog *(Pterodroma phaeopygia sandwichensis)*; tombs of ancient Hawaiians; Pele's Paint Pot, an area naturally tinted by minerals; and a bottomless pit some say extends to the sea.

You can explore great areas of 28,000-acre **Haleakala National Park,** which includes the crater, two wilderness camps and three cabins. Take a day hike, an overnight camping expedition or ride in on horseback.

One of Maui's best kept secrets is **Hosmer Grove Campground and Nature Trail** near the park headquarters at 7,000 feet.

"It's hardly ever full," said Haleakala Park Ranger Melissa England. "Nobody knows about it."

Stalking the Wild Nene

The high desert lava moonscape of Haleakala is home to two of Hawaii's most unusual native attractions that thrive in harshness—the claw-footed Hawaiian Nene goose (*Nesochen Sandvicensis*), which happens to be the endangered state bird, and the rare silver sword plant (*Argyroxiphium sandwicense*), a silvery sort of sunflower.

The Hawaiian goose is featured on the cover of *The Birds of Hawaii and the Tropical Pacific* which I highly recommend to birders. The bird has a black face, buff neck with deep furrows and claw feet. It is called Nene because of its two-syllable, high, nasal bark, *nay-nay*, which is similiar to the call of the Canadian goose, I am told.

Only about 1000 Nenes are left and they may only be seen on Maui and the Big Island of Hawaii, although I have never seen one there.

This is the best place to spend the night in a tent if you want to see the Haleakala sunrise. Tent camping also is permitted inside the crater at Paliku and Holua.

With advance planning you also may stay in one of three hike-in wilderness cabins maintained by the National Park Service inside the crater. They are **Paliku cabin**, which is at 6,380 feet; **Kapalaoa cabin**, at 7,250 feet; and **Holua cabin**, at 6,960 feet. Each cabin sleeps 12 maximum. All are in great demand from honeymooners.

To get a cabin, you've got to mail your request three months ahead of your requested dates. On the first day of each month the Haleakala park rangers hold a lottery and pull names out of a Smokey the Bear hat. If you're a winner, you get three nights in The House of the Sun. You will be notified by mail.

For cabin reservations write: Haleakala National Park, P.O. Box 369, Makawao, Hawaii 96768. There is a minimum charge of $15 per cabin, plus $3 per person for wood.

Cabins are supplied with wood, water, candles, kitchen utensils and Presto logs. Bring your own food. No open fires are allowed in the crater so bring a camp stove.

No reservations are required at two back-country campgrounds; it's first-come, first-served and permits are issued at park headquarters on the day you want to hike.

Whether you are camping or in a cabin, you may only stay a maximum of three nights. That's just the way it is.

Get prerecorded camping information by calling (808) 572-9177 or call Haleakala National Park headquarters (808) 572-9306. For the latest, prerecorded weather information in the crater, call 572-7749.

Two trails lead down to the crater floor 3,000-feet below. You may take **Sliding Sands** trailhead at the **Puu Ulaula Observatory** (10,023 feet) and head down 3.9 miles to the floor of The House of the Sun. Horse and mule pack teams enter and exit the crater at

Stalking the wild Nene—with a camera, of course—is possible at the Haleakala National Park ranger station where the geese often show at sunset. Lay prone with your camera and try to snap off a couple of shots before they run away or charge at you.

I once spent an hour flat on my stomach hidden in pili grass with my zoom lens trying to get the perfect shot of a camera-shy Nene, who kept an eye on me while making its weird goosey call; finally it flapped its wings and opened its beak, uttered something that sounded like "moo" and began to chase me. Talk about endangered! The silversword is a lot easier to photograph.

Maui 93

Halemauu Trail, a 3.9 mile switchback from park headquarters.

Most of the hikes are vigorous; you should be in good shape. Even so, your "downhill" leg muscles are going to ache the first night. Be prepared for all kinds of weather and the altitude. Remember, you are starting out nearly two miles high.

Except for day hikes, you must plan well ahead for this adventure, especially if you plan to stay overnight.

If you don't want to hoof into Haleakala, take **Charley's Trail Rides & Pack Trips**, an overnight guided horseback excursion, which travels up Haleakala's southern slopes to the crater from private stables with a professional guide.

Charley Aki, a real Hawaiian *paniolo* (cowboy), guides overnight trips into Kaupo Gap. Write him c/o Kaupo Store, Kaupo, Hawaii 96713 or (808) 248-8209. Parties of two or three, $200 a person; four to six people, $150 each. Includes meals, cabin fees, camping equipment.

✪ *Akamai Tip:* If you're already on Maui and want to camp in Haleakala, call 572-9306 *only between 1 and 3 p.m.* to check for cancellations. You may be in the crater *li'dat!*

Sunrise on Haleakala

When the sun comes up at The House of the Sun, it's one of the great natural wonders of the world. It happens at the summit of **Haleakala** where hundreds come to "embrace the gift of each day."

The best sunrise viewing spot is **Puu Ulaula Observatory**, a three-sided glass wind shelter at the very peak. Take a sweater or a parka, wear blue jeans and bring a thermos of hot coffee.

On a clear day, you can see 29.6 miles across the Alenuihaha Channel to the majestic, often snow-capped, peak of Mauna Kea on the Big Island of Hawaii.

The best way to do it is to go up the day before, pitch a tent at **Hosmer Grove Campground** (named for Ralph S. Hosmer, the first forester), spend the night at 6,800 feet, then wait for the sun to come up. You won't miss it.

Or you can get up in the middle of the night, around 3:30 a.m., and try to find your way up the mountain in the dark with a map and a flashlight.

Drive up windy Crater Road through 38 miles of climate change—from tropical to alpine—to the 10,023-foot summit. You may drive through clouds, have to slow for geese and pheasants and may even get woozy on the switchback turns. Drive straight to the **Puu Ulaula Overlook**, which is open 24 hours, offers a 360-degree view and serves as a windbreak. Wait for the dawn.

For the latest weather reports call 877-5124 or the Ranger Station at 572-7749. The Maui News also reports sunrise and sunset times daily.

Bicycling Up (or Down) Haleakala

While everyone hitches a ride up Haleakala in a van and then coasts down, a few still do it the old-fashioned way—they earn it. Now that's a great adventure.

"One of the most challenging rides in the world," said Robert ("Bicycling In Hawaii") Immler, who took eight hours to pedal 40 miles from sea level to 10,000 feet, and one hour for the downhill leg.

Take two water bottles, wear a windbreaker, use low gears. Start your assault on Haleakala at the intersection of Routes 36 and 37 near Sprecklesville. Ride through sugar cane fields to Pukalani—last stop for supplies—turn left on State Highway 377. The sugar gives way to pineapple, eucalyptus and fields of commercially grown flowers for leis.

At the midway point, about a mile high, fill your water bottles at restaurants and take a lunch break. Next water and rest rooms are available at the ranger station 10 miles and 2,500 feet higher. After lunch go left on Road 378 that twists up the mountain across Haleakala Ranch. (Be careful crossing the bone-rattling, rim-bending cattle guards.) You will ride through clouds, see ring-necked pheasant and maybe Nene, the Hawaiian state bird.

You may even see the **Spectre of Haleakala**. It's the natural phenomenon of seeing your own shadow on a cloud, surrounded by a rainbowed halo. It is said to occur only here and on Germany's Mount Brocken (where it's known as the Spectre of Brocken) under unique atmospheric conditions similar to those that combine to create rainbows. (See "Chasing After Rainbows" on Page 53).

Nobody has seen the Spectre of Haleakala for years. If you see it, take a picture and send it to me. I'll put it in the next, updated *Great Outdoor Adventures of Hawaii* under something called "Enigmas of the Pacific" and send you a free, autographed copy. We may even tell Time-Life Books.

You definitely will see the silversword, a six-foot plant that looks like an anemic artichoke plant, and, as you continue to climb, the first slagheaps of lava that last erupted out of Haleakala in 1790. At last, the summit is reached. Many outlooks offer great vistas; on a clear day you may see 100 miles. After a good rest, push off the volcano for the longest, fastest downhill ride in the world—after all, you've earned it.

❂ *If you didn't BYOB...* several Maui cycle shops rent new mountain, racing and touring bikes by the day or week, including The Island Biker (877-7744), Fun Bike Rentals (661-3053), and Paradise Pedaling Inc. (874-5303). Go Go Bikes (661-3063) offers free shuttle service.

In the Kaanapali resort district, Dollar Rent-a-Car rents bikes by the hour (two-hour minimum), day, or week. They have 15-speed mountain bikes, 12-speed racing bikes, tourers, tandems and cruisers. (808) 661-3037.

The less adventurous can simply hop on a bike and coast. Everyone who does it loves it, but me. Somehow, coasting down Haleakala on a bike doesn't make it even if you do drop 10,000 feet in 38 miles, pass through seven different climatic zones from subarctic to subtropical and hardly ever have to pedal. Somebody must like this, though, because since **Cruiser Bob's Original Haleakala Downhill** opened in 1983, he's booked more than 100,000 rides down the volcano.

His heavy-duty 19-inch Schwinn cruiser bikes with 26-inch wheels feature his own special "mega-brakes."

Best thing about Cruiser Bob's is his "weather insurance." If, for any reason, you don't like it—too many clouds, not enough oxygen—you get $1 back for every mile you didn't do.

Three Rainy Day Places on Maui

It hardly ever rains on Maui (the average annual rainfall at Lahaina is only 15 inches) except in Hana, where it rains 69 inches a year; but if it does you need to know where to find indoor adventures.

When sugar was king, Alexander and Baldwin were god. Now that the world sugar market has gone to hell, about all an old Big Five firm can do is diversify, sell off land to subdividers and open a museum. The **Alexander & Baldwin Sugar Museum**, in a 1902 plantation house at 3957 Hansen Road, sits next to Hawaii's largest and most productive sugar factory in Puunene. A visit here reveals Maui's bittersweet past before tourism. (808) 871-8058.

Makawao used to be a cowboy town, but now looks like Carmel, California on a volcano. This upcountry town of clapboards once had shops that sold saddles Dan Quayle, who finished, thought the downhill coast was the best thing about Maui. It figures.

Get up when it's still dark (an adventure for some). Ride a shuttle van 38 miles to Haleakala's summit. Get on a bike and coast down the world's longest, steepest paved road. The nearly six hour ride includes the bike, an escort, gloves and breakfast or lunch at Kula Lodge, for $92.70, including tax. Reserve a ride at Cruiser Bob's office, 505 Front St., Lahaina, Maui 96761 or call (808) 667-7717.

On the Hana Road

For many Maui visitors, the drive to **Hana** is the big adventure, the Hawaiian version of Chaucer's Canterbury Tales, and as many times as I've made the trip, it always feels like the first day of summer vacation to me.

The first time I drove to Hana almost 20 years ago, was with my uncle Ben Keau Sr., Maui-born and raised on the Keanae peninsula, and we did it Hawaii-style in a new, blue Datsun pickup with all the kids in the back, including me.

Going to Hana is great fun. The little village sits at the end of a 30-mile wiggle of a road with 600 breathtaking hairpin turns, 54 bridges, and more tropical flowers, waterfalls and coastal views than anyone can count.

It takes a day to drive round-trip (plan on three hours each way) if you stop to sniff the exotic flowers and swim in the pools—and you should—so start early.

The tropical village itself is more a state of mind, where one day seems like another, than it is a place on the map. It has a church, a school, a post office and a fancy resort where the rich and famous seek escape.

In "heavenly Hana," famed aviator Charles Lindbergh found peace (he is buried on a seacliff near the Hoomau stone church). Carol Burnett, George Harrison and Kris Kristofferson keep island retreats on the Hana coast. My first and spurs, but now it's been boutiqued into quaint shoppes with cute names, art galleries and such. If you end up in Makawao because of your mate, go directly to Casanova's at 1188 Makawao Avenue where you can sit at the open-air street-front cafe and watch the pickup trucks go by. Casanova Italian Restaurant & Deli (808) 572-0220.

When whalers hit Lahaina in the 1800s, they found strong drink, sweet-smelling girls and the tattoo parlor. You may still find them all in Lahaina, including the tattoo parlor, **Skin Deep**. The last time I stopped by, a Kona boat captain was having a shark etched on his ankle and an ex-fighter pilot from the Netherlands was getting a sea chart of the seven inhabited Hawaiian islands tattooed in four colors on his left shoulder. Drop by Skin Deep at 6266 Front Street and watch folks get etched with a lasting souvenir of Hawaii. Skin Deep Tattooing (808) 661-8531.

summer in Hana, we stayed in a big old beach house near the police station where Keith Keau then served as one of Hana's two policemen, whose chief mission seemed to be rescuing tourists in rental cars who had missed a turn while admiring the scenery.

Beyond Hana, the big adventure is attempting to swim in the **seven pools** that cascade down the mountain to the sea at Kipahulu.

That summer, I swam in five icy pools with one eye on the clouds in case of a cloudburst, shook breadfruit out of trees, ate *poi* pancakes with tree-ripe bananas from our yard, dug an *imu* for a luau of *kahlua* pig, picked *opihis* on the reef, hiked to the white cross on the hill, visited Lindbergh's grave, learned half a dozen old Hawaiian songs, made leis of flowers so bright they looked unreal, attended Sunday mass sung in Hawaiian, hiked to Red Sand beach, body-surfed at Hamoa Bay, set reef nets at sunset and plunged into the sea at sunrise to pick *pupus* of bright, tropical fish and, of course, shopped Hasegawa's General Store. It was the best of times in Hawaii, that summer in the 70s in Hana and, wonder of all, two decades later, this vestige of old Hawaii is as it was. Oh, there's been a few changes: Hasegawa's burned to the ground last year. The Hana Hotel got a $1 million face lift. There's a parking lot at Kipahulu now and by noon it's as full as a rental car lot. Wild pigs don't run across the road as often but you can still buy those juicy mangos for giveaway prices at roadside stands and everyone smiles if you do. Life in Hana is still wonderful.

From Kahului Airport, take State Highway 36 which becomes State Highway 360, a.k.a. the road to Hana.

Most people drive up and back in one day and they miss the point: the secret of the Hana road lies in what you do and who you meet along the way. Take your time, leave early in the morning (the tourist commute begins about 10 a.m.), stop by **Twin Falls**, visit the peninsula of **Keanae**, enjoy a picnic lunch at **Waikamoi Ridge** and take a hike in a bamboo forest that sings when the wind blows.

When you set out on the road to Hana, take a cooler full of beer, sandwiches, Maui potato chips and suntan lotion. Don't forget your swimsuit and beachtowel.

If you plan to spend a few days in Hana, and you should, call ahead to make reservations. For the best deal on lodging, call Zenzo and Fusae Nakamura at the Aloha Cottages ($45 and up), Box 205 Hana, Maui 96713, (808) 248-8420. Or Stan and Suzanne Collins at Hana Bay Vacation Rentals ($55 and up), Box 318, Hana, Hawaii 96713, (808) 248-7727. Or blow the budget on the Hotel Hana Maui, $335 and up. Hotel Hana Maui, Hana, Hawaii 96713, (808) 367-5224.

◉ *Akamai Tip:* Hasegawa's used to sell T-shirts that said, "I Survived the Road to Hana." You can probably find them somewhere else. If you do, don't wear them until you get home. You'd be surprised how many people in Hawaii have "survived" the Hana Road.

Stargazing in Kaanapali

Under Maui's star-spangled night sky, Brian O'Connell tapped a desktop computer and a huge telescope spun around to zoom in on the moons of Jupiter. "Welcome to recreational astronomy," said O'Connell, director of astronomy at the Hyatt Regency Maui on the Kaanapali Coast.

We stood on the roof of the nine-story seaside resort looking at the night sky with our naked eyes, waiting for a close-up look at the moon, stars and planets through the world's first "user-friendly" telescope. It's the best free show in Hawaii for hotel guests—others pay $5 to explore the heavens for 90 minutes.

"I want to expose a lot of people to space," said William Leighty, who created the first recreational telescope that looks like a big blue steel cylinder attached to a pair of binoculars linked to a desktop computer with a video game joystick. The system relies on a 16-inch diameter primary f-12 Coude'-Cassegrain reflector for its optics which are strong enough to bring the rings of Saturn into clear view.

Inventor Leighty, who earned engineering and business degrees at Stanford and took up sidewalk astronomy in San Francisco as a hobby, spent three years developing the scope with architect/designer Brent Gordon of La Jolla, California.

First shown at the 1989 American Association for Advancement of Science convention in San Francisco, the telescope made its operational debut in 1990 on Maui where the stars are bright and the climate perfect for outdoor viewing. The fact that Maui attracted more than 2 million visitors last year was also a factor, he said.

"The primary advantage to Maui observing," Leighty said, "is the benign climate, so you can sit at a telescope outdoors year-round." Maui's night sky is also free of light pollution. "The seeing is good," Leighty said, "which means things don't look wiggly through the scope."

He anchored the 150-kilogram system to the Hyatt's roof, fitted the scope to an equatorial mount and hooked up the personal computer with the video game joy stick to track the moon and stars.

Amateur astronomers now "drive" around the surface of the moon with the joystick while peering through stereo-oculars, a special eyepiece beam splitter that eliminates squinting. "There's minimum time fumbling around in the dark trying to find what you want to look at," Leighty said.

A full moon rose over the West Maui mountains the night I stood on the roof looking at the cosmos with other amateur astronomers. We took turns peering at the Milky Way, with hundreds of billions of stars; the rings of Saturn; a star cluster near Orion, and, finally, the Sea of Tranquility on the moon itself.

"The most satisfying and meaningful objects to people," Leighty said, "are the moon and Jupiter because you can see the four Galileo moons, first seen in 1608 by Galileo with a crude telescope."

"My hope," he said, "is that people will look at the stars and come away with a better understanding of who, where and what we are and then do a better job of taking care of Planet Earth and each other." Not to mention Maui.

Call the Hyatt Regency Maui at (808) 661-1234 and book a 90-minute look at the stars. Three shows nightly after sundown; it's only $5. The Hyatt Regency Maui is at 200 Nohea Kai Drive, in the Kaanapali resort area of Lahaina.

Cruising the Whales

The best way to see a whale is to take a cruise with one of the outfits that benefits whales, like **Pacific Whale Foundation**. This non-profit foundation supports its research and lobbying by offering cruises, snorkel tours and even trips to Molokini and Lanai.

They operate a 53-foot motor vessel *Whale I* and a 50-foot sailing ketch *Whale II*, and their rates for a three-hour whale watch cruise would make Moby Dick smile. Adults $30, children $15, December through May. Put your money where the whales are.

Pacific Whale Foundation, Kealia Beach Plaza, Kihei, Hawaii 96753. Call (808) 879-8811 or from the mainland tollfree 1-800-942-5322 (which spells WHALE 1-1.)

Of Whales and Maui

If the whales didn't come back to Maui each year to see the tourists, Lahaina's whaling industry would probably collapse.

No mammal on earth is celebrated in so many ways as the whale. There are whale posters, whale pins, whale T-shirts, whale jewelry, whale paintings, and whale murals, some of them quite awful. One "artist" has defaced more public buildings in the name of the whale and made more money than the best New Bedford whaler ever did.

The funny thing is that most of the 2 million people who come to Maui never see a whale. They see a spout or a splash about a mile out to sea and then they jump up and down, waving their arms and saying things like "Thar she blows!" I have seen this happen more than once in Lahaina.

If you don't see a whale, you haven't seen Maui. Don't waste your money on whale stuff, go see the real thing.

The humpback whale *(Megaptera novaengliae)* commutes to Maui from Alaska each winter and is protected as Hawaii's official state mammal. It's also the star of the annual whale watch season in the islands that begins in December and lasts, sometimes, until May.

The best way to see a humpback whale is to spot your own. You don't have to leave shore to see a spout. I once saw a whale come straight out of the water a quarter-mile off Oahu's New Otani and it stopped everyone cold.

Adult humpback whales are 45 feet long, weighing 40 tons and when they splash it looks like a 747 has hit the drink.

During their annual migration from Alaska, I watch them daily, parading a mile offshore of my beach house as they head over to Maui in November and then back up north to Alaska late in April. The whales come to Hawaii each year to give birth to a single, 2,000 pound calf, then head home. The best time to see them is between

Where to Watch the Whales

Maui:

On the **Puu Olai Cinder Cone** overlooking Makena Beach, you will have the right elevation in the right place to see whales as they dodge Molokini and cruise around Kahoolawe in the glassy calm. All you need is the right time to see the whales.

Kauai:

On the road to **Ke'e Beach** there are several turnouts at high vantage points that make good whale watch spots. If you don't see one along the road, go to Ke'e Beach and park. Walk down to the beach and on around the point, then climb up about 100 yards to a grassy knoll, known as **Laka's Hula Platform**, and have a seat. If you're here in whale season, you can't miss.

January and April from any island, but especially Maui, Kauai and Oahu.

There's no best time of day for whale watching, but I've noticed that when the sea is glassy and there is no wind, I always see more. A Scripps Institute marine biologist told me that's because whales are the only mammals without hair and they don't like wind on their body when they leap out of the water.

Once you see one, keep watching in the same vicinity; they may stay down 30 minutes. Bring a book.

The most I've ever seen in one place at one time in Hawaiian waters was in late April from the south shore of Niihau, where I spent the day snorkeling the crystal clear lagoons in search of lobster with chopper pilot Tom Mishler. Suddenly the blue water began to boil. Scores of whales began spy hopping, chin slapping, tail slapping and fluking and jumping straight out of the water. To our delight this great performance lasted more than an hour. It was a whale of a party. Tom even bagged a two-pound lobster.

Snork Molokini

It sits like a crescent moon fallen out of the sky just off the Makena coast of Maui, attracting thousands of fish who attract hundreds of snorkelers on scores of boats.

The only thing wrong with **Molokini** is the same thing that's wrong with Hanauma Bay—it's too popular.

Go early to snorkel here, catch *Kai Nani*, the first catamaran out of **Makena Beach**, and you'll have the islet all to yourself for almost 30 minutes before the Molokini fleet out of Ma'alaea Harbor drops anchor and turns this marine preserve into a churning froth of first-time gogglers.

Once everyone arrives, you are limited to exploring this submerged crater in the company of strangers, many of them quite anxious about actually getting in the water with fish. The odd thing is most neophytes spend exactly 15 minutes snorkeling (I know because I've timed them), then haul out and head for the sandwiches and cold beer on the aft deck. If you keep an eye on the divers, you may experience Molokini when there are more fish than people.

The best way to snork Molokini is to go on the *Kai Nani*, a 46-foot catamaran skippered by Sid Akiona that sails at 7:30 a.m. daily from Makena Beach in front of the Maui Prince Hotel. Call the Maui Prince at (808) 874-1111 and ask for the Ocean Activities Desk. You don't have to be a hotel guest. The five hour excursion costs $65 for adults and $40 for children 12 and under. Bring a towel and your swimsuit. Everything else—fins, mask, snorkel, boogie boards, and floats are provided. Once underway, the crew serves Continental breakfast with coffee and juice and an *apres-snorkel* buffet lunch at Molokini.

❂ *Akamai Tip:* During whale season (November to May), you may double your fun by taking a Molokini cruise since the whales like to cruise Molokini, too. I once saw 20 whales on the voyage to Molokini—at no extra charge. Go by sail and you'll see more; whales like sailboats best.

Hunting Adventures of Maui

If you want to bag a wild pig or a Spanish mountain goat, the best way on Maui is to join a "fair chase" hunting excursion on more than 100,000 acres of private ranch land out of **Haiku**.

They hunt from sunrise to sunset year-round here and everything's provided: a 4-wheel drive, guns and ammo, meat storage and packing for shipping, even taxidermy service, if you bag a trophy tusker.

Pigs and goats are a real nuisance in the islands; they'll eat the island to the waterline, so you're actually doing the right thing ecologically by shooting them. In order to save, you have to destroy. It isn't like shooting Bambi.

If hunting isn't your *kuleana* (Hawaiian for thing), you can hire a 4-wheel drive and take pictures or simply sightsee, but it won't be the same.

Fly Hookipa Beach

The aerodynamics of Maui are perfect for windsurfing. Big, wide U-shaped **Kahului Bay** acts as a funnel at the windward mouth of the isthmus which narrows and empties on **Ma'alea Bay** on the leeward side. The wind doesn't just blow here, it sucks, and those who go down to the sea with a surfboard and a sail love it.

Since the pros abandoned the fluky winds of Oahu's Kailua Bay a few years ago, **Hookipa Beach** is the Aspen of windsurfing, and home to an international jet-set that drops in to catch the 30 knot gusts in wind alley.

The wind has blown up a multi-million dollar cottage industry dedicated to the sport. Under "Windsurfing," the Maui Yellow Pages lists 58 shops dedicated to the sport, including sailmakers, mast repairs, a "ding" repair shop, lesson-rental-accommodation packages and a photographer to catch you in action.

World class professional sailors like Hugh England and Alan Cadiz will coach you on the best techniques if you aim to be a pro.

Beginners should investigate **Windsurfing Tours Maui**, which offers a three-hour lesson with equipment, a picnic lunch and round-trip hotel shuttle.

Or try **The Maui Windsurf Company**, which uses waterproof remote phones to coach students under sail and guarantees that "you will be sailing in just one lesson."

Hookipa is home base for a squadron of board sailers, known in these parts as the Maui Air Force, who get their kicks up in the air upside down. They slam head-on into waves big as whales to gain hangtime—up to five seconds in the air—before somersaulting back into the surf, usually right side up. Even if you don't try windsurfing, you'll want to catch the Maui Air Force in action.

From Kahului Airport, turn left on Kuihelani Highway (State Highway 380), go to the Y–intersection, turn left on Haleakala

Call **Hunting Adventures of Maui** at (808) 572-8214 or write them at 645-B Kaupakalua Road, Haiku, Maui 96708.

Rates are $400 first person, $200 each additional, three max (nonhunters free). Airport or hotel pick-up and drop-off.

Riding the Sugar Cane Train

Everybody should ride the **Lahaina-Kaanapali & Pacific Railroad** once, I guess. This 1890s narrow-gauge train which actually hauled sugar cane from the fields to the sugar mill, now shuttles sightseers between the Kaanapali resort area and the Lahaina tourist quarter, a distance of 12 miles.

It's a nice hour-long round-trip ride that appeals to small children, their grandparents and railroad freaks. If you're staying at Kaanapali, catch the trolley shuttle to the train station at your hotel. If you're not, you can catch the train at Lahaina station. Go down the main highway to the Pizza Hut light, come down Limahana Street, then make a right at the stop sign and drive to the cul-de-sac. Round trip: $9 adult, $4.50 children 3-12. One-way: $6, $3 children.

Road (State Highway 37) and then left on Hana Road (State Highway 32) and head for the old sugar town of Paia, now the world center of windsurfing. Hookipa Beach is on the road to Hana, about one mile past Paia town on the eastern edge of Kahului Bay's Spartan Reef.

Walking Tour of Old Lahaina

Gone are the glory days when salts came ashore for a night on the town in search of adventure after plying the Pacific in search of humpback whales. Now, tourists in small craft shoot whales with video cameras and take home whaletale trophies on gold necklaces. The *Carthaginian II*, a 19th century brig, rides at anchor on the Lahaina waterfront, the sole nautical reminder of this whaling port's rowdy past. Come, look; history is on every corner in old Lahaina.

Start the walking tour of Lahaina's historic and cultural sites at the coral block headquarters of the **Lahaina Restoration Foun-**

dation, corner of Front and Dickenson Streets. The building, Maui's oldest, served as the Master's Reading Room for sea captains in 1834.

Get the free map and walk back in time past **Government House**, the **Courthouse, Waine'e Church, Hongwanji Mission,** the **Lahaina Prison, U.S. Seamen's Hospital** and the **Seamen's Cemetery.** Several buildings serve as museums, like the two-story coral block house of Dr. Dwight Baldwin, a Protestant medical missionary; Hale Pa'i, the 1831 print shop; and the Wo Hing Temple.

Lahaina Restoration Foundation, P.O. Box 338, Lahaina, Hawaii 96761, (808) 661-3262.

Lahaina-Kaanapali & Pacific Railroad, P.O. Box 816, Lahaina, Maui, 96767, (808) 661-0080

HAWAII

BIG ADVENTURES IN PARADISE

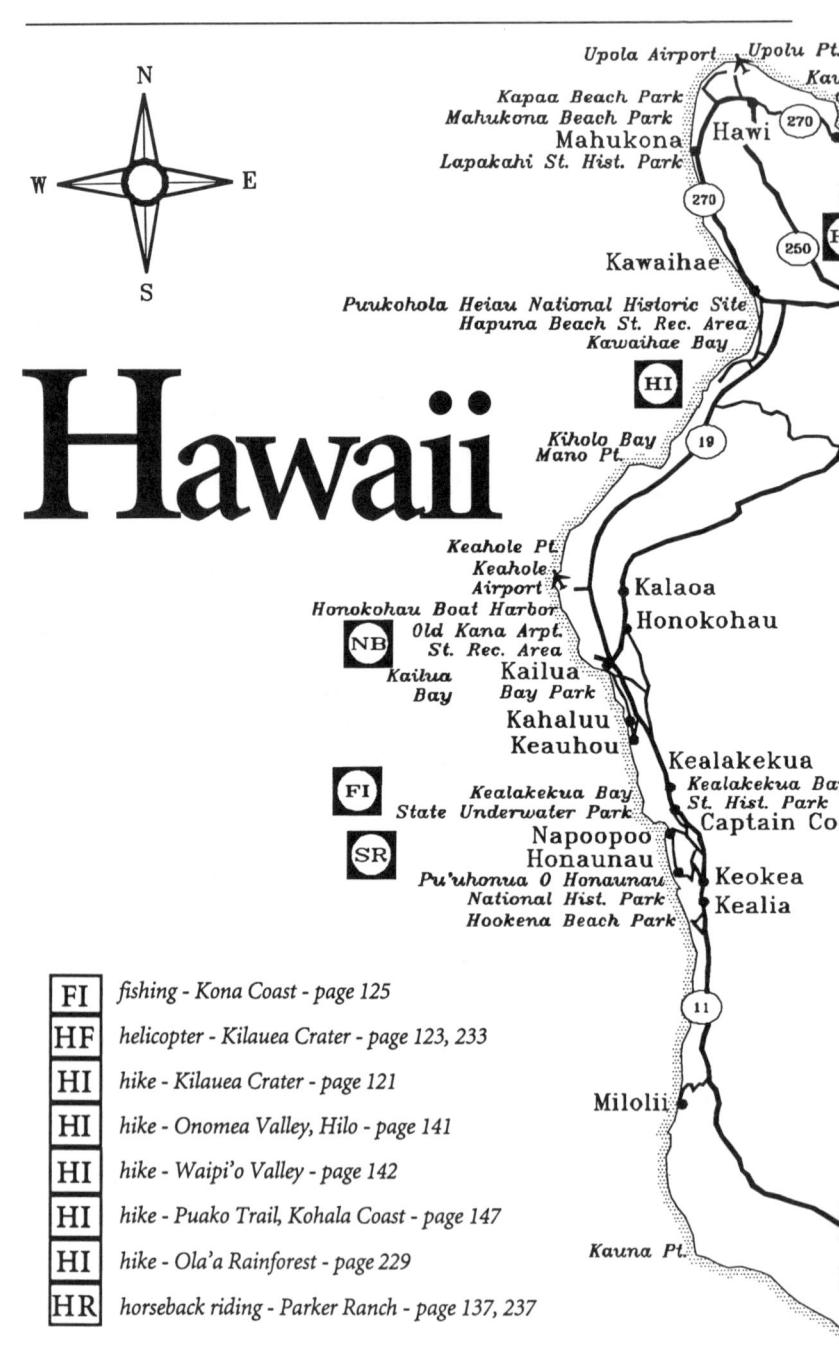

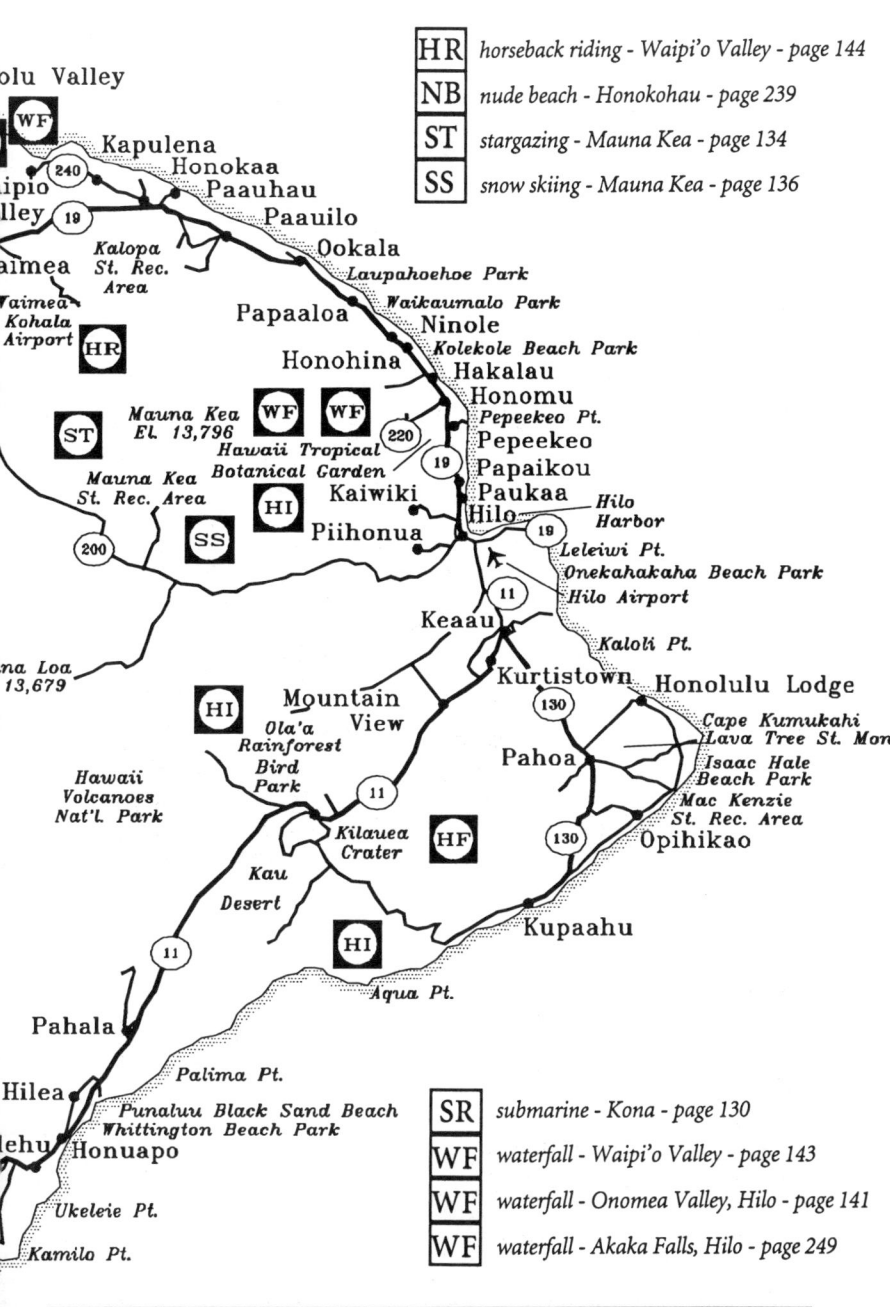

HAWAII

BIG ADVENTURES IN PARADISE

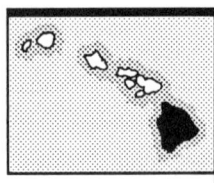

Hawaii
(ha-vi-ee)

Nickname
the Big Island

Flower
Lehua, blossom of Ohia tree

Color
Red

Capital
Hilo

Area
4,039 square miles

Population
105,000

Highest Point
Mauna Kea
13,796 feet

It is the biggest tropical island not just in Hawaii but the whole Pacific, if you don't count New Zealand and Australia, and I don't.

The Big Island is best described in superlatives. It is nearly twice the size of all the other Hawaiian islands combined (4,039 square miles with 300 miles of coastline); it has the state's highest peak, Mauna Kea (elevation 13,796); and the nation's biggest private ranch, the 225,000 acre Parker Ranch.

It grows the most exotic flowers (proteas, anthuriums and orchids) and tropical produce (papayas, macadamia nuts and coffee) and is home of the Wao Kele O Puna, the last endangered lowland rainforest in the United States.

It has the greatest number of climatic zones in one place (12); the world's most observatories (nine nations are represented at Space City observatories); and the world's biggest telescope, the W.H. Keck, which is 33 feet in diameter.

The Big Island has the most volcanoes (five), including Kilauea, the most active on earth. Still forming, the Big Island is the youngest in the Pacific.

The first surprise as you fly into Kailua-Kona airport is that the Big Island looks like hell—a scorched earth landscape of lava cinders that belong in a BBQ pit. On days when *vog* and *laze* (the two descriptive words used for volcanic emissions) are in the air, a kind of gloom takes over "like campfires of a great army far away" and the whole place appears to be something out of Dante's infernal imagination.

The source of all this eeriness is Kilauea Volcano which since 1983 has churned up 650,000 cubic yards of lava daily. This is enough lava, as my Hawaii geophysicist pal Fred Duennebier once figured out, to build a four-foot-wide, four-inch-deep sidewalk from Honolulu to New York in two days.

Some people come to chase marlin, others to enjoy "the huge sluttish pleasures of Hawaii's Nipponized beachfront hotels," but the volcano, which daily gives birth to the newest land on earth, is, perhaps, the greatest natural attraction and source of adventure in the islands.

And now a second one is erupting, out of sight, under the sea, but erupting just the same. Hawaii's newest volcano, Loihi, is bubbling up from the 3,000-foot depths of the sea 23 miles southeast of the Big Island. A dimple in the sea floor venting lava, it may join the island chain, oh—in 50 to 100,000 years or so. While everyone waits, there are plenty of other adventures.

The Big Island hosts golf tournaments, a $1 million billfish tournament and Hilo's annual three-day hula contest, the Merrie Monarch Festival.

Super athletes run/swim/bike around the Big Island at the three-day Ultraman endurance challenge while ordinary mortals march into Halemaumau, the bubbling cauldron at the center of Chain of Craters road, hike hellish Devastation Trail or explore the evergreen Wao Kele O Puna rainforest.

Gazing at the Volcano

Forget Yellowstone, even Yosemite, this park's got something going for it, namely the world's most active volcano. You can have Old Faithful and Half Dome, **Hawaii Volcanoes National Park** is happening.

Hawaii Volcanoes National Park is 250,000 acres of wilderness that is still being created by a live volcano that has erupted 27 times since 1920. There are 19 miles of roads and hiking trails, some periodically covered by hot lava; three volcanoes, two endangered rain forests, and an historic old hotel on the rim of **Halemaumau crater** that looks like something dreamed up by Dante. This is one national park not to miss.

Since 12:31 a.m., January 3, 1983, the beginning of **Kilauea's** current eruption, lava has flowed from the summit caldera on the southeast rift zone seven miles into the Pacific Ocean at **Apua Point.**

On March 25, 1984, **Mauna Loa** began to erupt and five days later Kilauea resumed fountaining. It was the first time in 116 years both Kilauea and Mauna Loa erupted at the same time.

Madame Pele, as Hawaii's volcano goddess is reverently known, has created more than 75 square miles of new island and a new, bigger black sand beach, a half mile long and 25 yards wide, at **Kamoamoa** where molten lava meets the cooler sea.

She also has destroyed 74 homes and caused more than $20 million damage. Nothing is sacred. Lava has forced the removal of the Painted Church, smothered the National Park Visitors Center, consumed the village of Kalapana, destroyed the old black sand beach and is inching toward the Waha'ula Heiau, built in the 13th century by the Polynesian navigator Pa'ao, who, incidentally, introduced human sacrifice at the temples.

Hawaiians believe the volcano is the work of Pele, the goddess of fire, who creates and destroys. They bring her gin, mostly Gilbeys, to slake her thirst, an arcane custom that challenges the faith of Martini lovers all.

I am happy to report that a more contemporary sacrifice is now accepted here; mere flowers or ti leaves well-placed often will suffice. I am told that they used to toss young and beautiful maidens into the volcano but such wastefulness seems so un-Polynesian that I think this to be an impractical Hollywood invention. Whatever, the volcano continues with alacrity, despite all offerings, including gin.

Of all America's national parks, this one's my favorite; it's got Fourth of July fireworks everyday, some of the weirdest landscape this side of the moon, a real tropical rain forest full of exotic birds called honeycreepers, no long lines of cars waiting at the toll booth and best of all—the cheapest tickets in the nation. I don't know how they do it.

A'a, Pahoehoe and Vog Explained

A'a and *pahoehoe* have entered vulcanology's lexicon. They are the Hawaiian words for molten lava.

A'a is crinkly and broken and looks like a melted parking lot. *Pahoehoe* is shiny and smooth and looks like devil's food cake frosting.

Vog is the hazy volcanic smog that is made up of volcanic gas and smoke from forests set on fire by lava.

Three Great Volcano Books

Volcanoes in The Sea by Gordon Macdonald, Agatin Abbott and Frank Peterson, University of Hawaii Press, 1983.

Volcano Watching by Robert and Barbara Decker, Hawaii Natural History Association, 1984.

Road Guide to Hawaii National Park by Barbara and Robert Decker, Double Decker

There are many things to do here. You can drive through it, hike it, smell it, or just stand there with your mouth open and watch it burn. There's nothing like it anywhere on earth.

Yet only 1.8 million people checked in at the **Kilauea Visitor Center** last year and those numbers are probably skewed since I know several people who went three or four times.

You have to because it keeps changing all the time. The Chain of Craters Road dead ends in a lava bed, a whole town disappears, things like that.

Make of that what you will, but make sure you see Kilauea. Forget maidens. Bring a bottle of gin, if you believe. Or to soothe your soul, if you don't.

The first surprise is this: volcanoes stink. They smell like rotten eggs. No matter, Kilauea, the earth's most active volcano, is one of Hawaii's main attractions today. You can fly over it in a helicopter, sail by it on a ship, or hike to the red hot burning edge of Earth. Forget your flip-flops, they'll melt down in place.

From Hilo Airport (General Lyman Field), take the Airport Road to Kanoelehua Avenue which becomes Hawaii Belt Road (State Highway 11). Drive 28 miles up to Volcanoes National Park. Admission is $5 a car or $2 per person, walk–in or drive–in. A $15 annual pass is good for all Hawaii State Parks. (808) 967-7311.

To see the volcano by foot, it's a hot and sweaty, strenuous 1.5 mile hike across two-year-old lava beds to the coast near **Apua Point**.

From the Park entrance, take **Crater Rim Road** around the yawning crater of Halemaumau to **Chain of Craters Road**; it's the junction on the right. Drive 30 miles to the end of Chain of Craters Road where the trailhead begins. It's a mile and a half to the viewing area—200 yards from the action.

Is it safe? "Yes and no," a Volcanoes National Park Ranger told me. "You just never know."

More than 1,000 people a day hike to the viewing area, which is

Press, Mariposa California, 1986.

Volcano Videos

The Hawaii volcano video market is erupting; there are more than a dozen Kilauea videos out now. The best on film are *VolcanoScapes I* and *VolcanoScapes II*, photographed by Emmy Award-winning Mick Kalber. *VolcanoScapes II* includes the incredible underwater sequence by Sharkbait Productions that shows red hot molten rock growing snakelike in the sea.

Available for about $29.95 (prices vary) at Honolulu Books, most hotel gift shops, or write Tropical Visions Video Inc., 62 Halaulani Place, Hilo, Hawaii 96720.

Hawaii

Thurston Lava Tube

The Thurston Lava Tube is a natural wonder created by a volcano that will amaze and delight those who like to explore dark, dank subterranean places. Lava tubes are formed when liquid lava, called *pahoehoe* even by vulcanolgists, cools on its surface but pressure continues and the liquid center runs out, leaving a hollow cylinder.

Inside, you feel, as Victoria Nelson wrote in "My Time in Hawaii," like you are "traveling up the intestinal tract of an extremely large fossilized creature of unknown species."

These tubes are so large, early Hawaiians used them as refuge caverns during wars and battles. It is believed that King Kamehameha, whose burial sight has never been found, may be entombed in a lava tube–who knows?–either on Lanai, where he kept a summer place, or on the Big Island where one near the old Visitor Center that was consumed by lava in 1989.

When the wind is offshore and the plumes of smoke lean out to sea, the viewing is spectacular. You can see chunks of new earth erupting out of the fiery volcano. Best time to go is after sundown. Bring a flashlight. Respect all signs, stay on the trail, bring a canteen of water, wear sturdy boat shoes; volcanic steam makes the trail slick. Bring binoculars.

If you plan to shoot pictures, pack a zoom lens and a tripod. The earth shakes a lot here. So will you.

Call Volcanoes National Park to get the current volcano eruption update. Call (808) 967-7977 for 24-hour recorded information on the volcano. Or Volcanoes Park Headquarters at (808) 967-7311.

These volcano eruption updates are unlike any weather report you have ever heard. The day I called, it went like this: "Lava is entering the ocean at Apua Point about a mile east of the established trail from Chain of Craters Road. There are visible lava fields. Conditions may change."

To see the volcano by air, go by chopper, not fixed-wing aircraft, for three reasons: you can get *real* close—within 10 feet—to all the action, you see more and there's less turbulence. Sure, a chopper costs more but you didn't come to Hawaii to save bucks. Or get air sick. Take a chopper. It's the closest you can get to Madame Pele without burning in hellfire.

Every Big Island helicopter agency offers daily flights over the volcano. All are about the same price. The biggest and best, Papillon, is my choice. It has four flights daily at 7 a.m., 9:30 a.m., 12:30 p.m. and 3 p.m. Go early, when skies are clear.

You can also see the volcano by sea. "If you don't have a volcano in your back yard and most of us don't," the late Captain Donald D. Bennett used to tell his passengers aboard the *S.S. Constitution*, "then you won't want to miss this." This is, for most, one of those once-in-a-lifetime adventures.

of the biggest lava tubes contains skeletons of ancient Hawaiians that even Bishop Museum archaeologists dare not touch. Apparently there are all sorts of *kapus* and political reasons not to.

All islands in Hawaii have lava tubes, but the Big Island's Thurston Lava Tube in Hawaii Volcanoes National Park is the most famous. You might want to have a look.

From Park Headquarters of Volcanoes National Park, take Crater Rim Road 1.8 miles to a parking lot and the trail head by the Interpretive Display and a bench. The 0.3-mile loop trail takes you up stairs through a fern forest full of red birds, to the dank cavern where ohia tree roots dangle from the ceiling, past blind albino insects, until you re-enter the real world out the lava tube's skylight.

It happens, volcano willing, every Tuesday around midnight when the 682-foot *Constitution* and her sister ship, the *S.S. Independence*, pass a half mile off the black lava coast where Kilauea volcano erupts into the sea, one of the greatest natural shows on earth.

"You are eyewitness to a living, breathing history, science and geography class," says Christiane Walsh, director of passenger services. "There's fire in the sky, the land and the sea."

It's the best free show in Hawaii. The cruise, of course, is extra—$1,000 to $3,000 a week, depending on accommodations.

The *Constitution* and *Independence* are the only two American flagships cruising Hawaii's waters and the Big Island's volcano coast.

Each ship makes a one-week cruise to the islands of Oahu, Maui, Kauai and Hawaii. For information: American Hawaii Cruises, 550 Kearny St., San Francisco, California 94108, (800) 227-3666.

On the edge of Kilauea crater, **Volcano House** is an old granddad of a lodge which drew big crowds in the 1920s when Halemaumau was a bubbling cauldron. The chilly lodge, which still heats its rooms with volcanic steam, is a major stop for tour bus travellers. You may want to stop for a cup of coffee or something stronger at **Uncle George's Lounge** (opens at 5 p.m.) and take in the great view of Kilauea.

Volcano House, P.O. Box 53, Volcanoes National Park, Hawaii 96718, (808) 967-7321. Rooms $75 to $125.

Volcano Bed & Breakfast, a three-bedroom country inn, is one of the most popular Big Island bed and breakfasts thanks to island-born hosts Jim Pedersen and his wife, Sandy, who dispense local lore and serve a full breakfast. $50 and $55 a night. In the village of Volcano, it's on Keonelehua Street, the third street mauka of Highway 11.

Volcano Bed and Breakfast, P.O. Box 22 Volcano, Hawaii 96785. Telephone: (808) 967-7779. Fax: (808) 967-7619.

The **Kilauea Lodge and Restaurant** is a 52-year-old, 11-room lodge and cottage operated by Albert Jeyte, an ex-Hollywood makeup artist for *Magnum P.I.* It offers pleasant overnight lodging and breakfast for house guests only. Open to the public for dinner from 5:30 to 9 p.m. $75 and $95 for a cottage and a honeymoon suite. One block off Highway 11 on Volcano Road.

Kilauea Lodge and Restaurant, P.O. Box 116 Volcano, Hawaii 96785. (808) 967-7366.

In Search of Great Blues

"I know about myself and why I troll for marlin. It is a rite, a chosen boredom that can be electrified by intense excitement; a catnap bursting into pandemonium with the strike; the taste of cold beer from bottles; deliciousness of slapped-together sandwiches; conquest, many things...."

Ed Sheehan

Out of **Honokohau Harbor** at sunrise, the water is smooth as blue glass and it gives no clue to what lies ahead, out there in the deep cold water in the always June weather off the **Kona Coast**.

Take A Free Kona Coffee Break in Kona

If beer always tastes better at the brewery, imagine what coffee tastes like fresh from the tree.

Sample fresh roasted Kona coffee at the Royal Kona Coffee Mill and Museum in South Kona from 8:30 a.m. to 4:30 p.m. Admission is free at this old coffee plantation which has been tweaked into a museum, souvenir shop and coffee bar.

On the way to Captain Cook, just above Kealakekua Bay, take Napoopoo Road off Highway 11 in South Kona. Call (808) 328-2511 for information.

○ *Akamai Tip:* Join the java jubilee every November at the Kona Coffee Cultural Festival, an old-fashioned weeklong county fair celebrating caffeine with food and crafts, coffee-picking contests and the coronation of Miss Kona Coffee Queen.

There are other fishing grounds in other places—Mexico's Sea of Cortez, and the Great Barrier Reef of Australia—but day in and day out, nothing anywhere can match the action that lies just below the mirror-like surface here.

It all has to do with the volcano which blew out of the Pacific floor 500 million years ago, leaving an underwater slope that finds its roots nearly four miles deep on the ocean floor. In that cold vastness big pelagic fish roam at will, following currents and thermal bands in such close proximity to shore that a fast boat like a Bertram or Hatteras under a smart captain can find the marlin stream in under 10 minutes.

Other elements combine to make Kona such a prime fishing ground—seas are small, the wind light and the weather summer-like year-round.

This rare combination of geologic and meteorologic features on the Big Island's southwest coast has earned Kona the title of blue marlin capital of the world since 1934, when Captain Charlie Finlayson first took anglers out all day for $25.

"If you want to catch fish," says Captain Tom Armstrong, "it doesn't get any better than Kona." They catch Pacific blue marlin daily off the Kona Coast but the best months are January through September, according to Captain Armstrong, who has fished the Kona coast since 1959. The best months are June, July, and August. The worst month is October.

The largest marlin caught off Kona to date was a 1,649-pound monster hooked aboard skipper Bart Miller's boat *Black Bart* on May 16, 1984.

The only decision any day is whether to go north to OTEC or to "the grounds"—south to C buoy or VV buoys or go out to F buoy or the current line.

A kind of nautical commute occurs just after dawn as charter boats with names like *Bill Collector, Li'l Hooker* and *Catchem!* race out of the harbor on half and full day runs to destinations decided by captains who read the day and rely on knowledge gained in daily pursuit of big fish. The right bait and a little luck never hurts.

In the morning calm, you'll hear the fishermen chattering friendly and nervously to each other. They sound like high school boys discussing stolen kisses, only most of these old boys have been kissed before and they are looking for something wetter and wilder.

A hookup can happen anytime; this time it happens while trolling to Captain Cook. It has happened to me before in the Sea of Cortez and on the Kona coast and there is no greater adrenaline rush. It just never fails.

Serious anglers come to Kona with three goals: set a world record, catch a "grander", a fish over 1,000 pounds, and win the International Billfishing Tournament.

In 1986, Gil Kramer did it all with one fish, a 1,062-pound marlin, aboard the *Ihu Nui,* under the helm of Freddy Rice, who is something of a legend in Hawaii.

In the last 20 years, more than 40 "granders"—20 tons of fighting fish—have been nailed off Kona. The names of the victors are etched in brass under their photographs on Grander's Wall, a local monument to sportfishing on Alii Drive's Waterfront Row, a crate and barrel shopping center with a good early-morning coffee bar.

Some come to Kona looking for a "grand slam"—a blue, black and striped marlin all in one day. It happened aboard Kona Captain Bill Casey's charter boat *Pacific Blue.* Others come to Kona seeking the rite of passage to manhood, for nothing separates man from boy like a big fish in Kona.

When the sun is low, the boats return and some fly triumphant flags from the halyards that call attention to the catch of the day. The monsters are hung by their tails and weighed on the **Kailua Pier** in town and at the **Kona Marlin Center** in Honokohau Harbor.

Real sportsmen and sportswomen tag and release these magnificent fish so they can live to fight another day, but trophy hunters still claim their catch for wall mounts and International Game Fish Association record seekers need a "proof-of-catch" photo after an official weigh-in.

Whether you are a novice or an experienced angler, it's easy to charter a boat and fish Kona. You don't even need a license.

There are two types of charter—private or share. If a private charter costs $500 a day, a share will cost you one–sixth of that (about $80) since most big boats take only six passengers. You can go half or full-day, most go full.

Rates vary by size of boat and crew; while most boats have a captain and crew, vessels vary in size from 24 foot to 54 foot. Twin engines cost more than a single. The bigger the boat the bigger the engines.

Book directly with the vessels or at any fishing activity desk in Kona. Don't waste time shopping for a deal. All agencies work together to get as many people out on the boats on any day.

Kona boats provide ice, coolers, tackle and bait. Most boats use top of the line Penn or Fin Nor tackle and custom rods. If you've got your own gear, let the captain know and he'll see if you've got the right stuff. Most Kona boats are well equipped to catch big fish.

Wear a swimsuit or shorts and a T-shirt. Wear rubber-soled boat shoes so you don't scar the boat deck. Bring a camera, sunglasses, a cap or visor, your lunch and beverage. No hard liquor, please. Beer and wine are okay. Some boats provide lunch and beverage, so ask.

If you just want to see a marlin, go to Honokohau Harbor between 11 a.m. and noon or between 3:30 and 5:00 p.m. any day of the week for the marlin weigh-ins at Kona Marlin Center.

From Kailua village, go north three miles on Queen Ka'ahumunu Highway (State Highway 19), look for the entrance to the harbor on the left, take South Inner Harbor Board to the left and head for the Kona Marlin Center across from the Harbor Master's office. Look for the Texaco sign. A deli packs box lunches and sells beer, soda, film, sunscreen and other important stuff everyone usually forgets. Open 6 a.m. to 6:30 p.m. seven days a week. (808) 329-7529.

Dive with Sharks

If you want to dive with sharks without getting cold and wet and scared, this is the only way.

Atlantis Submarines does a night dive from **Kona** that's both safe and interesting from several different view points. You submerge in the 65-foot sub to 108 feet below the surface just before sunset, so you can observe the diurnal/nocturnal changes: the day-time fish nod out and the night shift takes over. Then, the real adventure begins. Above you, on a surface boat, a deck hand starts chumming marlin bellies and out of the deep come the creatures of darkness—six to eight foot sharks and a barracuda everyone calls Barry.

Some nights a 40-foot-long whale shark glides into view and blanks out the 13 port holes on either side of the sub. You may also see octopus, free-swimming eels, huge ulua and other deep water predators on this, the only night dive in a sub in Hawaii.

The Atlantis sub departs from Kailua-Kona Pier at 5:30 p.m. nightly. It costs $74 for adults, $48 for children who, by Coast Guard safety regs, must be at least 36-inches tall. Meet at the ticket office in the Hotel King Kamehameha lobby. Call (808) 329-6626 for reservations.

Best Place to See the *Humuhumunukunukuapua'a*

At **Kealakekua Bay** on the Big Island of Hawaii, of course. The *humuhumunukunukuapua'a* was proclaimed the official state fish of Hawaii in 1986 but it may be in danger of losing its official status. Some complain it has no claim to fame except that it's cute, fun to say and is featured in a *hapa-haole* song.

The words to the song were written in 1925 by Tommy Harrison and Bill Cogswell, based on an old pop melody entitled, "Back In Hackensack, New Jersey."

The Hawaiian version was first sung on the 4th of July, 1933, at the Kona canoe races. It didn't become nationally famous until Los Angeles bandleader Ted Fio Rito at the Ambassador Hotel's Coconut Grove ballroom played it on his radio show later that year. The song became one of the all-time most popular *hapa-haole* songs. The fish appears in the last lyric, which goes like this: "*I want to go back to my little grass shack in Kealakekua, Hawaii, where the humuhumunukunukuapua'a goes swimming by.*"

From Keahole Airport, drive 18 miles south on Queen Kaahumanu Highway (State Highway 19) which becomes Kuakini Highway (State Highway 11) to the Napoopoo turnoff at the Manago Hotel in Captain Cook. Take the narrow road down to the beach park on the southern crescent of Kealakekua Bay, which is a State Historical and Underwater Park and Marine Life Conservation District.

Going to the Summit

You can't get higher in Hawaii than Mauna Kea, the Everest of the Pacific, which looms 13,796 feet (4,205 meters) above sea level—more than two and a half miles high!

The rest of the mountain is 19,680 feet *below* water. The *Guinness Book of World Records* calls it "the world's tallest mountain measured from its submarine base (3,280 fathoms) in the Hawaiian Trough to peak... with a combined height of 33,476 feet, of which 13,796 feet are above sea level."

This majestic snow-capped volcano whose Hawaiian name means "white mountain," last erupted more than 3,600 years ago and has never been declared extinct, so the possibility still exists.

If you are going to the top of Hawaii, be prepared for the altitude and the cold. Bring sunglasses to avoid snow blindness and sunscreen and lip balm; the extra ultraviolet burns quickly. Bring more clothes than you think you need.

It may be 82 degrees and sunny at the beach but up there it's probably snowing. Weather conditions change radically at two miles high and deteriorate to 20 degree temperatures, 70 miles per hour winds and blowing snow. Expect high winds, freezing fog and snow. Be prepared.

Air at the summit is very thin. Most people will feel short-term effects, such as light-headedness,

Prep for the Summit

To go to the summit, for your comfort and safety you should have:

wool hat
mittens or gloves
thermal Long Johns (top and bottom)
wool sweater
windproof parka
sturdy walking shoes & wool socks
sun screen & lip protection
dark sunglasses

Stay Warm. Layer up. T-shirt, sweatshirt, wool shirt, parka. You can always take extra clothes off but you cannot put them on if you don't bring them.

Star Watch on Mauna Kea

At 9,000 feet, the stars above the Big Island gleam like the Hope diamond. The air is cold and clean and the stars are so bright you almost need sunglasses. Just 4,000 feet below the world's largest telescope on the slopes of Mauna Kea, Eddie Mahoney, an ex-college professor who serves as the astronomy manager at the Hyatt Regency Waikoloa, brings the heavens down to earth five nights a week.

He's the informed host of one of the most fun adventures you can have on the Big Island after dark. He calls it "Starwatch." It's an exploration of the Hawaii night sky from Mauna Kea, one of the best star gazing spots on earth because of the clear, high-altitude, mid-ocean air. While the skies darken, he builds a fire, unwraps a picnic and sets up a telescope to view the galaxies. Bring parkas or blankets; baby, shortness of breath, headaches, increased frequency of urination, increased flatulence and dehydration. Scuba divers must wait at least 24 hours after their last dive before heading for the summit.

Children under 16, people with heart, respiratory and severe overweight conditions and pregnant women are advised not to go higher than the **Onizuka Center for International Astronomy's Visitor Information Station** which is 9,300 feet above sea level. Gas, food and supplies are not available on Mauna Kea.

The road to Mauna Kea begins at the 28-mile marker of the **Saddle Road** (across from the hunter's check station) and leads north to the summit. You will reach the Onizuka Visitor Information Center 8.5 miles below the summit.

The center, which opened in 1989, is named in the memory of Hawaii's only astronaut, Ellison Onizuka, who was killed in the Challenger space shuttle explosion.

Official summit tours are free and conducted by the University of

Hawaii's Institute for Astronomy every Saturday and Sunday at 2:30 p.m. at the university's 88-inch telescope on the summit. If you plan to go, stop at the VIS at least 45 minutes before the tour to get directions and a report on road conditions. You can reach the VIS in conventional automobiles, but anyone traveling to the summit (including on the tours) must have their own four-wheel drive vehicles to reach the summit.

On weekends, the **Visitor Information Center** hosts an educational program, followed by stargazing until 9 p.m. on Fridays and 10 p.m. on Saturdays (weather permitting) using an 11-inch Celestron telescope. Children are encouraged to participate.

The center is open Friday through Monday year-round; it is closed Tuesday through Thursday. Call ahead for information at (808) 961-2180. There is no admission charge for any programs.

Some of you, with no desire to be caught in a tropical blizzard, may feel more comfortable on a it's cold up there. Hot chocolate served with the cosmos.

This is free, if you are a guest at the Hyatt Regency Waikoloa. Otherwise, call Kim Marshall at the Activities Desk (808) 885-1235 and tell her you've come all the way from Oshkosh and that you'll only be on the island one night and you really want to see the stars and I'll bet they make a special deal for you.

Hawaii 135

guided tour. The best is called **Summit Tours**, a six-hour, $75 trip in a four-wheel drive with an experienced mountain guide who even serves a picnic lunch. Tours leave Parker Ranch Shopping Center in Kamuela. For reservations call (808) 775-7121 or write P.O. Box 5128, Kukuihaele, Hawaii 96727.

Hawaii is the home of the world's largest telescope. The **W.H. Keck telescope**, which is 33 feet in diameter and has 36 mirrors, is now in place at **Space City** at the peak of 13,796–foot Mauna Kea on the Big Island. A second telescope, similar in size, soon will join the Keck, giving the peak two big eyes to peer into the cosmos.

Ski Hawaii

I know a ski area where only a couple hundred skiers go each year. They have 100 square miles of snow all to themselves, with five–mile–long runs on four to six feet of fresh powder six months out of the year.

No tropical resort in the world can offer skiing except Hawaii, thanks to **Mauna Kea** which is usually snow-capped from Thanksgiving to Memorial Day, and sometimes until the Fourth of July.

This is the stuff of real adventure as skiing starts at the 13,796-foot summit where there's 38 percent less oxygen. Oh, and don't forget your swim suit because if you're like most Hawaii skiers, you'll snorkel a coral lagoon in the afternoon. That's called "ski to the sea."

Chris Langan, Hawaii's only licensed ski guide, came out to the islands 13 years ago from Jackson Hole, Wyoming, saw snow on top of Mauna Kea, rubbed his eyes at what appeared to be a tropical mirage, then wondered if you could ski the volcano.

Now, he guides a select few down the slopes each year. You can ski Mauna Kea without a guide, but you must get a permit. The best time to ski Hawaii is usually February, when the annual "Presidents' Cup" ski race is held over Presidents' Day weekend. Skiers come from all over the world to compete in this unusual event.

Write Chris Langan at Ski Guides Hawaii, P.O.Box 1954, Waimea, Hawaii 96743 or call him at (808) 885-4188.

Horseback Riding Way, Way Out West

To ride across this ranch is to be lost in time and space; it looks familiar and foreign all at once, stretching as it does from sunrise to sunset under the volcano out here west of the moon. Cows and tuff cones, longhorns amid lava—it all mixes up on the Big Island of Hawaii where the first cowboys rode herd on wild Mexican longhorns introduced by a well-meaning Brit.

The year was 1793. Explorer George Vancouver delivered seven randy head of cattle to King Kamehameha I as a gift that quickly got out of hand. These cows, warm and content under the tropical sun, ate everything in sight. By 1832, a worried King Kamehameha III, eyewitness to vast roaming, ravaging herds of longhorns consuming his kingdom, sent an ambassador to California to find something called cowboys to teach young Hawaiian boys the fine art of a rowdy new occupation that could bring cows to heel.

The cowpokes who came out west to Hawaii to deal with the problem were Mexicans, from Baja, California; Spanish-speaking *vaqueros* known as *espaniolas*, but Hawaiians quickly changed the unpronounceable word to *paniolos*.

The name stuck and so did the real old west traditions—braided rawhide lariats and unique, high-horned Mexican saddles with special pegged rigging for work on rugged lava slopes.

Paniolos added their own local style—colorful shirts and wide-brimmed hats with woven flower leis—and embraced this new adventure with the same zeal their ancestors took to canoes.

While Hawaii's *paniolos* roped, branded and held roundups like their cowboy counterparts "back east," their daily duties took unusual turns, especially when it came time to ship cattle to market.

First, the cattle were herded into the surf or lassoed and dragged through shark-infested waters to waiting longboats to be towed beyond the coral reefs. There, anchored steamers hoisted each cow in a sling for the final journey to Oahu. All this was done by *paniolos* on horseback.

Roundups by sea ended in the early 1950s as technology changed the profession, but Hawaii's cowboys still ride the range on the **Parker Ranch**, the world's largest privately owned ranch, a 227,000-acre spread under the volcano in the middle of the sea.

Now, the Parker Ranch is open to guided trail rides. Excellent horses are available at **Mauna Kea Stables** for guided trail rides over scenic Parker Ranch uplands. You do not have to be a guest at the hotel. Call (808) 882-7222.

The horses are available from 9 a.m. to 3 p.m. daily except Sundays and reservations must be made at the hotel's travel desk, which also arranges a shuttle to the stables. Children must be eight years or older. Rates are $26.50 a person for the first hour of ride, $48 a person for a two hour ride. Guides are provided on all rides so you don't get lost on the Parker Ranch.

The trail begins at the cool 3,000-foot elevation; wear long pants, boots, long-sleeved shirts and a jacket.

◎ *Akamai Tip:* Each year at the tail end of August, Big Island *paniolos* hold a rodeo that is the Western-most of them all. Calf-roping, wild cow milking, bull riding and a horse race relay are a few of the events held during the big Parker Ranch Round-up. Contact Elaine Scott at (808) 885-7311 for information on how to see it.

The Ultraman: World's Greatest Endurance Adventure

While the rest of America stuffs itself with turkey and watches televised football games over Thanksgiving weekend, a select group of international athletes is testing the outer limits of human endurance.

Forget Marine Corps boot camp, big city marathons, "Ironmans," and all other physical challenges. This international athletic event of epic stamina is the most beastly endurance test known to humans.

Each year, on the day after Thanksgiving, a small band of otherwise normal men and women from around the world gather in Kailua-Kona to engage in a three-day 320-mile event, begun in 1983 by ex-jock Curtis Tyler III, to "push the envelope" of athletic endurance.

The **Ultraman** course is the 4,039-square mile island, and it involves a six-mile swim, a 261.1 mile bicycle ride, and a 52.4 mile run.

They chase each other across the burning Ka'u Desert, past smoldering lava fields, over the hulking shoulder of 13,677-foot high Mauna Loa, into the county seat of Hilo, along the rain-swept cornice of the Hamakaua Coast, over the western slopes of 13,796-foot-high Mauna Kea and into the coastal hamlet of Hawi, before setting off on a double marathon across the lava fields of Kohala to the finish line under the Hotel King Kamemameha's banyan tree. There is no prize money, no gold medals, no cereal box fame. To finish the Ultraman is enough.

The best way to see the Ultraman is by car, chasing after the contestants, which is a test of endurance, itself. Be prepared for every kind of weather from tropical heat to snow and even lava flows.

On Day One, less ambitious spectators watch the start and finish of the six mile open ocean swim from Kailua Pier. Action begins at 6:30 a.m. when entrants take the plunge, then set off on ten-speeds on the 261.1 mile bike ride.

On Day Three, the biggest crowds gather in mid-afternoon at the Kailua-Kona finish line under the banyan tree where an ultra-party ensues.

Contact Ultraman director Curtis Tyler III at P.O. Box N, Kailua-Kona, Hawaii 96745. Telephone: (808) 326-SWIM. Fax: (808) 326-7474.

A Garden of Eden Hike Anyone Can Do

Take a walk on the wild side in Hawaii and you will discover it is pretty safe. No snakes, no crocodiles; only Happy Face spiders and Honeycreepers, each endangered. Not you. There is no poison oak, no poison ivy, no brambles or thorns in the jungle. So what are you waiting for? No excuses.

You will be rewarded by the silence of the jungle, the thickness of the canopy, the strong primeval scents, the sensual beauty of the exotic plants. You may even spot a rare bird, like the *o'o*.

Hawaii is "the best theater for evolution in the world," scientists say, and the best place to watch the drama unfold. Nine out of 10 of Hawaii's flowering plants, animals and birds live nowhere else on the planet, as you shall see.

Dan Lutkenhouse, a San Francisco green thumb, did his part to save Hawaii's endangered rain forest; he bought one and planted it with more than 1,800 species of tropical plants, then named it the **Hawaii Tropical Botanical Garden.**

Nearly all the exotics of the world thrive on 17 acres of botanical splendor in the lush Onomea Valley on the outskirts of Hilo. It is said to be the world's largest selection of tropical plant species. The site is spectacular, nestled between crashing surf and a thundering waterfall on the Hamakua coast. The flora includes a torch ginger forest, a banyan canyon, an orchid garden, a banana grove and bromeliad hill.

Some endangered Hawaiian specimens like the gardenia are flourishing with a little help in this natural habitat. If mosquitos bother you, bring your own jungle juice. If you forget, it's OK;

they provide complimentary bug spray and umbrellas at the trailhead in case there's a blessing of rain.

From Hilo, drive two miles north on Highway 19 to Onomea. Turn mauka or left to Onomea and stop at a burned-out shell of a church, which serves as headquarters for the Hawaii Tropical Botanical Garden, P.O. Box 1415, Hilo, Hawaii 96721. A van will take you the rest of the way. Call (808) 964-5233 for information.

Waipi'o Valley

> *"There is something fearful about the isolation of this valley, open at one end to the sea and walled in on all others by palis or precipices, from 1,000 to 2,000 feet in height..."*
>
> Isabella Bird, "Six Months in the Sandwich Islands"

Centuries ago Hawaiians lived in the **Waipi'o Valley**, farming taro in the rich soil. Some say they were kings and if that is not so, it is believed that Waipi'o was often visited by royalty, including King Kamehameha, himself. It is a very ancient place; you can feel it in your bones, especially when the cathedral walls close in to create a splendid isolation.

If you seek tranquility, go to **Waipi'o**, not just to the overlook like most people, but down into the valley of the curving water, which is what Waipi'o means. Go cross its streams, hike to its waterfalls, soak up the solace in this old Hawaiian place on the **Hamakua Coast**.

Waipi'o Valley is the largest on the island of Hawaii—one mile wide and six miles deep. It also has the highest waterfall,

1,200-foot Hiilawe Falls that cascades down a 3,000-foot cliff.

The population of Waipi'o, never more than 15,000, declined after the first white men arrived in this secret place in 1823. Today, nestled amid 900-foot high cliffs, the valley looks much as it did a century and a half ago; a garden of Eden amid evergreen taro, red bananas, wild guavas and waterfalls. Only about 50 people live in the valley today, tending taro, fishing and soaking up the ambience of this special place. It is the last remnant of an ancient Polynesian way of life. A three night stay here isn't long enough to explore the valley; a lifetime may be too brief.

From the black sand bay at its mouth, Waipi'o sweeps back six miles between vertical walls laced by 2,000-foot high twin falls. From the 1,200-foot overlook, the Waipi'o Valley reveals itself like a yawning abyss. You've seen its picture in magazines and on postcards; it's a cliche shot no shooter can resist.

An easy hike (all downhill), it is only a mile to the valley floor down a one-lane road with a 25 percent grade, steeper than San Francisco's Lombard Street. If you dread the uphill return leg, take the Waipi'o Valley Shuttle that loops into the valley on 90-minute tours.

From Kailua-Kona Airport, it's about a 90 minute drive north on Queen Ka'ahumanu Highway (State Highway 19), through lava fields along the Kohala Coast to Kawaihae. Turn right at Kawaihae Road to Waimea. Turn left on Mamalahoa Road at Waimea and drive about 12 miles to the Honokaa turnoff. Turn left, drive to Honokaa, turn left again and drive past the village of Kukuihaele to the end of Highway 240 where you will see the Waipi'o Valley lookout.

The **Waipi'o Valley Shuttle** tour departs from the wooden bench on the makai side of the parking lot. It costs $20 a person, roundtrip; children under 12 cost $10. (808) 775-7121.

You may take a four-hour horseback ride for $60 with **Naalapa Trail Rides** (775-0419), or take a mule-drawn surrey with a fringe on top on the two-hour **Waipi'o Valley Wagon Tour** operated by Peter Tobin and his mules, Lehua and Nui, who have pulled their wagon from California to New York and back again—without leaving Waipi'o Valley. The tour begins at the company's office in Honokaa, at the end of the main street next to the hardware store. A shuttle takes you down to the valley. Tours are four times daily, at 9:30 and 11:30 a.m., and 1:30 and 3:30 p.m. Tickets are $35. Waipi'o Valley Wagon Tours, P.O. Box 1340, Honokaa, Hawaii 96727 or call (808) 775-9518 for reservations.

For accommodations, there is the **Araki Hotel** with no electricity, no refrigeration, no hot showers. It's not the Ritz-Carlton, yet there's always a problem getting reservations at Tom Araki's rustic lodge on the valley floor. $30 a night per couple. (808) 775-0368.

If you prefer, there's the **Waipi'o Valley Treehouse**. A shipwright built a 200–square foot treehouse 30 feet up in a huge monkeypod tree for Linda Beech's unique bed and breakfast in the valley. She taps the nearby 1,000-foot waterfall and solar heats it for drinking and the *piece de resistance*: a Japanese *ofuro* soaking tub. $125 a night per couple. (808) 775-9518.

There is also the **Waipi'o Wayside Inn**, a 1938 sugar plantation manager's house living on as a bed and breakfast operated by Jacqueline Horne, a Silicon Valley refugee, and great cook. The five-room inn is two miles outside Honokaa (about a 10 minute drive to Waipi'o). Rates $50 to $70 a night. (808) 775-0275 or toll free (800) 833-8849. P.O. Box 840, Honokaa, Hawaii 96727.

◉ *Akamai Tip:* To camp in the Waipi'o Valley you need a permit from Hamakua Sugar Company. Call (808) 776-1511.

See Mo'okini Luakini

"E ola na mamo o Kohala aina ali'i."

"Our descendants will live forever."

from the Mo'okini family chant

Ancient Hawaiians first settled on the **Kohala Coast**, which is the birthplace of King Kamehameha the Great and home of Hawaii's oldest, largest, most important ancient religious site, the 1,500-year-old **Mo'okini Heiau**.

A *heiau* is a Hawaiian temple used for fasting, praying and offering human sacrifices to their gods.

This three-story basalt stone chief's temple, dedicated to Ku, the Hawaiian god of war, was built in 480 A.D. under the direction of High Priest Kuamo'o Mo'okini, according to the Mo'okini genealogical charts.

Each stone is said to have been passed hand-to-hand from the Pololu Valley 14 miles away by 18,000 men who worked from sunset to sunrise to complete the task.

The *heiau* was the focus in Kohala of religious life and order for the Polynesians. It is about 1,000 yards from the birthplace of Kamehameha the Great, who was born in approximately 1758 at Kapakai, Koko'iki and then taken to Mo'okini Heiau for his birth rites.

He returned as a young man to worship at Mo'okini until he rebuilt Pu'ukohola Heiau near Kawaihae.

The two temples provided a spiritual staging ground for Kamehameha's unification of the Hawaiian islands into the first kingdom. The **Mo'okini Luakini** was designated a National Historic Landmark in 1963. (Luakini is the Hawaiian word for the sacrificial *heiau*.)

Kahuna Nui Leimomi Mo'okini Lum, a direct descendant of the first high priest, often recreates ancient ceremonies at the temple but thankfully omits all sacrificial details.

Take a bumpy road to Upolo Airfield. The Mo'okini Heiau is near Upolu Point in the North Kohala District on the northern tip of the Big Island.

Drive North to Hawi on Queen Kaahumanu Highway (Highway 19). Turn left on Akoni Pule Highway (Highway 270). Drive along the Kaiwaihae Coast to the Upolu Airport turnoff. Follow it along a row of ironwood trees 1.8 miles to a dirt road, turn left, take the washboard road 1.8 miles to the *heiau* which sits on a high bluff.

Best time to go is late afternoon when the sun strikes the lava rock walls and creates a spiritual mood guaranteed to give you "chicken skin" — the pidgin colloquialism for goose bumps.

Pu'uhonua O Honaunau

They call **Pu'uhonua O Honaunau** the place of refuge, but I always thought of it as the great escape for misadventurers. Supposedly, the concept worked like this: if you'd been caught sleeping with the king's mistress or stealing one of His Majesty's pigs, all you had to do was run like hell to this place and yell, *"ollie ollie oxenfree"* —or the Hawaiian equivalent—and then everything would be all right. Since Hawaii got annexed to the U.S. and became the 50th state, it doesn't work like that anymore. To avoid the downside of misadventure in Hawaii these days you need a Honolulu lawyer. Don't miss this 180-acre national historical park on the lava coast that dates to the mid-1500s to see how early Hawaiians managed somehow without lawyers.

From Keahole Airport in Kailua-Kona, drive south about 30 miles on Kuakini Highway (State Highway 11) past Kealakekua and Captain Cook to the well-marked turnoff at Highway 160. Turn *makai* (toward the sea); go 3.6 miles to the park.
Go early to avoid crowds and experience the *mana* (power) of this sacred place. The park's open at 7:30 a.m., closes at 5:30 p.m., and costs $1. Under 17, and over 62 free. Take the self-guided tour. Hookena Beach Park, open from 6 a.m. to midnight, is nearby and worth exploring.

On the Puako Trail

A groove in the dirt three feet deep runs along the Big Island's **Kohala coast** for miles. It looks as if somebody ran a unicycle along the shore until you realize this path was cut by thousands of bare feet very long ago. This trail of ancient Hawaiians has one of the finest and largest concentrations of stone symbols in the Pacific; more than 3,000 petroglyphs line the route like old graffiti.

For no other reason you should visit the 233-acre **Puako Petroglyph Archaeological District.** It used to be hard to find, but not anymore, so there's no excuse not to see the petroglyphs.

From Kailua-Kona Airport drive 23 miles on Queen Kaahumanu Highway to the still developing Mauna Lani Resort. Turn left and then veer to the right toward the new Holoholokai Beach Park. Park your car, walk back a few yards to the entrance to Puako Petroglyph Park. A local artist has recreated 29 petroglyphs (turtles, fish, centipedes, warriors) suitable for rubbing if you want a semi-authentic souvenir.

It's a short hike, 1.4 miles round trip, but the heat and the stillness will make it seem longer. For your safety, stay on the trail; it is marked with little *ahus* through a dense kiawe forest that covers the lava beds like a canopy.

Don't wear rubber flip-flops because the razor-edge lava can shred your feet. Dress for extreme heat. Lava beds radiate heat and it can hit 110 degrees in the shade. No water is available on the trail or at the viewing site. Bring your own. The kiawe forest is tinder dry so no smoking.

Best time to do this is early morning or late afternoon when the sun is low and the heat of the day has passed, which probably was when the petroglyphs were carved in stone.

Big Island's Best Restaurants

Roussel's
60 Keawe Street
Hilo, Hawaii (808) 935-5111

Soft shell crabs in Hilo? N'awlins-style remoulade, too. Man, this is living. Roussel's has catfish, crawdads, and gumbo, and even serves a passable *beignet,* thanks to two good ol' boys from Louisiana who quit the bayou for paradise and now serve some of the best food on the Big Island in a defunct city bank. They use the vault for a wine cellar and, of course, feature live jazz. Reservations are a must.

Huggo's
75-5828 Kahakai Road
Kailua-Kona, Hawaii (808) 329-1493

It's not the seafood (okay) or the service (ho-hum) that makes Huggo's a singular attraction, it's the location—on the waterfront in Kona. At *pau hana* time, marlin hunters crowd the open-air bar, which features blowups of big fish, including "The 940 Pound Marlin," taken by the late millionaire big game-fisherman Morton "Buster" May. You can see the same shot at New York's Metropolitan Museum, but it's not the same as being here.

A Small Hotel on the Big Island

Hotel King Kamehameha
75-5660 Palani Road
Kailua-Kona 96740
(808) 329-2911
$99-$165, suites $275-$485.

The King Kamehameha, a funky old 1950s beachfront hotel near the waterfront, is close to all the action in Kailua-Kona, a tropical Carmel-by-the-sea. The 455-room hotel has 28 shops, two restaurants, six tennis courts and a poolside bar on a sandy beach. It's also the final resting place of the World Record Pacific Blue Marlin, a 1,062.5-pound, 14-foot-six-inch whopper landed on 50-pound test line by Gil Kraemer of the Laguna Niguel Billfish Club, aboard the *Ihu Nui* on August 8, 1986, after one hour and 20 minutes. He used a doorknob for a lure.

Great Places to Stay on the Big Island's Kohala Coast

The barren Kohala "gold coast," first developed by Laurance Rockefeller, is becoming Hawaii's newest playground. More than $8 billion worth of luxury hotels have risen out of the coal black lava beds on this gilt-edged seacoast, and more are planned, like the Four Seasons, the Regent Beach Hotel and the Mauna Kea Prince at Kohala.

Kona Village is still the top destination on this once lonely coast, but the neighborhood is changing and you should take a look.

Explore the grounds, take a look at the art and architecture, spend the day at the beach, enjoy a sunset cocktail, maybe even splurge on dinner created by a Michelin chef from Lyon, France.

Remember, in Hawaii the beach belongs to everyone — up to the mean high tide line. Some of the best things in life are still free.

Hyatt Regency Waikoloa
1 Waikoloa Beach Drive
Kohala Coast, Hawaii 96743
(808) 885-1234
$235–$395, suites $575–$3,000.

When the sleek silver train pulls into the grand lobby of the Hyatt Regency Waikoloa and your travel-weary kids spring to life at the sight, you know you're on the right track for fantastic family adventures. The perfect destination for families, the Hyatt Regency Waikoloa is spread over 62 acres of awesome coastline on the Kohala Coast of the Big Island of Hawaii with plenty of great adventures, like swimming with dolphins.

Maybe you don't always want to ride the silver train to your room. So catch a yacht instead, and cruise the grand canal in style. You can also walk through halls filled with a $3.5 million collection of art works from the Pacific in a kind of linear museum, past scarlet macaws and other exotic birds who might just say "Aloha" as you pass. Regardless of which transit mode you choose, you're already having fun. And so are your kids, because no hotel was ever like this. This is Hawaii's Disneyland.

Mauna Lani Bay Hotel and Bungalows
One Mauna Lani Drive
Kohala Coast, Hawaii 96743
(808) 885-6622.
$260–$425, suites $700, bungalows $3,000, ocean villas: one bedroom $325 (three night minimum); two bedroom $395 (three night minimum).

Cowabungalow, the Mauna Lani Bay Hotel and Bungalows is Hawaii's first resort with its own suburb. It has five 4,000-square-foot bungalows with 24-hour butler service. For only $3,000 a day. Which is probably why Robin "Lifestyles of the Rich and Famous" Leach called it "the #1 U.S. Resort" in 1990.

Mauna Kea Beach Hotel
1 Mauna Kea Beach Drive
Kohala Coast, Hawaii 96743
(808) 882-7222
$250–$420, suites $440–$880.

The cornerstone of Kohala, the 25-year-old Mauna Kea resort is top choice for captains of industry who take annual holidays in this open-air art museum on a crescent bay.

Ritz Carlton Mauna Lani
50 Kaniku Drive
Kohala Coast, Hawaii 96743
(808) 885-8886
$250–$2,500.

For no other reason than Philippe Padovani, the former

head chef of the Michelin-starred La Tour Rose in Lyon, France, you should visit the Ritz Carlton at Kapalua. He's the star of the Ritz' culinary show at this 542-room world class hotel that looks like Ralph Lauren's island home.

Royal Waikoloan
P.O. Box 5000
Kohala Coast, Hawaii 96743
(808) 885-6789
$125–$300, suites from $400.

The Royal Waikoloan is the adventurers' choice. This unluxury hotel sits amid her platinum sisters like an undiscovered Cinderella with a half-mile-long beach, very friendly staff and excellent location, all at one-third the cost of her glitzy siblings. It's the perfect headquarters for anyone who seeks to explore the Big Island. The open-air Petroglyph Bar is like an oasis in the lava fields, the Garden Cafe opens at 6 a.m. with Japanese breakfast, paniolo eggs and hash, and Swiss muesli, and closes with Keahole abalone and other local treats. Sure, the Holiday Inn-ish rooms lack chocolate swans on your pillow, but you didn't come to Hawaii to sleep. Best bargain on the Kohala Coast.

Kona Village Resort
P.O. Box 1299
Kailua-Kona, Hawaii 96745
(808) 325-5555
$390–$640.

The first time I heard people would pay $500 dollars a night to stay in a grass shack on a lava field in Kaupulehu, I chuckled. Then I went to Kona Village myself. It's a seaside village of individual *hales* (houses) in various South Seas architectural styles, with no phone, no television, no radio—only the sound of the wind, surf and distant laughter. Previously accessible only by seaplane, this primal place was once the site of an early Hawaiian village, and when drums beat across the lava after dark you can feel the link to the past. Other resorts are swell but Kona Village remains the great escape.

Kauai
The Mystique Endures

Kauai

CA	camping - Koke'e - page 161
FI	fishing - Koke'e - page 164
HF	helicopter - Na Pali Coast - page 225, 233
HI	hiking - Laiwi - page 168
HI	hiking - Awaawapuhi Trail, Koke'e - page 161, 162, 231
HI	hiking - Kalalau Trail, Koke'e - page 158, 227
HR	horseback riding - Waimea - page 169, 236
HU	hunting - Koke'e - page 166
KA	kayaking - Na Pali Coast - page 164, 253
KA	kayaking - Huleia River, Lihue - page 167
NB	nude beach - Kauapea Beach, Kilauea Point - page 238
WF	waterfall - Wailua Falls - page 249
WW	whale watch - Ke'e Beach - page 105
WI	windsurfing - Anini Beach - page 241

156   *Great Outdoor Adventures of Hawaii*

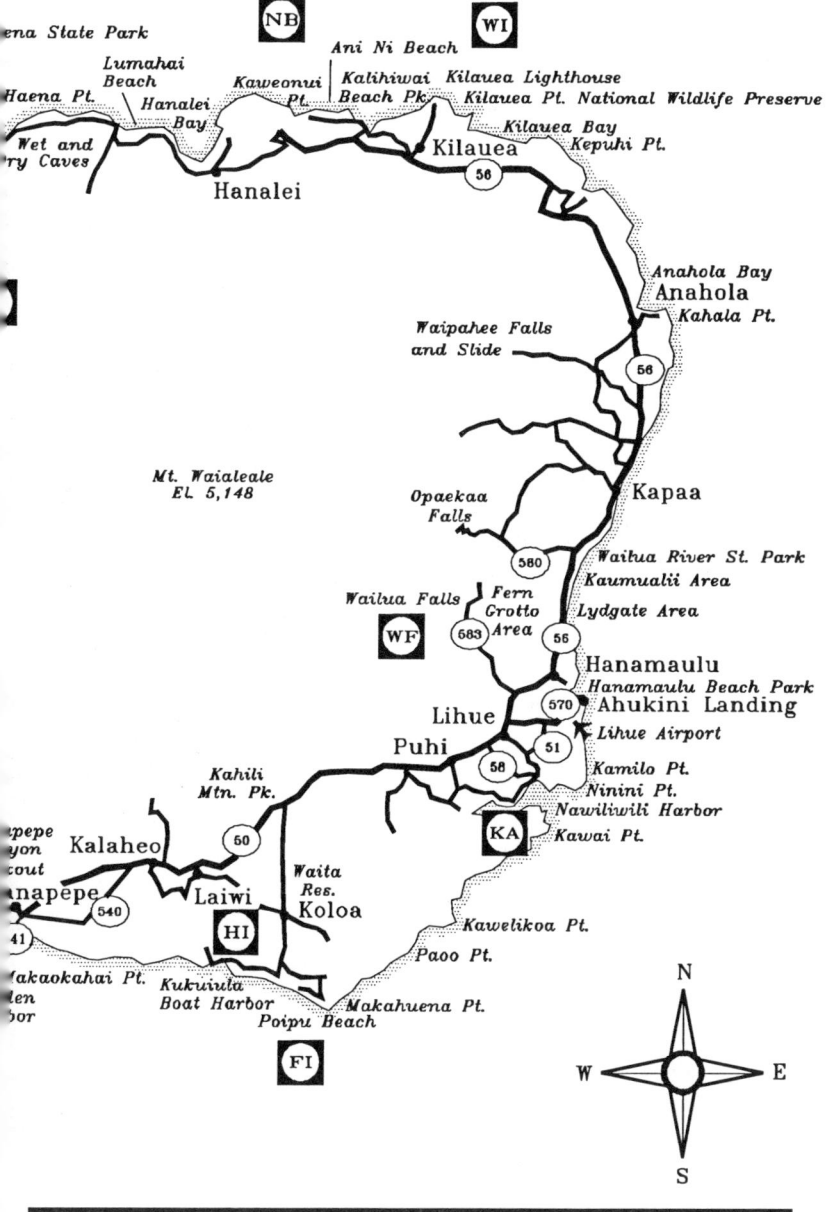

Kauai 157

KAUAI

THE MYSTIQUE ENDURES

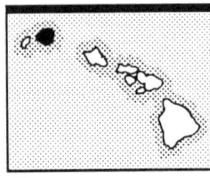

Kauai
(cow-eye-ee)

Nickname
The Garden Island

Flower
Mokihana

Color
Green berry

Capitol
Lihue

Area
549.4 square miles

Population
45,000

Highest Point
Mt. Waialeale
5,243 feet

ON its wild north shore, Kauai rises like a mythical sea castle with tropical birds flitting at its towers and wild goats clambering up its turrets.

This island is beyond dull care. California is 2,300 miles east, Japan north by northwest and the great world a distant memory.

Some opt for choppers to ply the steepled cliffs like swarms of bees, soaring in and out of canyons, hovering before waterfalls, dipping across white crested combers that lap against the ramparts.

Others ride the wild waves on inflatable crafts called Zodiacs, coming face to face with whales, splashing inside sea caves and hauling out on remote beaches to stand shivery naked under icy waterfalls.

Still others hike the sheer and splendid **Kalalau Trail** on ancient Hawaiian foot trails that crease this wild coast. And who is to say which way is best to see Kauai?

Of all the islands, Kauai stands aloof, out of sight of the others. It is called "the separate kingdom." It was the last to be dominated by King Kamehameha's rule.

Up on the North Shore, the village of **Hanalei** evokes the independent spirit of old Kauai. Dogs sleep in streets named for fish. People smile and wave beneath a score of waterfalls that crease the Bali Hai ridges.

Half-moon **Hanalei Bay**, where sloops anchor and surfers play, opens wide as a Saturday yawn to a beach made for kids of all ages.

On Kauai's sun-washed south shore, **Poipu Beach**, devastated by Hurricane Iwa in 1982, is a fully recovered retreat of low-rise hotels which, by law, stand no higher than a coconut tree, about four stories. That restriction kept Kauai a great, green place even as mega-buck fantasy resorts appeared on the island.

The jewel in the crown here is the new $250 million Hyatt Regency Kauai, a C.W. Dickey-inspired hotel in the California Mission style, which stands like a rich uncle's island retreat, rekindling the romance of the era when sugar was king and tourists came by steamship.

Today's Kauai is a series of sugar cane corridors that stretch like an inland sea. Visitors drive through a world so green they act bewildered when they emerge.

Here, old plantations give way to new suburban houses, while historic plantation houses enjoy a second life as restaurants with Sunday polo matches on the green.

At **Waimea**, not far from Captain James Cook's first Hawaiian landfall in 1778, the past has been preserved in a collection of real tin roof plantation houses. Once home to Filipino cane field workers in the early 1900s, these authentic guest houses offer a rare glimpse of Hawaii's yesterday.

Thousands peer into the striated mile-wide, 3,000-foot deep rift of **Waimea Canyon,** the so-called "Grand Canyon of the Pacific," home to feral goats and long-plumed tropical birds, which was carved over millions of years by water flowing from Mount Waialeale. Now, riders on horseback ride the canyon rim.

At **Koke'e State Park,** stay at a rustic lodge or cabins in California-like redwood groves. They offer extra blankets and pot belly stoves to ward off the chill of misty high-country nights. That tropical contradiction is a central part of beautiful Kauai. In the end, this island always plays back in your memory like a dream, and the mystique of Kauai endures.

Koke'e: Hawaii's Yosemite

Ansel Adams came to Hawaii in the 1950s to photograph its peaks and valleys, but the light was wrong and the weather diffident and, although he illustrated a book, *The Islands of Hawaii,* he left, discouraged, claiming Hawaii's mountains somehow didn't measure up to his favorite California subjects. He should have spent more time in Koke'e, but then so should everyone.

If **Waimea Canyon** is the Grand Canyon of the Pacific, then **Koke'e** is Hawaii's Yosemite. A natural upland wilderness, 3,600 feet above sea level, Koke'e offers a Hawaii so seldom seen, it almost qualifies as a secret place.

A true tropical rainforest, it receives 75 inches of rain a year, enough to keep the streams flowing and forest evergreen with rare plants, native birds and Hawaii's only native land mammal, the Hoary bat *(Lasiurus cinereus)*, which came from continental shores before man arrived. You may never see it (good thing, some of you are saying) but it's likely to be spotted at sunset on any of the 45 trails that crisscross Koke'e.

The well-marked trails take you into the 4,345-acre forest in a variety of ways, from a brief nature hike to a 10-mile slog in the **Alaka'i Swamp**.

The forest is full of native plants, such as *maile* vine, *mokihana* berry, the *ohia lehua* tree, the *iliau* (similar to Maui's silversword), and imports like Australia's eucalyptus and even California's redwood.

Pigs, goats and black-tailed deer thrive in the forest but the *moa*, or Polynesian jungle fowl *(Gallus gallus)*, is the cock of the walk.

❂ *Akamai Tip:* A new trail guide, *Koke'e Trails*, is available for $1.50 at the Koke'e Museum. Or you may write Hawaii Nature Guides, P.O. Box 70, Kealia, Hawaii 96751.

The rustic **Koke'e Lodge** offers a dozen furnished cabins (complete with wood stoves) from $35 to $45 a night. Since Koke'e is a state park, you may stay only five nights, which is just enough time to enjoy this unspoiled wilderness.

The 12 cabins at Koke'e are very popular, so write or call now and make reservations, probably for next year. The cabins vary in size from one large room which sleeps three persons to a two-bedroom that can accommodate seven.

The Greatest Hike of All in Hawaii

After 26 years of hiking in Hawaii, Tom Kaser, the *Honolulu Advertiser's* great outdoors writer, has found what he claims is his "best hiking experience" in the islands.

It's a 10-mile hike on Kauai that combines the 3.25-mile **Awaawapuhi Trail** with the **Nualolo Cliff Trail** and the **Nualolo Trail** itself. I've hiked each separately but not all at once, which, I discovered, takes the average semi-fit hiker about eight hours. It's a great hike that takes in a two-tiered waterfall, a rainforest, sea cliffs, hanging valleys, feral goats, a spiny ridge with sheer drops on either side, and a unique reverse-view of the Na Pali coast. It will take your breath away.

Just above Koke'e Lodge on Koke'e Road (State Highway 550), the 3.25 mile Awaawapuhi Trail begins at the 4,120-foot elevation. Bring

Give the number in your party and dates you wish to reserve. One night's deposit is required for confirmation. Include a stamped, self-addressed envelope with your check. Your deposit is refundable if you cancel two weeks before your arrival.

Check-in is 2 p.m. or later (call ahead for arrivals after 5 p.m.) and check-out is noon. The lodge serves breakfast and lunch daily and dinners on Friday and Saturday nights. For reservations, call or write: Koke'e Lodge, P.O. Box 819, Waimea, Kauai, Hawaii 96796. (808) 335-6061.

Na Pali by Sea

Ride the wild **Na Pali coast** on a rubber boat. Come fly with Captain Zodiac to the valley of the lost tribes on Kauai's primitive North Shore. Clancy Greff is Captain Zodiac, and his fame is known beyond these islands. He's the son of a sea captain who turned his hobby into a livelihood on the water.

The adventure begins at the end of the road where the Na Pali coast begins. Clancy, who spent his boyhood exploring this brooding place, knows every nook, cranny and beach on the crenelated coast. He now runs a sea-going fleet of big black rubber Zodiac rafts that take 10,000 people a year in and out of the Na Pali coast. His band of young raft pilots bound over crystal waters 12 miles down the coast to the remote deserted beach of **Nualolo Kai**, where you may dive calm waters, explore an ancient fishing village, enter sea caves, see whales and dolphins, and always, drink in the majesty of Kauai's seacliffs.

All voyages depart from Tunnels Beach at Haena, the beach neighborhood beyond Hanalei. It costs $80 each for the full voyage; shorter three hour cruises in the morning or late afternoon are $50. Charters are available. Contact Captain Zodiac Expeditions at P.O. Box 456, Hanalei, Hawaii 96714 or call (808) 826-9371.

your own water, a rain slicker, and expect—thank you Lewis Carroll—to gyre and gimbol in the slithy toves of Koke'e. Oh, and bring your good balance or you may come face-to-face with *limu*, Hawaiian seaweed.

In summer, when the ocean is calm, many kayak down the wild coast, a singular adventure that is becoming very popular on Kauai.

Contact Outfitters Kauai, which rents kayaks and offers guided expeditions. (808) 742-9667.

Best Place to Catch Rainbow Trout

Most sport anglers come to Hawaii in search of trophy marlin and overlook the fresh water streams and lakes that offer anglers some of the greatest fishing adventures in the Pacific.

No self-respecting fisherperson can rest until he or she has landed a rainbow trout *(Oncorhynchus mykiss)* in the high mountain streams of **Koke'e** on the island of Kauai.

The trout, introduced in 1920, is found only on the islands of Kauai and Hawaii, where its habitat is cold water streams with a moderate flow—the tail end of tropical waterfalls.

Hawaii's rainbows generally are under three pounds, but have unofficially reached eight pounds; the state record is six pounds and it's mounted on the wall at Koke'e Museum. The world record, landed in Alaska, is said to be 42 pounds, three ounces.

Hawaii's rainbow trout are bluish or olive green above, fading to silver below, with a broad pink lateral stripe; back, sides, dorsal and caudal fins are marked with small dark spots.

Limited spawning occurs in Hawaii because water temperatures are too high; what spawning does occur takes place from about November to February.

Annual stockings of the Koke'e region on Kauai are accomplished with eggs from California, hatched and raised on Sand Island in Oahu's Honolulu Harbor.

The young feed on small insects and crustaceans; adults feed on fish eggs, minnows and other small fish including other trout. Small spinners or flies are effective lures; salmon eggs are used with great success.

I don't have to tell you how tasty they are pan-fried or grilled on an open fire with fresh ginger and soy sauce.

The **Koke'e Public Fishing Area** is 10 miles north of the town of Kekaha on Kauai. The fishing area is at 3,000 feet above sea level in the vicinity of Koke'e Park and Waimea Canyon. It includes 13 miles of fishable streams, two miles of fishable ditches and a 15–acre reservoir. The only specie available is rainbow trout, which may be taken during an annual open season during 16 days in August and on weekends in September. The State Division of Aquatic Resources issues permits at Koke'e Park Headquarters during trout season. Contact State Division of Aquatic Resources, 1151 Punchbowl Street, Honolulu, Hawaii 96813 or call (808) 548-4002 for more information.

◉ *Akamai Tip:* A freshwater game fishing license is required, and the daily bag limit per fisherperson is seven trout. Fishing is allowed between the hours of 5:30 a.m and 6:45 p.m.

Shooting Captain Cook's Goats

Since there is so little wildlife on Kauai and most of it is endangered or threatened, a Hemingway wannabe must content himself with taking potshots at Captain Cook's goats. I know it doesn't have the same macho appeal as bagging a trophy rhino in Africa, but after you see the natural habitat of Kauai's goats, you may change your mind. Before you stand up for animal rights and protest the wearing of kid gloves, let me explain that goat season is short and sweet and necessary to thin the herds, which otherwise might eat the island to the shoreline. On the island of Kahoolawe, feral goats long ago ate all the foliage, then pounded the earth to dust. The goats, first introduced by well-meaning Captain Cook, are considered sort of a picturesque nuisance; so ready, aim, fire.

Goat hunting on Kauai is an adventure that will test your fear of heights, sharpshooting ability, and patience with bureaucrats.

The blood sport is regulated by the State Department of Land and Natural Resources which issues permits, sets rules for muzzleloader-only and regular rifle hunting, and declares two seasons.

Muzzleloader season is only one weekend, usually in late July. Hunters are permitted to bag one feral goat per permit. You don't have to forfeit your regular rifle goat limit if you bag one with a muzzleloader.

The regular season usually begins the week after the muzzleloader hunt and lasts seven weekends, usually from late July to early September.

Hunting of feral goats with bow and arrow is permitted year-round in some areas.

Contact the Public Information Office of the Department of Land and Natural Resources at (808) 548-6957, or write Forestry and Wildlife Division, Hawaii Department of Land

and Natural Resources, 1151 Punchbowl Street, Honolulu, Hawaii 96813.

Up the Huleia by Kayak

Of the world's great rivers, the Nile, the Amazon, the Tigris and Euphrates, the **Huleia** is probably the least known but best recognized by movie fans, everywhere.

It's the river Indiana Jones narrowly escaped with his life under heavy native pursuit while racing to the seaplane in the opening scene of "Raiders of the Lost Ark."

Now, anyone can voyage quite safely through the jungle on the Huleia, which is a lot friendlier than Hollywood made it appear.

For one thing, it's in the **Huleia National Wildlife Refuge**, a 240-acre wetlands preserve, and last stand for the endangered Hawaiian gallinule *(Gallinula chloropus)*, known elsewhere as the Common Moor Hen.

You may see the gallinule, as well as the Great Blue Heron, *(Ardea herodias)*, the Hawaiian Shearwater *(Puffinus newelli)*, and the Cattle Egret *(Bubulcus ibis)*, which, along with the Bell Ranger *(Noisy helicopteris)*, is Kauai's most common bird.

You voyage up the Huleia in a "royak," a 12-foot long pirogue that is a cross between a kayak and a canoe, which is easy to paddle and virtually unsinkable.

The three-hour voyage on this picture perfect little river, which also starred in *King Kong* and *Uncommon Valor*, is ideal for all, but especially movie buffs and great adventurers under 12.

From Lihue Airport, take State Highway 58 or 51 to Wilcox Street, fronting Nawiliwili Harbor in Lihue. Make a left hand turn into the entrance of Small Boat Harbor and follow the dirt road past the private sailboats until you see the Island Adventure office. Say you want to book a trip up the Huleia. It costs $37, starts at Nawiliwili Harbor and explores the lower reaches of the Huleia River in the Huleia National Wildlife Refuge. Lunch included. Wear a swim suit and boat shoes. The kayak trips depart at 8:45 a.m. daily. Call (808) 245-9662 for information. Island Adventure, P.O. Box 33780, Lihue, Hawaii 96766.

National Tropical Botanical Garden

On the way to Waimea, in the village of **Laiwi**, is a 300-acre tropical garden worth a look even if you flunked Botany 1-A.

This little known **National Tropical Botanical Garden**, which does no advertising or promotion, hosts a three-hour, two-mile walking tour which is a flower lover's dream, along paths of ginger, heliconia, 600 species of palm trees, ferns, orchids, cinnamon trees, allspice, jack fruit, breadfruit, kapok, pandanus and bamboo.

Tours are held twice daily, at 9:00 a.m. and 1:00 p.m. They are limited to groups of 26, and include a visit to the beachfront estate of the late Robert Allerton whose privately held gardens, begun in 1870 by Hawaii's Queen Emma, wife of King Kamehameha IV, include statues, pools, fountains and gazebos, the queen's own summer cottage and bougainvillea planted on the hillside by Her Majesty, herself.

From Lihue Airport, take Kaumualii Highway (Highway 50) beyond the Poipu resort area toward Waimea to the little town of Laiwi, about three miles west of Koloa.

Tours originate at the visitor center at the end of Hailimi Road. (808) 332-7361.

On The Beach at Sunset with Smoky

As the sun sets in the west over the "forbidden" island of Niihau, my trusty steed Smoky and I gallop in the surf of **Waimea Bay**. It is a scene out of every western movie, except this adventure on horseback is in paradise. It's even called "Paradise on Horseback."

Trail guide Les Milnes, an island boy who started riding before he could surf, knows every trail on Kauai. He keeps a string of 12 steeds—quarter horses, Appaloosas, Arabians and Palominos—that are virtual pets, so if the last horse you rode was at the merry-go-round, you'll be okay in the saddle.

The two-hour sunset beach ride is popular for riders of all ages and experience levels. He also offers rim rides along the Grand Canyon of the Pacific, treks into the 3,000-foot canyon with a picnic beside a crystal pool, and a unique four-hour fishermans' trail ride through a tropical rainforest to a bass pond, with lunch and tackle provided. The fish are up to you.

Take Highway 50 to Waimea, the small sugar plantation town at the mouth of the Waimea River. **Garden Island Ranch** is just west of Waimea, adjacent to the turn-of-the-century Waimea Plantation Cottages. Call (808) 338-0052 before you go, because all rides require 24-hour advance reservations. Rates range from $100 an hour for two on the Sunset Beach Ride, to $175 for the four-hour Tropical Fishing Foray.

Two Great Places to Bird Watch

In the half light of the forest, a wing flash of shadow plays against ostrich-necked ferns. Honeycreepers, bright as jewels, crowd a flame red ohia blossom to sip nectar. Everything seems perfect here in Paradise, but things aren't always what they seem.

Now that the Big Island's Wao Kele O Puna rainforest is being invaded by bulldozers and geothermal wells, the 4,345- acre **Koke'e Wilderness Forest** of Kauai is one of the last sanctuaries for Hawaii's endangered birds—and one of the best and most easily accessible places in all of Hawaii to see them. Other places include the **Kamakou Preserve** on Molokai and the **Ola'a Rainforest** at Volcanoes National Park. Thanks to man and mongoose, which eats bird eggs, Hawaii is the "endangered bird capital of the world." More species of native birds have become extinct in Hawaii in the last 200 years than anywhere else. Of 87 native species of birds in Hawaii, 23 are extinct, 29 are endangered and one is threatened. Only 11 are left on Kauai. Even the Hawaiian crow *(Corvus hawaiiensis)* is on the brink of extinction here.

The most recent casualty may be the Kauai O'o, a tiny jet-black honeycreeper bird with yellow thighs *(Moho braccatus)* whose haunting flute-like song was last heard in the Alaka'i Swamp in 1986. It was probably saying aloha, which in this case, means goodbye.

Up here you may still see the 'apapane *(Himatione sanguinea)*, a red bird with black wings and a curved black bill; and the 'i'iwi *(Vestiarai coccinea)*, a red bird with black wings, orange legs and a salmon-colored bill.

Other frequently seen native birds are the 'amakihi *(Hemignathus sagittirostris)*, a plain olive green bird with a long straight bill, and the 'anianiau *(Hemignathus parvus)*, a tiny yellow bird with a thin, slightly curved bill.

These birds are among the 22 species of native honeycreepers who sing like canaries and deliver complex concerts in the forest.

Often visible here is the 'elepaio *(Chasiempis sandwichensis)*, a small, active gray flycatcher with an orange breast that perches with tail up. This bold, curious bird is easily "squeaked up" by imitative whistles.

The most common native bird at Koke'e is the Moa, or red jungle fowl *(Gallus gallus)*, brought as domestic stock by ancient Polynesians to every inhabited island of the Pacific. Ordinarily shy, they are quite tame at Koke'e.

From Lihue Airport, drive west on Kaumuali'i Highway (State Highway 50) to Waimea, turn right at Waimea Canyon Drive (State Highway 550), drive 20 miles up the curving road with spectacular overlooks to Koke'e State Park.

Large colonies of seabirds nest on Kauai's north shore at **Kilauea Point.** You can easily snoop on the red-footed boobies *(Sula sula)*, and wedge-tailed shearwaters *(Puffinus pacificus)*

How to See the O'o

Kauai isn't the only place to see the rare Kaui o'o, (also known as the o'o'a'a). You may see it any day of the week in the Bishop Museum under glass, mounted like an old ladies hat. At least you will know what to look for when you go birding in the field.

The Kauai o'o bird is sooty black with a short tail, white eye and yellow thighs. It has a polka dot throat and a short, pointed tail frequently cocked up. A fancy bird with an attitude, in other words.

An acrobatic bird, according to *The Birds of Hawaii and the Tropical Pacific*, it dominates all other nectar-feeders and will defend a favored ohia tree against all comers.

It looks like no other bird in the Alakai Swamp and has a distinct call that sounds like *take-a-looky-now* and may remind birders of the song of the Western Meadowlark, but with without causing a great disturbance.

And you may see other Pacific seabird species, such as the great frigate bird *(Fregata minor)*, red-tailed tropic bird *(Phaethon rubricauda)*, and the Laysan albatross *(Diomedea immutabilis)*.

The Laysan albatross is an incredible bird with an immutable homing extinct that makes pigeons look like pikers. As an experiment, albatrosses were blindfolded and flown to Alaska, San Francisco, Los Angeles and Australia and released. Within 10 days, they flew back to Midway Island, 1,500 miles west of Honolulu.

Exhibits at **Kilauea Lighthouse**, built in 1913, describe the wildlife and habitats of seabirds on Kauai and the remote island refuges like Nihoa, Pearl and Hermes Reef and Howland Island. Howland Island is 1,800 miles southwest of Honolulu, where aviatrix Amelia Earhart was bound on her last mysterious flight in 1937.

From Lihue Airport, drive north on Kuhio Highway (State Highway

56) about 25 miles. Turn right at Kilauea, look for the sign to Kilauea Lighthouse, go down a dirt road until you see the lighthouse.

Kilauea Point is open to the public daily from 10 a.m. to 4 p.m. Entrance fee is $2. Several days a week, the National Wildlife Refuge offers a two-hour docent-led hike along the rugged Crater Hill coastline. Call (808) 828-1520 for information and reservations.

Four Rainy Day Places

If it rains only for a few minutes it's called a blessing, if it rains for more than a few minutes it's a squall, if it rains for more than three days it may be a disaster, especially on Kauai. Don't let it dampen your spirit. Kauai is the home of Mt. Waialeale, the wettest spot on earth (it means rippling water), with more than 450 inches of rain a year (that's 37 feet!). Chances are good that it will rain on you. Here are three great rainy day adventures on Kauai:

fewer slurs, i.e.: *kay-kittle-keedle-o-coo.*

If you happen to be in England, you may also see the Kauai o'o in yet another form at the Pitt-Rivers Museum at Oxford University, where some British acquisitor in the late 1700s somehow obtained a cape once worn by Hawaiian kings, made of 20,000 bright yellow o'o thigh feathers. It's not the same as seeing an o'o on the wing, but Simon Winchester of the *Manchester Guardian* called the o'o cape "certainly one of the most remarkably lovely things in any museum in England."

Get into your rainy day, Polynesian-style, by grabbing a *punee* on the *lanai* and ordering a Hinano, the beer of Tahiti. Or one of Christian Marston's world famous Mai Tais. Then kick back and watch giant bullfrogs dodge cars that splash down the highway. The **Tahiti Nui**, the last true Polynesian place in Hawaii, is a real thatched-roof South Seas neighborhood bistro presided over by a hulking Tahitian hostess, Louise Marston.

Order some *poisson cru*, that great Tahitian pupu made of raw fish marinated in coconut milk and lime juice. Play a little ukulele, talk story, enjoy the rainy day.

Drive Highway 56 to Hanalei. Just before the first turn to the right you will see the bamboo sign, "Tahiti Nui" and know that you have arrived.

Most mission houses are small, dark, inappropriate transplanted Boston cottages that wholly ignore aspects of tropical architecture. But the **Waioli Mission House Museum**, a two-story dwelling built and occupied by Abner and Lucy Wilcox of New Bedford, Mass., is a redeeming example of how heathens managed to convert the Christians, at least in architecture. The wood frame house, which cost $2,000 in 1836, features a lanai on both stories, with the cookhouse in a separate building, according to Hawaiian practice.

Builders used lava rock for its chimney, hard *ohia* wood for its planks, and then furnished it with Hawaiian *koa* wood pieces, including a bookcase by William C. Parke, the first American cabinet maker in Honolulu.

The white house sits in a green field against steepled cliffs that sing with waterfalls, which inspired the house's name: *Waioli* or "singing water."

Drive a mile beyond Tahiti Nui, past Ching Young's new market on the right and the green church on the left.

If it rains for more than a day, go directly to **Stevenson's Library** at the Hyatt Regency Kauai at Poipu. You have never seen a library like this, sort of an English gentlemen's club with big, soft, embracing chairs, a *koa* wood bar with a real brass rail, a line of single malt Scotch and Port, including a Fonseca 1963 at $49 a glass, two billiard tables, a reading room with important newspapers like the *New York Times* and *The Wall Street Journal*, and a smoking lounge although the barman doesn't vend either cigarettes or a good cigar.

About the library: it's named for Robert Louis Stevenson but there are no books of his to be found; the library also lacks good Hawaii and Pacific books, which leads me to believe an interior desecrator bought them by the yard, without due concern to gentle readers. Stevenson's Library looks like a library but it really is just another fancy bar. Good place to hang out on a rainy day, though, if you bring your own book.

Walk through the Grand Lobby of the Hyatt Regency Kauai, turn left, and then go right to the entrance of Stevenson's Library. The Hyatt Regency Kauai is at 1571 Poipu Road, Koloa, Kauai. (808) 742-1234.

I hate to go shopping, but it's okay if you're looking for the perfect aloha shirt. Do this on a rainy day, so you don't miss anything. The best place to look for an aloha shirt on Kauai is The Only Show in Town, where all manner of vintage Hawaiiana flotsam seems to have washed ashore.

Drive to the outskirts of Kapaa, look for a green, two-story building with overdressed mannequins waving from the lanai. You won't miss it. 1495 Kuhio Highway, Kapaa. Open 10 a.m. to 6 p.m. (808) 822-1442.

Visit the First Fantasy Resort

The mother of all fantasy resorts in Hawaii was created by an ex-astrologer's assistant from Atlantic City, New Jersey, who came to the islands in 1948 and saw the future of Hawaii in kitsch.

In the early 60s, Grace Buscher Guslander took a two-story roadside motel by a busy highway across from Wailua Bay and turned it into one of the world's most popular destinations, **The Coco Palms.**

She created thatched cottages around a man-made lagoon in the coconut grove and found the simple native structures appealed to guests from around the world.

She used "killer" clam shells for bathroom sinks, put a live water buffalo in the lagoon, named a caged gibbon "Little Grace," inaugurated African snail hunts on Wednesdays to keep the grounds pest-free (and guests occupied), and installed ceramic frogs in the bath tubs.

First to revive the ancient torch-lighting ceremony, she narrated it in her own "legendary" voice as native Hawaiian runners dashed in loin cloths through the 45-acre coconut grove lighting tiki torches as a sign of Hawaiian hospitality. The free show (at 7:30 p.m. nightly) is still a crowd pleaser.

"For thousands of Hawaii visitors, her concept of a Polynesian vacation defined Paradise," critics wrote.

The Coco Palms became one of the most successful resorts in Hawaii. Elvis sang "The Hawaiian Wedding Song" to Joan Blackman as he floated down a lagoon to his screen wedding in the 1961 film, *Blue Hawaii*. Ricardo Montalban welcomed "Fantasy Island" visitors from a bridge across a fish pond here. Rita Hayworth got married in the wedding chapel in *Sadie Thompson*.

Hundreds of young couples still get married a la Elvis on a raft that floats down the canal. The Blue Hawaii Wedding special at $1,895, includes raft, flowers and three nights of romance in a thatch–roof bungalow under the palms.

The "death" of Grace Guslander, mistakenly reported by the *Honolulu Advertiser* on August 19, 1987, only enhanced her status as the living legend who originated the fantasy resort concept. Now in her 80s, Grace and her innovative Coco Palms live on.

From Lihue Airport, take Kuhio Highway (State Highway 56) to the Coconut Coast, about six miles north to Kuamoo Road by the Wailua River. Turn left and park in the visitors lot. Enter through the open air lobby near the roast pig on a spit.

The Legendary Tahiti Nui Mai Tai

The Mai Tai, bright as a tropical moon, smooth as summer surf, rich as old Lurline passengers, is Hawaii's favorite drink. One sip and it's paradise.

Nobody makes them better than Christian Marston at the **Tahiti Nui** in Hanalei. Unless it's his mother, Auntie Louise.

How to Mai Tai One on Your Own

The original recipe is reprinted here for your drinking pleasure.

Trader Vic's Original Mai Tai:

Pour only 80 proof J. Wray & Nephew Rum from Jamaica over shaved ice.
Add juice from half a fresh lime.
Some orange curacao.
A dash of rock candy syrup.
A dollop of French orgeat.
Shake vigorously.
Add a sprig of fresh mint.

The world's record at Tahiti Nui, incidentally, is 12. I hit seven, one rainy Friday night and the next day learned that not only was I playing the ukulele but singing falsetto, neither of which I can do under ordinary circumstances. Be careful—and get somebody to drive you home.

The recipe is a secret and it's just as well because, like *poisson cru* in Papeete, some things taste better close to the source. Tahiti Nui's Mai Tai bears no resemblance to those sickly sweet pineapple things foisted off on Waikiki tourists for $5 a bucket.

The Mai Tai is Polynesian in origin (the word itself is Tahitian for good), although exactly who created this refreshing rum drink remains in doubt.

Many years ago, I set out to find the inventor of the Mai Tai, a journey which took me on assignment from San Francisco to Honolulu to Tahiti, where few had ever heard of such a drink. In Tahiti they drink Hinano beer and Pernod, although not together.

My research began with the late Vic Bergeron, creator of Trader Vic's restaurants, who claimed he invented the drink in his Oakland establishment in 1944.

"There has been a lot of conversation over the beginning of the Mai Tai. And I want to get the record straight. I originated the

Mai Tai. Many others have claimed credit. Some claim it originated in Tahiti. All this aggravates my ulcer completely. Anyone who says I didn't create this drink is a dirty stinker.

"I took down a bottle of 17-year old rum. It was J. Wray & Nephew from Jamaica—surprisingly golden in color, medium bodied, but with the rich pungent flavor particular to the Jamaican blends.

"The flavor of this great rum wasn't meant to be overpowered with a heavy addition of fruit juices and flavorings. I took a fresh lime, added some orange curacao from Holland, a dash of rock candy syrup, and a dollop of French orgeat for its subtle almond flavor. I added a generous amount of shaved ice and shook it vigorously by hand to produce the marriage I was after."

He added half a lime for color, a branch of fresh mint for garnish and the Mai Tai was born.

"I gave the first two to Eastham and Carrie Guild, friends from Tahiti who were there that night.

Carrie took one sip and said, 'Mai tai roa ae.' In Tahitian this means, out of this world, the best. Well, that was that. I named the drink 'Mai Tai.'"

He took the Mai Tai to Hawaii in 1953 and introduced the drink at the Royal Hawaiian, Moana and Surfrider hotels, where it was revived by bartender Danny DePamphillis in 1986.

After I quoted Bergeron in a *Honolulu Advertiser* article on his creation of the classic Polynesian cocktail, I received a personal invitation to lunch from Donn (The Beachcomber) Beach who said he, not Trader Vic, invented the drink at his Hollywood establishment in 1932, but named it the QB Cooler after the QB Flight Squadron of World War II.

He said Trader Vic may have come up with the name but that he created the drink. A few days before we were to investigate this controversy in depth in his Banyan Tree House at International Market Place, Donn Beach died.

I honestly don't know who created the Mai Tai, but reasonable facsimilies of Trader Vic's version live on at better drinking establishments, like Tahiti Nui.

Kauai's Best Restaurants

Tahiti Nui
Kuhio Highway
Hanalei
(808) 826-6277

In Tahiti, tropical roadhouses that serve excellent food are common; in all of Hawaii there is only one: **Tahiti Nui**. Host-chef

Christian Marston serves authentic Tahitian cuisine at this celebrity haunt where the Mai Tais are equally famous.

A Pacific Cafe
4831 Kuhio Highway - Suite 220
Kapaa, Kauai
(808) 822-0013

On May 16, 1990, Kauai entered the age of gourmet dining thanks to chef Jean-Marie Josselin, who presides over A Pacific Cafe, where the cuisines of East and West are married nightly. No one should miss this excellent restaurant. This is the Roy's of Kauai.

Jimmy's Grill
4-1354 Kuhio Highway
Hee Fat Building
Kapaa, Kauai
(808) 822-7000

Forget all that nouvelle stuff, when you want a cheeseburger you want a cheeseburger. The best on Kauai are served at Jimmy's Grill, a funky roadside surfer's cafe with sand on the bar floor, tradewinds in the open air dining room and "solid drink and good food" on the menu.

Tidepools
Hyatt Regency Kauai
One Poipu Beach Road
Poipu Beach, Kauai
(808) 742-1234

Tidepools is a unique thatch–roof restaurant on stilts over a lagoon that's already cornered the market for escapism, ro-

Hotel Paradise

Kauai's last big resort is the first to pioneer a new way of experiencing Hawaii directly. It takes you there.

"We are dedicated to creating the magical experience of old Hawaii for all our guests," says general manager Morrie Graves of the 600-room Hyatt Regency Kauai on Keoneloa Bay in the Poipu Beach district.

"The tourism industry as a whole has a responsibility to protect the environment, heritage and culture that make Kauai such a distinctive place to visit," said Graves, a Chicago hotelier who learned his ecology in Sacramento, California. This new, "responsible" tourism enables guests to learn why the Hawaiian monk seal is endangered, see native plants preserved in the resort's landscaping, and take a naturalist-led dune walk to archaeological sites.

Oh, yes, taste two-fingered poi and taro mance and South Seas nostalgia but needs to tweak its seafood menu; along with fresh mahi and ahi, they still serve "surf and turf" this late in the 20th century.

Places to Stay on Kauai

Hyatt Regency Kauai
1571 Poipu Road
Koloa, Kauai, Hawaii 96756
(808) 742-1234
$300–$390, suites $475–$1,800.

The Hyatt Regency Kauai is a nostalgic retro-style hotel which appears on Poipu Beach like a mirage of the 1920s when travelers arrived on the Lurline or West Coast seaplanes. The hotel recalls the timeless style introduced by C. W. Dickey, the father of Hawaii's architecture, who, inspired by grass shacks, adapted the California Mission style to Hawaii's tropical climate. Enter the vaulted lobby and step back in time. It's like visiting a rich uncle's grand and comfortable island retreat, except no one ever had it this good. Not even

William Randolph Hearst had a five-acre lava rock swimming pool with three waterfalls, its own island, a lagoon and water slide by a white sand beach. Of six restaurants, my favorite is Tidepools, a collection of open-air thatch huts on a lagoon that needs only monkeys to recall steamy tropical nights down in old Zamboanga.

Waimea Plantation Cottages
P.O. Box 367
Waimea, Kauai, Hawaii 96796
(808) 338-1625
Fax (808) 338-1619
$75–$325.

The Waimea Plantation Cottages are not a hotel, but a collection of 40 brightly painted turn-of-the-century cottages that are remodeled relics from Kauai's sugar plantation era. They live again under a Waimea beachfront coconut grove and are so popular they are booked ahead six months—often by descendants of their original occupants.

chips. Play the nose flute and ukulele. And really learn to hula from a real *kumu hula* (hula teacher) from Na Hula O Kaohikukapulani, one of Kauai's most respected *hula halaus* (hula schools).

"Kauai by Design," takes you out the front lobby deep into the ecological and cultural heart of the island. You can visit Niihau, trek Kaui's rainforest with naturalists, ride the Waimea Canyon with a local trail guide and explore the sea with marine experts.

Book a stay at the Hyatt Regency Kauai. Activities are exclusively for guests and range from $150 to $400 a person. Transportation, food and beverages, including wine and cheese, are included.

Kauai Vacation Rentals
P.O. Box 3194
Lihue, Kauai, Hawaii 96766
(808) 245-8841
Fax (808) 246-1161

Hanalei Bay is high on everyone's list of the World's Most Beautiful Places. It's hard to wrench your eyes from the spectacle of jagged green mountains gushing with waterfalls all around the taro fields and breathtaking bay.

The best way to enjoy Hanalei is to rent a beach house for a week or a month from Kauai Vacation Rentals and really get to know the place. The houses range from simple Gauguin-like cottages under the palms to architectural gems that go for $4,000 a week.

Molokai
True Adventures in Old Hawaii

Molokai

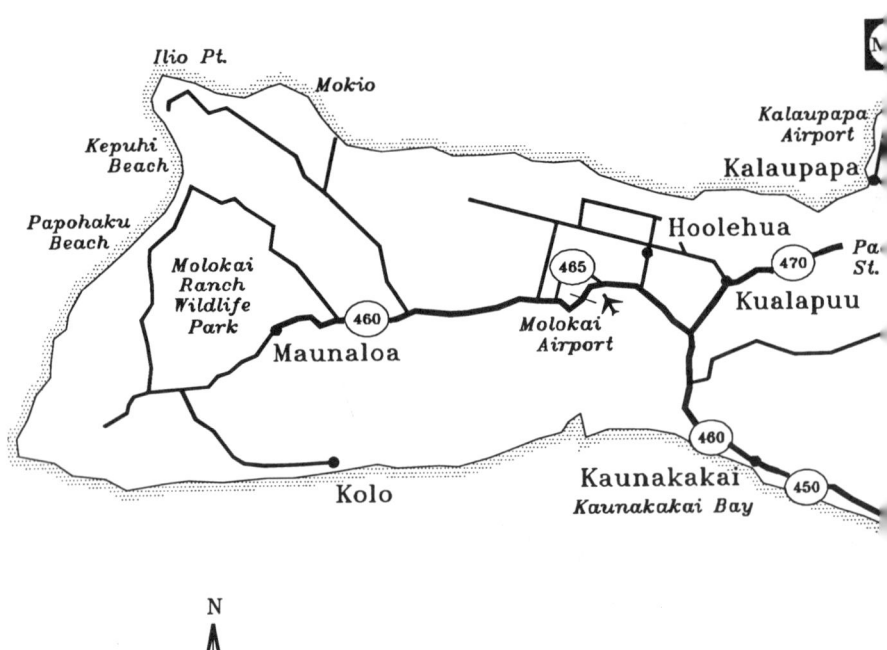

CA	camping - Waikolu, Kamakou Preserve - page 191
HI	hiking - Kamakou Preserve - page 190
HI	hiking - Halawa Valley - page 194
KA	kayaking - Halawa Bay - page 254
MR	mule ride - Kalaupapa - page 192
WF	waterfall - Halawa Valley - page 194

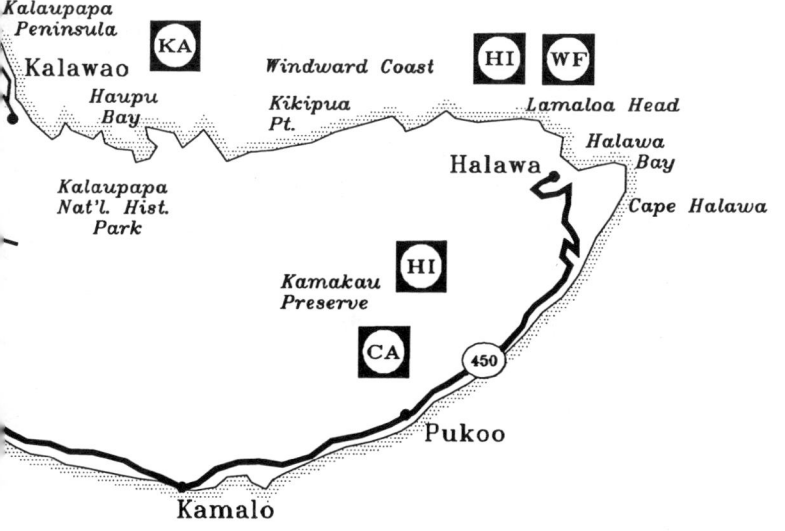

MOLOKAI
TRUE ADVENTURES IN OLD HAWAII

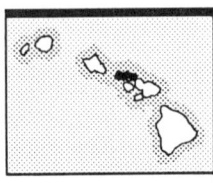

Molokai
Mow-law-ka-ee

Nickname
the Friendly Island

Flower
Kukui,
a small white
blossom from the
candle nut tree

Color
Green

Capital
Kaunakakai
(Cow-naw-caw-ki)

Area
260.9 square miles

Population
6,300

Highest Point
Kamakou
4,970 feet

UNDER the mango trees at sunset, on Molokai's south shore, the islands of Maui and Lanai show like separate nations across the blue gulf.

All three islands are related politically—they comprise Maui County—but each one has different goals. While Maui embraced tourism like a prima donna, her shy sisters waited in the wings. Molokai is still waiting.

A sleepy, rural island, known for ancient fish ponds and the world's highest sea cliffs, Molokai clings to its past and seems to exist in its own time zone, offering a clue to what all the islands must have been like before contact with The Outside World.

It got its first taxi last year. Now, there are two. But there are still no stoplights, an ironic indicator of island progress. However, the Japanese have purchased one-third of the island from American landlords, so it might be smart to hurry to Molokai before it's reincarnated as another Tokyo honeymooners' retreat like glitzy Okinawa or Guam.

Only 26 miles across the Kaiwi Channel from the bright lights of Honolulu via twin-engine plane, Molokai has yet to be visited by 747s, which may be its salvation.

Adventure here is singular and personal. Once here, a sort of tropical malaise sets in and you either fall in step with people who go about life at their own island pace, or flee to Waikiki or Lahaina where the beat goes on.

Molokai is where Honolulu people get away from it all, taking weekend retreats that sometimes become longer. The rural lifestyle of **Kaunakakai**, tropical kin to an old West town, is contagious; it inspires urban refugees to make life changes. A California architect became an onion grower. A "valley boy" from Encino runs a kite factory. A New York heiress owns a cattle ranch. Hawaii state senator Bill Pfeil is the island's best known watermelon grower.

The great adventures of Molokai are simple pleasures, often old-fashioned or personal in nature. Or sometimes they are real white-knucklers—a kayak adventure on the wild coast of Molokai, for example.

The chief attractions are natural and fantastic, such as an incongruous wildlife park where African lions and giraffes gambol on a mock veldt. Or the **Kamakou Preserve**, a 2,774-acre Nature Conservancy tract with more than 219 indigenous Hawaiian plants, an oasis for endangered birds like the Molokai thrush, *oloma'o,* and Molokai creeper, *kakawahie.*

The island's few tourists (only 20,000 visited the island last year) call on a lone resort that perches on Hawaii's largest white sand beach, three-mile long **Papohaku Beach** with its own pocket coves popular with skinny–dippers.

At the opposite end of the 30-mile long thin island, on the south shore, the idyllic **Halawa Valley** produces taro which is dried and pressed into tasty taro chips. They are quite addicting, especially with a cold beer.

Even the few tourist attractions are genuine adventures: mules daily traverse the world's steepest sea cliffs to **Kalaupapa**, where lepers once were banished and where Father Damien deVeuster spent his life, before modern drugs arrested what is now called Hansen's disease. A few victims of the disease remain and live on in the valley by choice.

Or wagons ride up a sacred valley to the *Iliilipae heiau*, a massive stone altar said to have been built in a single day by a human chain of 10,000 workers, and dedicated to Lono, the Hawaiian god of fertility and production. Good thing, too, because the *heiau* is famed for human sacrifice and the *mana* (power) of the ancients is still strong enough to lean on.

Molokai is a preserve not only of flora and fauna, but of the Hawaiian way of life, where a kiss still comes before a handshake when strangers meet. If you like Molokai, you would have loved old Hawaii. But hurry.

Hike the Wild Kamakou Preserve

From the lush rainforest near Molokai's nearly mile-high summit to the dry lowland forests, the **Kamakou Preserve** is like no other forest on earth.

This 2,774-acre forest, which supplies 65 percent of Molokai's water, is home to 219 Hawaiian plants which grow nowhere else and provide a home for Molokai's unique birds and insects.

The Molokai thrush, *oloma'o*, and the Molokai creeper, *kawawahie*, live only on Molokai and are extremely rare.

The vivid green *'amakihi* can still be seen and the abundant *apapane* sips nectar from ohia blossoms while the Hawaiian owl, *pueo*, takes night wing.

The Kamakou Preserve became a reality in 1982, when the Molokai Ranch Ltd. conveyed rights to The Nature Conservancy of Hawaii, which manages the wilderness area and permits hiking and even hunting under strict rules.

To get to the Kamakou Preserve you need a four–wheel drive vehicle. From the Molokai Airport, take Maunaloa Road (State Highway 46) to the Forest Reserve jeep road, about a half-mile south of the junctions of Highways 46 and 47 (Kala'e Highway).

A 45-minute drive on the jeep road brings you to the preserve entrance at **Waikolu Lookout**. The road is often impassable. Contact the preserve manager to check road conditions.

Hikers must stay on regular trails and roadways. Overnight camping is not permitted within the preserve but the nearby **Waikolu Lookout Campground** is available to campers.

Contact the Maui District Forester at P.O. Box 1015, Wailuku, Maui, Hawaii 96793. All visitors must contact the manager for access information prior to arrival.

Hunting of pigs, goats, Axis deer and introduced game birds is permitted subject to rules available from the Preserve

Going Pau Hana at the Pau Hana

The best place to go *pau hana* (end of work) in Hawaii is literally the **Pau Hana Inn** on the beach at Kaunakakai.

The best time is any Friday afternoon, but especially before a three-day weekend.

The seaside bar at the open-air **Banyan Tree Terrace** is cool and shady (thanks to a real banyan tree), and there's a delicious sense of being far away from it all.

From Molokai Airport, take Maunaloa Highway (State Highway 46) to Kamehameha Highway (State Highway 45) about eight miles southeast to Kaunakakai, the principal town. Drive through town until you see Pau Hana Inn on the right. Walk through the lobby to the Banyan Tree Terrace. Ask for one cold beer.

Pau Hana Inn
P.O. Box 546
Kaunakakai, Molokai
Hawaii 96748
(808) 553-5342

Manager. Hunters must check in and out at the Visitor Check Station.

Kamakou Preserve, P.O. Box 40, Kualapu'u, Molokai, Hawaii 96757. (808) 553-5236.

Molokai Mule Ride

You've seen the bumper sticker "I'd rather be riding a mule on Molokai" and now here you are, astride a mule you just met, edging nimbly down a nearly perpendicular 1,600-foot sea cliff to **Kalaupapa**, the former leper colony.

This is a white-knuckle ride for anyone with a fear of heights, but don't worry, they have never lost a sure-footed mule or a nervous rider yet. Although some call it a "once-in-a-lifetime" ride, Molokai muleskinners like Buzzy Sproat do it almost daily, weather permitting. The well-worn trail, cut in 1886, is three miles long with 26 switchbacks and takes about two hours, one-way.

The trail winds through lush rainforest and along sharp drop-offs with unparalleled vistas of Kalaupapa and the blue Pacific.

The Molokai mules go down the cliff at 8:30 a.m. and return at 3:30 p.m. The trail ride is limited to 26 people who must be physically fit and weigh no more than 225 pounds.

While leprosy, now called Hansen's disease, was abated in the 1940s, the state of Hawaii bans anyone under 16 from entering the settlement, which is still inhabited by 90 patients.

The trail ride costs $75 per person and includes a guide, saddle mule, picnic lunch and tour of Kalaupapa. Reservations are required. Call (808) 567-6088 or (800) 843-5978. Oahu tollfree: 537-1845.

Hike to Halawa Valley Falls

One of the most beautiful valleys in the islands is nestled on the east end of Molokai, where as early as

Kaunakakai's Musical Claim to Fame

This old Hawaiian town became famous in the 1930s in a popular hapa-haole song, "The Cockeyed Mayor of Kaunakakai."

The syncopated comedy hula song was written in 1935 by R. Alex Anderson, one of the most prolific Hawaiian song composers, who composed nearly 200 songs, including "Lovely Hula Hands," "I Will Remember You," and the humorous ditty "I Had to Lova and Leva on the Lava."

There is no mayor of Kaunakakai because Molokai, like Lanai and uninhabited Kahoolawe, is part of Maui County. Mayor Linda Lingle keeps office in Wailuku, Maui, the county seat.

650 A.D., farmers cultivated taro in terraced paddies. A tidal wave swept over the three-mile long valley in 1946, and scoured out the taro fields. The idyllic little valley lives up to almost every tropical expectation.

Two miles into the valley on a muddy path that crosses **Halawa Stream**, the cold waters of **Moaula Falls**, a twin-tiered waterfall, await hot and sweaty hikers.

If you see someone place a ti leaf in the pool, it's yet another test of the Legend of Mo'o, the lizard who lives here. If your ti leaf floats, Mo'o is happy and you may swim safely; if it sinks, good luck.

From Kaunakakai, drive 30 miles on Kamehameha V Highway (State Highway 450) to Halawa. You get your first glimpse of the valley at Mile Marker 26. Near the end of the road, look left for a green and white church and a sign that points the way to Moaula Falls. Park in the picnic area across from the church. Walk past the church down a dirt path that forks left. At the next fork, go right and cross the creek.

Molokai Ranch Wildlife Safari Park

Usually it's wise to avoid these roadside attractions, but since there's a paucity of them on Molokai, this one looks better than it is. You ride around in a van with 13 other people for two hours on a 50,000-acre ranch looking at nearly tame giraffes and zebras who think they're in Africa. Kids love the "giraffe lunch." You sit at a picnic table in a corral while giraffes graze over your shoulder. The $25 adult ticket and $15 youth ticket entitles you to refreshments and alfalfa pellets for the giraffes. Call (808) 552-2767 for reservations.

Big Wind Kite Factory

Every time I walk in here I want to buy six kites. Then I come to my senses and only admire the art of kites, created by hand by Jonathan and Daphne Socher, kite makers extraordinaire. They make and sell Hawaii's largest collection of original design, handmade and imported kites, and give free flying lessons. Shop at your own risk.

From Molokai Airport, drive 10 miles up to the old sugar mill town of Maunaloa. Turn right on Maunaloa Highway (State Highway 46) which leads to Maunaloa. Big Wind Kite Shop, P.O. Box 53, Maunaloa, Molokai, Hawaii 96770. (808) 552-2364.

Molokai's Best Restaurant

Dining on Molokai is a real adventure in local food. The **Mid-Nite Inn** *was* the best place in town, until it recently burned down. Try the **Pau Hana** restaurant for dinner now. See page 192.

Best Places to Stay on Molokai

Honomuni House
Star Route 306
Kaunakakai, Molokai, Hawaii 96748
(808) 558-8383
$75 and up for two, $10 a night for each additional adult.

At Molokai's Honomuni House, freshwater prawns play among the rocky pools of a nearby stream, and the legacy of old Hawaii is evident in the taro terraces and ancient stonework in Honomuni Valley. This cottage, nestled in a tropical garden within easy walking distance to the beach, sleeps four adults.

Guests may pluck fresh papayas and bananas from the garden and collect fresh eggs from jungle fowl.

Pau Hana Inn
P.O. Box 860
Kaunakakai, Hawaii 96748
(808) 533-5342
$45 to $90.

Under a century-old banyan tree next to ancient fish ponds, Molokai's oldest hotel, the **Pau Hana Inn,** is a favorite for locals and visitors alike.

LANAI
PINEAPPLES, PICKUPS AND PETIT FOURS

Lanai

HI	hiking - Munro Trail - page 205
HU	hunting - Lanai - page 206
SD	scuba - Hulopoe Bay - page 207
SW	swim - Hulopoe Bay - page 230

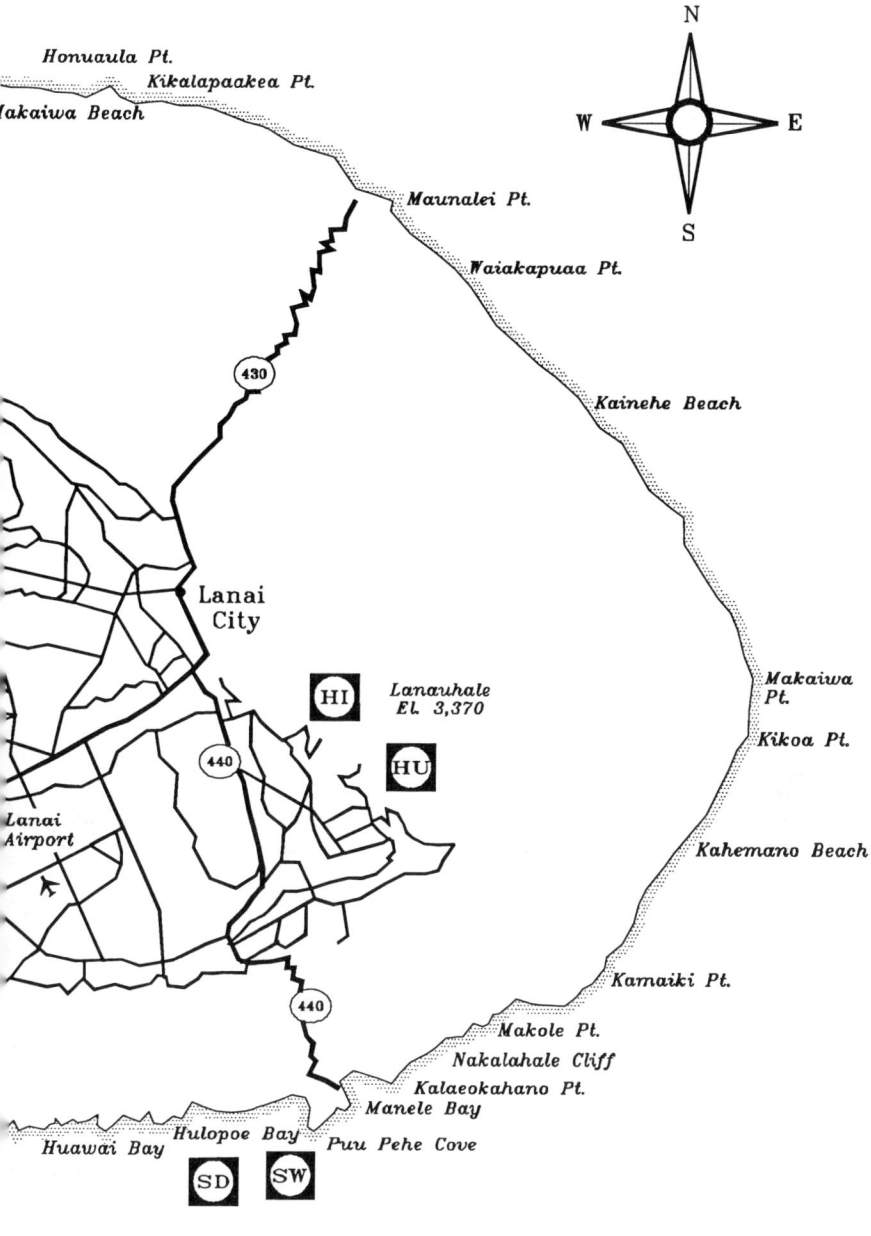

LANAI

PINEAPPLES, PICKUPS AND PETIT FOURS

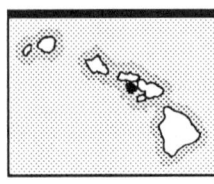

Lanai
(lah-nigh-ee)

Nickname
the Pineapple Island

Flower
Kaunaoa,
an air plant with
round flowers

Color
Yellow and
Orange

Capitol
Lanai City

Area
144 square miles

Population
2,000

Highest Point
Lanaihale
3,370 feet

From a passing cruise ship, Lanai looks like a desert island full of sheer cliffs, white sand beaches and pocket coves. From the air, it appears as a kidney-shaped island with precise rows of pineapples and a piney woods at its peak. Lanai is all that and more.

It is a stalking ground for wild deer and Mouflon sheep, a four-wheeler's paradise where every mile except the 40 paved ones are off-road, an archaeological treasure chest with more than 300 petroglyphs, and a nature lover's retreat for those who like to wander off the beaten path.

Lanai is the last major unspoiled island, thanks to pineapples which once proved more profitable than tourists. That is changing, though, since a Los Angeles developer claimed the island deed in a merger acquisition with Castle & Cooke, the former owner, who imported Filipino field hands and ran the island like a company store.

Once accessible from Honolulu only by twin-engine Sea Otter aircraft, this 144-square-mile island known as "the Pineapple Island" is being re-invented and re-marketed as "Hawaii's private island" to up-scale tourists in slick travel magazines.

The first jet service from Honolulu began suddenly last summer. So you better hurry if you want to see the last remnants of "old Hawaii, plantation-style" where folks still ride around in pickups with gun racks and shoot up their tin roofs on New Year's Eve. The alternative may be a mellow, tricked–up boutique version of "paradise" created by a Los Angeles architect.

Already, seven man-made lakes, several waterfalls, two golf courses, four tennis courts and a lawn bowling court have suddenly appeared, and this funky old town that calls itself **Lanai City** is about to be redone.

Formed by a single volcano, Lanai sits at the center of the Hawaiian islands, and from the summit of 3,370-foot **Lanaihale**, all the major Hawaiian islands are visible. For that reason, historians believe Lanai may have been the command post of kings who could keep an eye on canoe navigation in the sea lanes of the kingdom.

Seldom visited and little known, the island's Gibraltar-like cliffs, Tahoe-like pine forests and pocket coves are about to be discovered, along with its Polynesian ruins and myths.

Once the plantation headquarters of the Dole Pineapple empire, Lanai now cultivates another, more lucrative crop—well-heeled tourists who drop small fortunes to stay in splendid isolation at a European-like lodge, which looks like a nouveau riche Long Island transplant.

While they may take "high tea" and petit fours in the afternoon and dine formally every evening, you don't have to; there's still plenty of raw, red dirt adventure left on this island.

Despite all the upgrades, Lanai endures. The hunting on Lanai is the best in the islands. Lanai abounds with wild turkey, pheasant and the tiny Axis deer, which may be hunted in three seasons that include shotgun, rifle, and bow and arrow.

An archaeological treasure chest, Lanai once served as King Kamehameha's summer home and may be the lost burial spot of the monarch. Ruins of a 13th century Hawaiian fishing village are preserved here, along with the **Luahahiwa petroglyph field** with icons of a running man, deer, turtle, bird and goat.

The best way to see Lanai, most people say, is from the front seat of a bouncing four-wheel drive. One lane, red dirt roads lace the island and lead to Lanaihale's peak and **Shipwreck Beach** (with a real marooned freighter on the reef), or the **Garden of the Gods**, a netherworld cluster of lava rocks that change color at sunset.

Offshore, Lanai teems with tropical fish in submarine cathedrals of coral and lava, making these prized diving waters.

Lanai City, a turn-of-the-century plantation town of tin roof shacks, retains its folksy charm and clings to old Hawaiian ways, including "talk story" legends.

One story holds that evil spirits will take the life of anyone who spends the night in Lanai City, an old "kapu" disproved nightly by pampered visitors who, so far, are treated better than Hawaiian royalty ever were.

Adventure in Lanai may be as subtle as a morning hike on the **Munro Trail**, a two-mile long ridge path amid Norfolk pines, or a taste of fresh pineapple soup close to the source. Or it can be a dramatic chase in a 4 x 4 across a red dirt valley after a wild pig. Forget your white linen suit, unless you are staying at Koele Lodge.

Hiking the Munro Trail

New Zealand naturalist George C. Munro planted Lanai's peak with Norfolk pines *(Araucaria excelsa)*, which not only started an evergreen forest on this dry island but more importantly created a watershed.

Now rain clouds that scud across the 3,370-foot peak of **Lanaihale** drop their moisture in the forest of perfectly symmetrical pines.

The 8.8 mile forest trail, which takes eight or nine hours to hike, often may be muddy due to precipitation. Bring a poncho or a Hawaiian raincoat—a plastic garbage bag.

You will enjoy sweeping vistas; the 1,500-foot deep **Mauanalei Gulch**, prime source of Lanai's water; and the ubiquitous Axis deer. At the summit, about five miles up, you may see all other main islands but Kauai, and hike back through pineapple fields.

From Lanai City, drive north two miles on Route 44 to the end of town and bear right on Keomuku Road, past Koele Lodge. Take the first paved road to the right and drive up to Lanai Cemetery. A wooden sign points the way to the Munro Trail.

Stalking the Axis Deer

"One of the unintentionally best-kept secrets about Hawaii is that it is a veritable hunter's paradise..."

Euell Gibbons

Lanai City is an old West town that is a city in name only, where blue-jeaned folks ride around in pickups with guns racked, waiting for deer season to begin. Antlers hang next to marlin tails on trophy walls and fresh venison is served both on home dinner tables and in restaurants.

It may never rival Africa for latter-day Hemingways, but the island of Lanai is Hawaii's prime stalking ground for small wild game like Axis deer, Mouflon sheep and pheasant.

Anyway, they shoot to eat here on Lanai and all the guns go off (although not at once) during special hunting seasons set by the State Department of Fish and Game. The size of the herds and flocks are regulated and "damage control" hunts take place in addition to the regular season.

The Axis deer, an import from Japan, is a smaller, compact version of California's Mule Tail deer. It was introduced to Lanai by King Kamehameha's consul in Hong Kong. The herd, which ranges over the entire island but prefers the security of the eroded valleys, is known to feed on pineapple. The herd is estimated to number 20,000, which means there are more deer on Lanai than people.

The best way to hunt Lanai is to arrange a private hunt at The Lodge at Koele by contacting the concierge.

Four-Wheeling Lanai

With only 40 miles of paved road, no freeways, and a total area of 144 square miles, Lanai is, hands down, the four-wheel capital of Hawaii.

Only Niihau, where there are no paved roads, beats Lanai for off-road fun, but they ride horses there. When it rains, this red dirt island begins to resemble a mud wrestling pit. Almost everything here is off the road.

If you want to see Lanai, get a jeep and head out off the highway to check out the ghost town of **Keomuku**; the **Garden of Gods**, a weird bunch of rocks that look like badlands; **Shipwreck Beach**, with a real ship on the reef; the **Munro Trail** and petroglyphs above a pineapple field. Don't wear anything white if you plan to explore beyond your room.

Lanai City Service & Rentals, (808) 565-7227, rents jeeps for $100 a day, tows and pull-outs extra.

Diving Cathedrals

Off Lanai's splendid Hulopoe Bay, in 70 feet of water, there are two large caves known as the Cathedrals because the sunlight glints into them through the deep blue water like god-rays through stained glass windows of an old European church. The church reference may also derive from the litany of mumbled prayers of SCUBA divers who wend their way into these treacherous underwater grottos.

The Cathedrals attract experienced SCUBA divers from around the world. Veteran SCUBA diver Bob Moon, formerly of Lanai City, has led expeditions to the Cathedrals for nearly a decade.

The only way to reach the caves, he cautions, is by small craft, preferably a charter out of Maui, and then only on a breathless morning when the sea is calm and the swell is at ease.

The underwater caverns are about two miles apart, and linked by old lava tubes (probably full of blind, albino lobsters) that create a scary labyrinth for even the most daring divers.

Enter through narrow passageways into caves which open into huge cathedral chambers. If you look up, Moon says, you can see shimmering light on the dark walls. The dramatic effect is not unlike filling your face mask with water and going inside St. Andrews Cathedral in downtown Honolulu on a full moon night to look at the stained glass windows.

Contact Aaron's Dive Shop in Kailua, the oldest dive shop in the islands with the most experienced group of professional divers. If you want to go, definitely have somebody lead you into the Cathedrals.

Aaron's Dive Shop, 602 Kailua Road, Kailua, Hawaii 96734. (808)261-1211.

Best Places to Stay on Lanai

The Lodge at Koele
Lanai City, Hawaii 96763
(808) 565-3800 or (800) 223-7637
$275-$350, suites $425-$900.

The Lodge at Koele is a Euro-tropo gentleman's lodge in the pines, right out of *Architectural Digest*. It's a bit overdone for this red dirt island, but appealing nonetheless to big spenders who seek seclusion. Two very worldly new resorts are changing life for Lanai's 2,300 mostly Filipino residents, many of whom fled the grueling pineapple fields in favor of waiting tables and making beds. The mix of first-class hotelier and ex-field hands comes out surprisingly charming. It's like going to an island in the southern Philippines. Much of the food is raised on the island, including the venison. The Lodge at Koele is not your average Hawaiian experience—upcountry, cool and often misty under the Norfolk pine trees, kind of a British hill station with Filipino waitpersons.

The Hotel Lanai
P.O. Box A-119
Lanai City, Hawaii 96763
(808) 565-7211
$65 to $80.

The Hotel Lanai, an old 11-room hunters' lodge, is about to be redone a la Laura Ashley and turned into a cutesy B&B. Damn this world that won't hold still! Local people still meet here for ice cold Buds and raw fish poke. But you better hurry if you still want the old island-style ambience.

Manele Bay Hotel
P.O. Box 775
Lanai City, Hawaii 96763
(808) 565-7545
$295 to $500.

Down at the shore in sunny glitz, the **Manele Bay Hotel** is one ancient village ruin away from the island's best beach where spinner dolphins swim in the bay.

It's a 256-room Mediterranean style hotel, complete with green tile roof, with rates starting at $295 per day. It sits on a bluff at the end of Manele Road (State Highway 440) above Hulopoe Bay.

Niihau
"Forbidden" Adventures

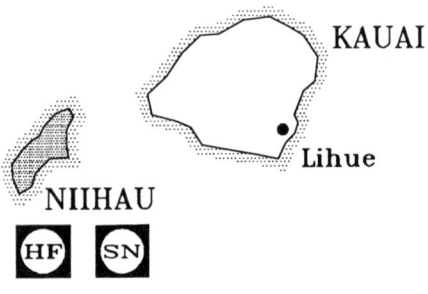
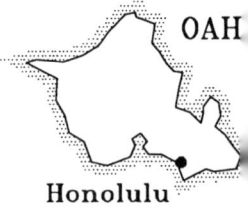

| HF | helicopter - page 216, 228, 235 |
| SN | snorkeling - page 217, 225 |

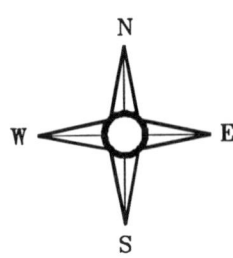

Niihau

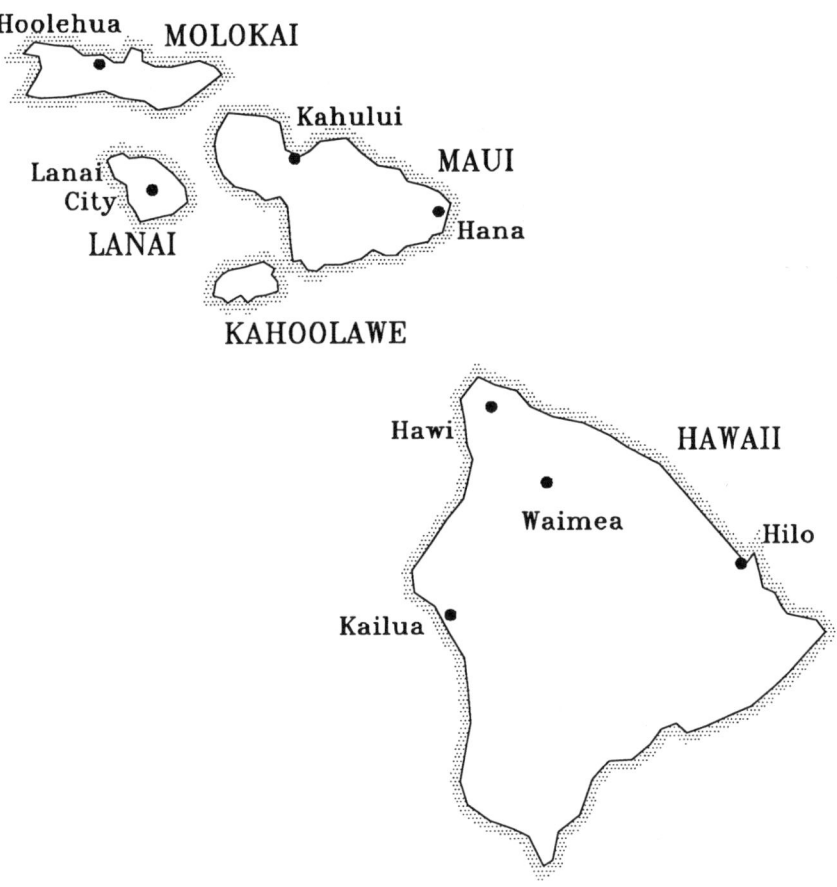

NIIHAU

"FORBIDDEN" ADVENTURES

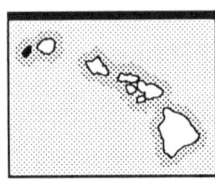

Niihau
(knee-ee-how)

Nickname
the Forbidden Island

Flower
(none) pupu shell

Color
White

Capitol
Puuwai
(Poo-oo-vy)

Population
226

Area
73 square miles

Highest Point
Paniau
1,281 feet

THE first time I saw Niihau, walked its empty beaches and plucked silver dollar-sized opihis from virgin tidepools, it seemed like a dream of a desert island.

Now, five years later, in this world that won't hold still, nothing on Niihau has changed. Absolutely nothing.

Except that you, too, may visit this long forbidden island that lies dry as a bone off the west coast of Kauai. Slowly, Niihau is opening to adventure.

We came swooping down from the sky in an Italian helicopter like some predatory bird that July, nearly five years ago, to set foot on this long taboo Pacific island. We knew each step we took would leave its mark and that nothing here would ever be the same again. Nobody turned back.

The quest for Niihau, for most of us, began that moment we first read or heard about this strange island bought for a pittance from a king 128 years ago, and since inhabited only by Hawaiians who choose a pure and simple life over 20th century trappings. It all sounded wonderfully arcane, the stuff of English shipwreck novels and Swiss Family Robinson, a six-mile by 18-mile chunk of lava slumbering in the late 18th century in the middle of the sea. It didn't help to know that the deed to Niihau is held by a man named Robinson.

Anyone with an ounce of adventure who has ever heard of Niihau secretly yearns to go there, if only to say they have been, and I am no exception.

Once off-limits to all but Hawaiians, this privately owned island 17 miles across Kauai's Kaulakahi Channel is now accepting visitors by special arrangement.

You may go there, as I first did, on a $1 million Italian chopper and land on one of the island's two deserted beaches, that probably look unchanged since the day Captain Cook dropped anchor in 1778.

Or, if you are a guest at the Hyatt Regency Kauai at Poipu Beach, you may snorkel the lagoons, pluck opihi from the tide pools, comb the beaches for glass ball floats lost from Japanese fishing nets and, perhaps, meet some of the people who live here.

The second time I visited Niihau, several residents of Puuwai came down to say aloha, talk story, play the ukulele.

If you are lucky—and I was—you may even buy a Niihau shell necklace on Niihau, direct from the craftswoman who made it. It's all possible now.

Niihau was bought in 1863 for $10,000 in gold by a Scottish family. The descendants, real-life Robinsons, now run a cattle ranch on Niihau where Hawaiian is the *Lingua franca* and horseback is the primary mode of travel.

There are no telephones, no jail and no tourists in the clapboard village of **Puuwai**, the island's only settlement. Sorry, the last true Hawaiian village is still off–limits until Niihau gets comfortable with its own new adventurous role as a host.

Fly to Forbidden Island

Over the years many people have tried different ways to go to Niihau, which has always been off-limits. Now, anyone can book a flight on **Niihau Helicopters**. The 20-minute flight takes you back a century or more to a museum-piece island right out of the pages of Captain Cook's journal. It's eerie and wonderful all at once.

Book a flight at Niihau Helicopters by calling (808) 335-3500 and checking the flight schedule, which is variable. The flight takes about 20 minutes, includes two landings, one at **Keamanu Bay**, the other on the lava beds of **Keanahaki Bay**, where Captain Cook first anchored. The flight, which usually includes a close-up look at the sharks in **Shark's Cove**, costs $185.

Snorkeling Niihau

It may be the best snorkeling in all of Hawaii. The fish are big and friendly, probably because they've never seen humans with rubber fins, snorkels and face masks. The water is crystal clear because there's no fresh water runoff into the lagoons. There are no crowds, usually only two people, you and your buddy.

The best place is the lava rock tidepools and lagoons off **Keamanu Bay**, the only snorkel spot, so far. The diving looks real good off **Lehua**, a submerged crater that's a twin to Maui's Molokini.

Shelling on Niihau

I am sitting on the beach on the "forbidden" island of Niihau plucking tiny white shells out of the sand with Momi Pahulehua. An island girl, she is eight years old and has keen eyes. She quickly finds the prized shells. Never before possible, this cultural encounter on the last, true Hawaiian island is one of the most memorable adventures designed by anthropologist Summer Harrison for the Hyatt Regency Kauai, which is pioneering a unique program, "Kauai by Design," which enables guests to visit Niihau, trek Kauai's rainforests with naturalists, ride the Waimea Canyon with a local trail guide and explore the sea with marine experts.

Unfortunately, "Kauai By Design" is available only for hotel guests, although anyone may make their own arrangements with adventure firms utilized by Hyatt.

Niihau Shell Leis

"*Pupu O Niihau,*" goes the Hawaiian song about the tiny seashell, symbol of this island. The little ivory, pink and brown Niihau shells, once worn by Hawaii's queens, are plucked from sand and strung into expensive necklaces, worth up to several thousand dollars. You may see some of the best collections of these and other shells in the main dining room of **Tahiti Nui** in Hanalei and at the **Hyatt Regency Poipu**.

Go at low tide, follow the tide line, look real hard. That's what Momi told me and she knows. The shells are red and white and yellow and not much bigger than this: °.

After you have found about 1,000, dig the sand particles out and then pierce each one with a needle to string them into a shell lei. All this is easier said then done. You don't have to be on Niihau to find Niihau shells; they sometimes wash ashore on Kauai, but they are still known as Niihau shells no matter where they turn up.

Kahoolawe
The "Target" Island

KAHOOLAWE

THE "TARGET" ISLAND

Kahoolawe

SINCE December 8, 1941, the day after the day of infamy, the United States Navy has conducted the longest air raid in military history on the Hawaiian island of Kahoolawe. It sits like a raw, red bleeding wound only 32 miles across the sea from Maui's luxury resorts.

Smallest of the eight main Hawaiian islands, Kahoolawe is 45 square miles, about the same size as San Francisco, with 11 miles of coast, two excellent beaches, some of the best fishing in the islands and tons of ordnance, some of it still "live."

Forget Beirut and Kuwait, Kahoolawe is the most bombed place on Earth, a fact that eluded even George Bush until he came to Hawaii last year. He stopped the bombing on October 22, 1990, a day of rejoicing in Hawaiian history.

Nobody lives on this "target" island, but it once was inhabited by wild goats and cats, which mostly have been bombed away. If cat lovers only had known the Navy was killing pussy cats, it's my guess the bombing would have stopped years ago.

The Persian Gulf War proved the precision of so-called "smart" bombs, yet the U.S. Navy insists it needs Kahoolawe to practice its bombing missions. It wants the island back.

Native Hawaiians have other ideas. They want to "heal" the island after the Navy cleans up its mess, then resettle Kahoolawe and restore it as a Hawaiian place of refuge and cultural learning center.

Few outside Hawaii know about Kahoolawe and the fight to save it; even fewer have set foot on the island. If you do, watch your step.

Six times a year a native Hawaiian group, *Kaho'olawe Aloha 'Aina*, which serves as the island steward, opens Kahoolawe to public access. You have to arrange your own transportation to Maui. A $75 fee includes ground transportation on Maui, round-trip boat transportation between Maui and Kahoolawe and all meals on the island. You swim ashore from a boat and camp on the beach.

Write Davianna McGregor at Protect Kaho'olawe Aloha Aina, P.O. Box 62012, Honolulu, Hawaii 96939.

GREAT HAWAIIAN ADVENTURES

All-Time Top Ten Great Hawaii Adventures

※

IF you only have two weeks and want to keep your adrenaline higher than your cholesterol, it's easy in the islands. All you have to do is hit five islands in 14 days and head for the most excitement you can find anywhere on Earth.

I've told you how to do them all in other chapters, but, as a summation of great adventure in Hawaii, here's my All-Time Top Ten list:

Helicopter Kauai

Enter the realm of tropical birds, where waterfalls splash to the sea on a 50 million-year-old island so rugged no road can ring it. Come, dream-fly over the spectacular wilderness of Kauai.

Snorkel "Forbidden" Niihau

Crystal lagoons, huge tame fish, and the silence of the land on this museum-piece island that is the last real Hawaiian place, all add up to a once-in-a-lifetime experience no longer forbidden.

See the Volcano on the Big Island

No matter how you see it, from the air, land or sea, see it. Hawaii's greatest natural attraction, the most active volcano on earth, is simply awesome.

Kayak to Desert Isle–Oahu

Row a solo kayak across an emerald lagoon to one of two pyramid-shaped islands off Lanikai Beach, known as the Mokulua. Go early, just as the sun climbs out of the Pacific, and you may be the only one on this desert island.

Sunrise at "The House of the Sun"–Maui

Rise before dawn and drive to the 10,023-foot summit to watch the sun come up like thunder at the volcano Hawaiians call Haleakala, The House of the Sun. One of the great natural wonders of the world.

Gallop the Hana Coast–Maui

Let others crawl up this jagged coast in a rental car parade, the best way to enjoy the Hana Coast is on horseback, past secret coves and hidden beaches and across the open range of Hawaii's most beautiful sea ranch.

Sail Waikiki at Sunset–Oahu

Come sundown, the best place to be is on a starboard tack off Diamond Head as the city lights of Honolulu begin to sparkle.

Take a sailboat and really get down to sea level on Oahu's Mamala Bay where dolphins and flying fish play.

Hike the Kalalau Trail–Kauai

Follow the footsteps of ancient Hawaiians along a cliffside path to the Valley of the Lost Tribe. Hiking the Kalalau is the most difficult and challenging hike in Hawaii and one you will never forget.

In Search of Marlin–Hawaii

More exciting than a new Ernest Hemingway biography, this is the stuff of raw high sea adventure where 1,000-pound marlin fight the hook by dancing on their tails along the Kona Coast, one of the world's best game fishing grounds.

Soar off Makapu'u–Oahu

If God had wanted us to fly, he would have made our brains small and bones hollow, but if you insist on trying your wings, jump off Oahu's windward cliffs and catch a Makapu'u thermal to new heights on a hang glider.

The Secrets of Hawaii

※

"What is the point of a secret if it is kept a secret?"
  Dominick Dunne, *An Inconvenient Woman*

THERE are several different Hawaiis: the imaginary paradise that exists in your mind, the postcard Hawaii tourists see, and the real Hawaii that reveals itself only after a long time in the islands. I call that the secret Hawaii.

Each version of Hawaii is satisfying, but none more than the last, because that Hawaii enables you to discover something special about the place. Years ago, I used to think I knew the islands well because I visited so often; now after nearly a decade here, I know this: there are so many secrets of Hawaii no one could know them all. I have no reluctance sharing these few because there are so many more.

Shark's Cove–Niihau

Years ago when the Hawaiians first loaded cattle onto boats bound for Kauai, the sharks came into this pocket cove on the south shore of Niihau and tried to bite some steak on the hoof. When the white-tipped sharks mate in this cove, the green water boils with action, which is why Jacques Costeau calls Niihau "the sharkiest place in the world."

The safest way is by helicopter. Captain Tom Mishler of Niihau Helicopters buzzes the lagoon in mating season so you can see this incredible spectacle. It's a bonus on the flight to the "forbidden" island. For flight schedules, contact Niihau Helicopters at (808) 335-3500.

Ola'a Rainforest–Hawaii

No tour buses go to the rainforest; it isn't advertised or mentioned in guidebooks. If you can find the rainforest on the Big Island map, it appears in very small type. So most people don't know there is a rainforest here. In fact, there are several, the largest of which are the 9,654-acre Ola'a in Volcanoes National Park and the nearby 15,000-acre Wao Kele O' Puna.

Enter and you disappear into a Hawaii that exists in the imagination of all who yearn for paradise. In misty sunlight, honeycreeper birds suck nectar from red ohia blossoms, ferns grow big as trees and the gray-green ohia trees form a canopy that shelters all.

All is not perfect in the rainforest. Wild pigs root up ferns on the spongy forest floor, and alien plants such as the banana poka choke out Hawaii's native species. Now, a geothermal plant is threatening "the last big rain forest in America," as the *New York Times* called it. The damage began the day the bulldozer sliced up access roads in the Wao Kele O' Puna rain forest, opening the earth for non-native plants, like strawberry guava, Hilo grass and Koster's curse (aptly named) to invade.

You may not be able to visit the Wao Kele O' Puna, which is a battle ground between Hawaiian activists, the Sierra Club and the RainForest Action Network, who oppose the state's $15 billion scheme to tap the volcano and turn its steam into electricity. You may visit the nearby Ola'a Rainforest in Volcanoes National Park, which is under the safekeeping of the National Parks System. From the Hilo Airport (General Lyman Field), take the Airport Road to Kanoelehua Avenue which becomes Hawaii Belt Road (State Highway 11). Drive 28 miles up to Volcanoes National Park and, just before the town of Volcano, turn right on Highway 148, which leads to the Ola'a Rainforest. A tree fern and ohia forest may also be visited inside the park.

Hulopoe Bay–Lanai

Now that there's a big, new, 250-room resort hotel on the cliff, the secret of this idyllic little beach on a seldom seen island may be lost forever.

Only a quarter–mile long, Hulopoe is a state Marine Conservation District and the fish must know it because the royal blue bay is full of polychromatic fish—but that's not the secret. The tiny bay is home to a pod of spinner dolphins and if you are lucky to be in the right place at the right time you can join them for a swim.

From Lanai airport, drive about a mile to Kaumalapau Highway (State Highway 440) and just before you reach Lanai City, turn right on Manele Road. Drive across the pineapple fields of the Palawai Basin about eight miles to Manele Bay. The beach park has picnic tables, outdoor showers and drinking water.

The Awaawapuhi Trail–Kauai

The Kalalau Trail gets all the headlines while the Awaawapuhi remains one of Kauai's best kept secrets and probably Hawaii's best hike, especially if you loop out along the Nualolo Cliff trail and come back on the Nualolo trail.

This eight-hour 10-miler for anyone in good condition takes you through Kauai's Green Mansion-like rainforests to the spectacular Awaawapuhi Lookout and then back along the Nualolo, past streams, waterfalls and aerial views of forbidden valleys. You will experience a Kauai few ever see, except from helicopters. The Awaawapuhi (it means "ginger valley") remains a local secret because *haoles* can't pronounce it. Say ah-vah-ah-va-poo-hee. Now, there's no excuse.

The trailhead is at the 17-mile marker of Kokee Road, about a mile and a half before the Kalalau Valley Lookout. Go early in the morning, hike counterclockwise to the Awaawapuhi.

Three Best Chopper Rides

❋

Pablo Picasso said the three greatest inventions of the 20th century were the blues, cubism and Polish vodka. Had he ever visited Hawaii, he might have added the helicopter.

If you go to Hawaii and don't get above it, you've never seen Hawaii. Only a helicopter can bring you face-to-face with volcanoes, waterfalls and remote beaches.

More than 50 helicopter tour operators fly everything from the $1 million Agusta 109 to the Hughes 500D high performance bird. A few are fly-by-night outfits; most, like Papillon and Inter-Island, are 110 percent professional, which means pilots take no chances, crews perform regularly scheduled maintenance, and the operations manager keeps a keen eye on Hawaii's always changing weather conditions.

Two rules-of-thumb: Never fly with a chopper pilot you meet in a bar after 10 p.m. Always book the first flight of the day.

You can go anywhere in Hawaii on a helicopter, but three adventures exist nowhere else on earth.

Fly the Volcano

We are hovering now, bee-like, only 10 feet above the earth's newest land, staring into the red hot heart of planet Earth as fast flowing lava meets the sea at Kalapana, the village lost to lava. Huge chunks of newborn earth explode out of the misty sulphuric smoke on this raw wave-lashed coast; it grows before our eyes. My palms are sweaty not from fear, but because 1,800-degree heat radiates out of the molten lava that runs to the blue sea like wildfire. In the beginning, this must be how the world began. We sit in awe behind a thin plexiglass bubble, with goosebumps in the heat, observing the very act of creation. At lift-off, you never know if Kilauea Volcano will be pumping, but since its current eruptive phase began in 1983, it's seldom stopped; so your chances are usually good to excellent.

The best ride (and most expensive: $295 a person) is a two-hour flight with a stop in Hilo that takes you to the Kilauea Volcano, into the Waipio Valley and along the Hamakua Coast.

Catch a Papillon helicopter at the new Waikoloa heliport, in the middle of a lava field, about one mile north of the entrance to Mauna Lani Bay Hotel. Flights are also available at Keahole Airport by special arrangment. Call (808) 329-0551 in Kona or (808) 961-9252 in Hilo. Or from the mainland U.S. and Canada call toll free (800) 367-7095.

Fly Kauai

Close your eyes and hold on, this is the big thrill ride, a real white–knuckler that takes your breath away.

More fun than the Santa Cruz roller coaster, the Hughes 300D takes you swooping across coffee and macadamia plantations at 2,000 feet into the 3,000-foot deep Grand Canyon of the Pacific at 110 miles an hour, then up and over the Kalalau Valley on the wild north shore and into the 5,200-foot vertical temple of Mount Waialelae, the most sacred place on the island and wettest spot on earth. If you are a waterfall buff, this ride's for you; there are more waterfalls than you can count.

Fly with Inter-Island Helicopters, which I think is one of the best of the 31 outfits flying Kauai. They do aerial photography tours, private charters and stand on 24-hour call for air-sea rescue. They use the high performance Hughes 500D Helicopters with the best seating configuration for visibility. Two in the front and two in the back. No middle seat.

Another good feature is a two-way intercom over David Clark's H-1066s, the best headphones for helicopters because they have a soft, fluid-packed earpiece and big stereo sound. The two-way is important so you can tell the pilot when you need to see more.

Splurge on the Kauai "deluxe" tour, a 60-minute joyride that begins and ends in Hanapepe and gives you the grand tour of Kauai.

Inter-Island Helicopters is located on Highway 50 in Hanapepe, next to the Green Garden Restaurant. Phone (808) 335-5009.

○ *Akamai Tip:* The first time I flew Kauai, with top L.A. adventure photographer Tom Grimm, we took the doors off so we could avoid "canopy flare," and my seat belt—the only thing between me and eternity—accidentally unsnapped minutes after liftoff. If you opt for the "open door" flight plan, wrap adhesive tape around your seat belt buckle, so it doesn't let go up there. Oh, and shoot at 1/500th or more; otherwise everything will come out jittery.

Fly Niihau

"Where we're going is a lot different than Waikiki," says Captain Tom Mishler as we lifted off Kauai in a $1 million Agusta 109 jet helicopter bound for the "forbidden" island of Niihau. The seven passenger Agusta is used for medical emergencies for Niihau residents and when there's no problem, it shuttles out to Niihau for a beach landing, snorkeling and sight-seeing on this island where 200 Hawaiians cling to the old way of life. This is like flying through a time warp back 100 years to a Hawaii which has disappeared elsewhere in the archipelago. You may see sharks, wild pigs, and even 100 percent native Hawaiians on the privately-owned island that slowly is opening its door to the outside world. Sometimes people come down from the village to meet you and they bring precious Niihau shells for sale. You never know when it will happen; it's like looking for a rainbow.

Special and personalized tours and charters are available to Niihau by contacting Niihau Helicopters at P.O. Box 370, Makaweli, Hawaii 96769. (808) 335-3500. The basic Niihau tour, which includes a beach landing, is $185.

Three Best Trail Rides

※

ONE of the best ways to really see Hawaii is to saddle up and ride across the Big Island's sprawling 227,000–acre Parker Ranch, gallop along Kauai's westerly shore at sunset, trek through the Grand Canyon of the Pacific, or meander through the tropical rainforests.

Sunset Beach Ride–Waimea, Kauai

We are galloping on the Waimea coast at sunset, splashing through the surf with wild abandon as a huge red sun sinks into the Pacific. This two-hour sunset beach ride is everybody's favorite on Kauai—thanks to wrangler Les Milne who keeps a string of seven horses ready to ride at Garden Island Ranch.

Take Highway 50 to Waimea, the small sugar plantation town at the mouth of the Waimea River. Garden Island Ranch is just west of Waimea, adjacent to the turn–of–the–century Waimea Plantation Cottages. Call (808) 338-0052 and reserve a horse 24 hours in advance. Sunset beach ride is $100 an hour for two.

On the Hana Coast–Hana, Maui

No more than six riders at a time can go on this five-hour guided trail ride on Maui. Wrangler Frank Levinson introduces his seven horse string and checks out your riding ability to find a suitable steed for the ride on the Hana Coast.

Meet at Hoolawa Bridge, on the Hana Highway, at 10 a.m. Follow down a dirt road to Levinson's sea ranch. For advance reservations, write Adventures on Horseback at P.O. Box 1771, Makawao, Hawaii 96768. Or call (808) 242-7445.

On the Parker Ranch–Big Island

Put on your boots and head for the biggest privately owned ranch in the U.S.—you can be a *paniolo* for a day (that's Hawaiian for cowboy). There's no wider range to ride in Hawaii than the 227,000-acre Parker Ranch that sprawls down the slopes of Mauna Kea into the emerald hills of Waimea, the upcountry ranch town. Contact Lehua Hoopai at Parker Ranch, (808) 885-7655.

Best Nude Beaches

✺

OH, I know it's supposed to be illegal. Tell it to everyone who goes naked everyday somewhere in the islands, mostly at these beaches.

Go Naked in Hanakapiai–Kauai

Some enchanted evening you will meet a (naked) stranger hiking in the remote valleys, but soon *au naturale* seems perfectly natural here. Maybe it's the sun, or the nature of the place, but something about Hanakapiai compels people to go naked. In this place as lush as Eden (we can only imagine), sooner or later you throw off your remnants of civilization and run, splashing down the sea.

Drive Kuhio Highway (State Highway 56) to the end of the road at Ke'e Beach, park and lock your car, begin the two–mile hike; it's one steep mile up and one steep mile down.

Secret Beach–Kauai

One of Hawaii's best known nudist beaches, it's ironic name is a joke; it's map name is Kauapea Beach. This long, wide sandy beach is also good for swimming, bodysurfing, surfing and fishing. High surf from October to April creates dangerous currents near the shore. If you're not careful you could lose your birthday suit.

On the Hanalei side of Kilauea Point, just before the entrance to Kalihiwai Road, turn off Kuhio Highway (State Highway 56) onto the dirt road—oh, you know the way.

Little Beach–Maui

Maui's morality police may still write up tickets for people who dress down at Little Beach (nudity is still against the law in post-missionary Hawaii), but so many people sunbathe nude here that it seems unlikely. This is the scene of the 1986 mass arrest of 100 sun worshippers who founded Friends of Little Beach to protest nudity arrests.

Drive past Kihei and Wailea, which is starting to look like Waikiki, to Makena Bay, near the Maui Prince Hotel. Park at Big Beach, take a short hike over the knoll to the thin crescent of sand edged by lava rock on either side. A bonus here is that, between November and April, whales come within 60 yards of the shore.

Kaloko-Honokohau–Big Island

Hard to say, hard to find, this popular Big Island nude beach may become Hawaii's first official "clothing optional" beach, under the auspices of the National Park system. It's on the Kona Coast of the Big Island in a new 1,300-acre National Historical Park between Kailua-Kona and Keahole Airport.

Drive three and a half miles south of the Keahole Airport to the Kaoko Industrial Park. Turn toward the ocean at the unmarked dirt road located opposite the industrial park warehouses. The access road is rough, so park near the entrance gate and walk three-quarters of a mile to the ocean. Follow the well-worn trail along this lava coast to the nude beach.

◉ *Akamai Tip:* I know this sounds silly this late in the 20th century, but the Boston missionary influence in Hawaii is such that it's still against the law for women to sunbathe topless, although Polynesian women have been doing so since Day One.

Women may be cited for topless sunbathing and men for letting it all hang out at Hawaii's beaches and state parks. However, since the Hawai Supreme Court overturned a 1987 nudity conviction, there's a live-and-let-live attitude and Hawaii may even get into the swing of things. In the meantime, be discreet, don't skinny-dip at Waikiki, cover your buns near churches and use high-test sunscreen everywhere.

Three Best Windsurf Spots

❋

THE windward shores of the Hawaiian islands are the best places to windsurf because the wind almost always is onshore, which means you won't be blown out to sea.

The water is warm and buoyant, and that's important to a beginner because you'll spend a lot of time in the water before you get it. It's amazing how many ways you can fall off something with only two sides.

Anini Beach–Kauai

On lazy afternoons at Anini Beach, what passes for wind is a warm breeze that's just enough to nudge a beginning windsurfer along. This is where I coached my long, tall friend Scott Blakey on the fine art of windsurfing and if he can do it, anyone can.

Lanikai Beach–Oahu

For beginners to intermediates, this is the best "trainer" beach in the islands. Steady, light onshore trades blow almost daily across this turquoise lagoon with two islands.

Hookipa Beach–Maui

The hard wind that blows daily at Hookipa Beach is the big draw for windsurfers from around the world. Definitely for advanced surfers, this is the home of the Maui Air Force, those high-flying aerialists who smash waves head-on to gain "hang-time" up in the air like junior birdmen and birdwomen.

Three Great Roads to Cruise with the Top Down

※

RENT a red convertible, put the top down, fill the cooler and pop a Gabby Pahinui cassette in the deck. Let's go cruising in the islands.

Whether you take the highway to Hana, or a Saturday night beach cruise in Waikiki, you are going to see a lot of Hawaii from the driver's seat.

Be prepared for unusual caveats, like this one on the Big Island map: "Some roads on the island may be closed due to volcanic activity; inquire locally of status." Or the sign on Maui near Kipahulu that warns: "Baby Pig Crossing."

In addition, watch out for "cane haul trucks," flash floods, and slick roads in mango season. It's all part of the tropical obstacle course that is Hawaii's strange road system.

You will meet first generation drivers, unidentified rusty vehicles and see roadside shrines of those who didn't make it home. Play it safe. If you drink, don't drive.

Nobody in the world drives like people in Hawaii. Stay alert and smile a lot. Be polite and take your time. On an island, why hurry?

◉ *Akamai Tips:*
> Nobody honks; it's considered rude.
> It's OK to turn right at a red light after a stop.
> Pedestrians always have the right-of-way.
> Top speed limit is 55 miles per hour.
> It's okay to drive barefoot.

Highway 11–Big Island

No road in Hawaii is like the one that goes all the way around the Big Island. It goes around erupting Kilauea volcano, along the wild sea, across the great Ka'u desert, across smoking lava fields, under the vog, past ghost towns covered by lava, through Kona coffee plantations, past South Point (the southernmost point in the U.S.), into the clouds, through the rainforest, past orchid farms, down the volcano into gloomy Hilo, under giant banyan trees, along the levee, past Akaka Falls, through sugar cane fields, along the nearly vertical Hamakua coast, across canyons over postcard bridges on stilts, through the world's biggest private cowboy ranch, past $8 billion worth of glitzy resorts, down the middle of coal black lava beds, past white-rock graffiti that tells you who got here yesterday, past the abalone ponds of the Ocean Thermal Energy Conversion Plant, and, finally, into Kailua-Kona town to end up at the pier where sport fisherpersons get their pictures snapped next to 1,000-pound marlin. Somebody should make a Grand Prix out of this.

Start in Kailua-Kona, drive counterclockwise around the island until you see something you want to see more of, get hungry, need gas or a pit stop. Go until you return to start and then stop. You can do it in a day—and I've done it—but it's a grind, so take two or three days.

From Kailua-Kona, take Highway 11 south and keep on rolling. If you make it an overnight, stay at Volcano Lodge (call ahead and make reservations at Volcano Lodge or Kilauea Lodge), visit the endangered Wao Kele O' Puna rainforest, hike Devastation Trail, browse the Volcano Art Center.

Spend the next day in Hilo, eat N'awlins-style soft shell crabs at Roussell's; walk through the Hawaii Tropical Botanical Garden; take a sidetrip to Hawi, one of the last great little Hawaiian towns; visit the Mo'okini *heiau*; pop into the new Ritz-Carlton for a $50 lunch; take a hike down the petroglyph trail at Mauna Lani.

Waimea Canyon Road–Kauai

On the Waimea Canyon Road, the island of Kauai reveals itself in all its rugged tropical canyon/waterfall/forest glory like one of those fast-forward time exposure films. This is a subtle ride full of unexpected natural pleasures like showers, god-rays of light, wild pheasants, fluttering bats at sunset, unexpected "oh, look!" lookouts, misty fern forests, and icy mountain streams of Koke'e State Park at 3,500 foot elevation. The Natural History Museum and Koke'e Lodge are worth exploring; you might book a stay at the lodge.

Your goal is the 4,120-foot Kalalau Lookout, which offers a view of clouds, tropical birds and an isolated beach out of your tropical dreams. On the way back, in the afternoon, the setting sun on the canyon walls creates a light show of designer earth tones in the Grand Canyon of the Pacific, carved by eons of run-off from Mt. Waialeale, the wettest spot on earth, which annually records 36 feet of rain.

Go early in the day. Turn mauka up Waimea Canyon Drive, just past Waimea town. Don't stop at the canyon lookouts like everyone else. Go directly to the Kalalau overlook so you can catch the 4,000-foot view to the sea by early morning light before clouds obscure the view. Then take your time on the way back and dodge the traffic. Make a day of it, bring your own lunch, cheese and wine are fine; take a sweater and surround yourself in Kauai's natural splendor.

Best place for a picnic is at Pua Hina Hina on a grassy bluff overlooking Waimea Canyon. It's on the right just before the Pua Hina Hina lookout.

Cruising Waikiki–Oahu

The ultimate see-and-be-seen Saturday night beach cruise is in Waikiki, a one-way ride down four big lanes of asphalt named for a king.

Bumper-to-bumper at 6 miles per hour, it's the perfect speed to show your stuff and nobody holds back in this parade.

There are red hot Ferraris and little deuce coupes, stretch Mercedes Benz limousines, chopped hogs, Porsche Speedsters, chopped and channeled Volkswagen bugs, sky-high 4 x 4s, pink T-birds driven by aging beach ladies and, once in a great while, a real old "woodie" surf wagon with a quiver of longboards jutting out the back.

The last time I cruised Kalakaua Avenue on a Saturday night was with Glenn Hodson who made the scene in his ermine white Rolls Royce Corniche convertible, which may be the ultimate beach cruiser. We had the Beach Boys on the Blaupunkt and did we get the eye, especially from young girls. Oh, to be 18 again, oh.

Go around 10 p.m. any Saturday night in Waikiki. Head down Kalakaua Avenue toward Diamond Head, turn left at Kapahulu Avenue, drive ewa on Ala Wai Boulevard, turn left on McCully Street and double back on Kalakaua. Repeat cycle.

Three Great Waterfalls

❋

THERE are hundreds, if not thousands, of waterfalls in Hawaii, mostly on Kauai. I counted 31 one rainy afternoon while crossing the Koolau mountains on Oahu's Pali Highway.

Many waterfalls are in remote, difficult to reach places, which is why resorts now replicate waterfalls. With a little effort and some hiking you can see the real thing.

Sacred Falls–Oahu

Up a narrow valley cut by the slippery Kaluanua Stream, past wild guavas and mountain apples, Sacred Falls is a 4.4 mile round-trip hike enjoyed by thousands who make a day outing in this cool, green canyon.

The 87-foot falls splash into a cold swimming pool which ancient Hawaiians reputedly believed was bottomless and led to another world inhabited by a demon. To go safely many believers and the superstitious still make a small offering of a stone wrapped in a ti leaf, which you may see along the trail.

You won't be the only one here, especially on weekends, but this is one waterfall that is gained by a gentle hike even kids can make without too much complaint.

From Honolulu, drive over the Pali Highway (Route 61), then left on Highway 83 to Hauula. Turn left at the sign on the left marked "Sacred Falls State Park." Distance: 28 miles.

Akaka Falls–Big Island

Akaka Falls on the Big Island, one of Hawaii's most scenic water features and most requested Hawaiian songs, cascades 442 feet into Kolekole stream, which is lined by red, white and yellow ginger.

Drive a few miles north from Hilo on Highway 19. Turn left at Honoimu and go five miles inland to the park. Signs point the way to the falls which are reached after an easy half-hour hike on a paved path. You'll see 100-foot Kahuna Falls first, then round the corner and see Akaka Falls.

Wailua Falls–Kauai

You've seen it on television, now see it in person. It's even more spectacular. The twin cascades of the 80-foot Wailua Falls on Kauai, which appear in the opening scenes of "Fantasy Island", may be seen from an overlook but not visited close up; it's impossible to descend the cliffs.

Drive 10 minutes from Lihue on Highway 546, turn left on Highway 583 and proceed four miles to the falls.

Best Sea Cruises

"Steaming westward from California, you've gloried in the lazy days and lovely nights of your voyage...then your pulse quickens for this moment—landfall at sunrise. For islanders, it's home, the most beautiful home in the world...for visitors, the first view of these fairy-like islands, rising rose-tinted in the tropic sea...and in a few moments, the flower-filled "Aloha" that Hawaii bestows on her beloved Lurline..."

1952 Lurline advertisement

THE Lurline is long gone; so, too, is the *S.S. Matsonia* and *S.S. Monterey*, but that doesn't mean you can't take a sea cruise in Hawaii.

American Hawaii Cruises offers year-round weekly cruises in the Hawaiian islands aboard two luxury ships—the *S.S. Constitution* and *S.S. Independence*.

I have sailed on both and they are the best way to see the best of Hawaii: the Honolulu city lights, the leaping humpback whales, the Big Island volcano at midnight, the far side of Lanai, sunsets at sea.

You call on the main ports of Hawaii—Honolulu, Kahaului, Hilo and Nawiliwili—and go ashore like liberty sailors to seek island adventures.

The bon voyage party is right out of a 40s movie. On our cruise, the Eugene LeBeaux Orchestra played all those old tunes as we threw leis out over the side. It is so romantic, people actually cry.

Life aboard isn't a series of lazy days in a deck chair with a novel. You can do that too, but there's a lot more going on—cocktail parties, dinner with the captain, meeting new friends. The nightlife/entertainment/parties aboard the ship are excellent—stage shows like "Phantom of the Opera" and musical revues.

The abundant food (five servings daily in four different restaurants) didn't surprise me but the pampering service did.

When you go ashore, all the island adventures await you. You can chopper over the volcano, explore Onomea Gardens, go up the Huleia river in kayaks or dance the night away down at Club Jetty.

If you want the Hawaii sea cruise, this is it. Contact American Hawaii Cruises, 550 Kearny Street, San Francisco, California 94108. (800) 227-3666.

Best Booze Cruise

If you must go on a Waikiki booze cruise, the best of them is the *Rella Mae*, the first cruise ship of the sunset fleet which joined the service on New Year's Eve, 1980.

Operated by Windjammer Cruises, the 283-foot vessel has four square sails, four head sails, four stay sails and one spanker sail for a total of 6,020 square feet of power. It carries a crew of 15 with 46 passenger attendants. It sails twice an evening year-round, weather permitting, from Honolulu Harbor, off Waikiki Beach to Diamond Head, then returns.

Best Yacht Charter

What's better than having your own private yacht in the Pacific? Any sailor will tell you, it's having access to one. Carol and Bob Hogan have sailed all over the Pacific on the *Discovery*, a 45-foot luxury cruiser out of Kailua-Kona, and they will take you and five others on a sea cruise.

You can call, write or fax Bob or Carol. Phone (808) 326-1011. Fax (808) 326-1011. Write 75-293 Aloha Kona Drive, Kailua–Kona, Hawaii 96740.

Kayaking the Islands

❈

"Today I tried again to write about Molokai but the sea was there beyond the open door..."

Audrey Sutherland, *Paddling My Own Canoe*

KAYAKERS are going down to the sea in bright, shiny small craft that open a new world of adventure in Hawaii.

Hundreds go down those coasts daily in rubber inflatables and new high-tech plastic hardshells. Any tranquil lagoon or bay will do for starters (**Kailua Bay** on Oahu's windward side is probably the safest place for first-time kayakers to wet a paddle), but inevitably kayakers are drawn to **Molokai's windward coast** or **Kauai's north shore**.

Not for the Sunday kayaker, the surging sea, dangerous cliffs and total isolation of each wild coast will test the skill and nerve of most kayakers, especially in the winter.

The best time for Molokai and Kauai is between May and September when seas are flat, but even in the calm of August, 10-foot seas can come up suddenly and put you in real danger.

On Molokai, kayakers launch from Halawa Bay and head down to Kalaupapa past 3,000-foot sea cliffs so high they're listed in *The Guinness Book of Records*. From Halawa to Kalaupapa it's an incredible 12 miles, especially from sea level.

Gary Budlong, who has led tours down Molokai's coast for eight years, claims the most seaworthy craft is an ocean kayak known as a Scupper or the Aquaterra's Prism.

Both 14-foot kayaks are made of high-impact, poly-plastics that can withstand high seas, huge boulders and coral reefs.

Several outfits used to lead guided tours down the Molokai and Kauai coast, but Hawaii's State Department of Land and Natural Resources banned commercial waterfront activity, so now you must go it alone—and that can be dangerous for anyone unfamiliar with Hawaiian water.

The safest way is to check out the local connection, like Go Bananas on Oahu, (808) 988-3913, which sells and rents kayaks and offers guided kayak tours to Fiji and Tonga. On Kauai, try local outfitter Kauai By Kayak, (808) 245-9662; or Outfitters Kauai at Poipu Beach, (808) 742-9667.

Beginners on Oahu should check out Bob Twogood Kayaks Hawaii, 171 Hamakua Drive, Kailua, Oahu (808) 262-5656.

◎ *Akamai Tip:* Audrey Sutherland recounts her epic paddle around Molokai in a nine-foot inflatable canoe in her book, *Paddling My Own Canoe*. She also appears in "Molokai Solo," an award-winning adventure film by Bob Liljestrand. Read the book or see the film before you go.

Three Great Adventure Resorts

※

TAP the Doric columns; they are hollow; worse, they are made of fiberglass. The waterfalls are man-made, even the lagoon.

Welcome to the glitzing of Paradise, where all your dreams come true, thanks to petrochemical by-products in hyper-real settings that would make William Randolph Hearst jealous. The swans, thank God, are real.

As if it isn't enough just to be in Hawaii, the pineapple is now gilded by world class luxury resorts. Some of these leisure malls by the sea are so gauche you'll think you're in Florida; others are indigenous, appropriate and somehow Hawaiian. All are dedicated to pleasure, one of life's great adventures, although it is doubtful you will experience any real surprise beyond a life-size chocolate nautilus shell on your pillow, until you get the final bill. Everyone has to be somewhere though, and these resorts are worth a look if only for the spectacular achievement in fantasy. In case you get tired of roughing it, these are a few of my favorite resorts, glitzy and otherwise:

Kauai Westin Lagoons, Kauai

If you like fantasy—and who doesn't?—you will love what Christopher Hemmeter did to the Kauai Westin Lagoons, changing an old dog of a resort to one that now resembles a tropo-Versailles, and for only $250 million. The funny thing is I like it, just as I like Hearst Castle, but not everyone does.

Rooms are small (except for the two-story Presidential Suite with spiral staircase), but the huge, scallop-shaped pool more than makes up for that and the romantic promenade along Kalapaki Beach is absolutely cinematic, especially when the *S.S. Constitution* steams out of Nawiliwili Bay.

The Westin has Kauai's first escalator, liveried chauffeurs in stretch Cadillac limos, Clydesdale-drawn carriages ala Central Park, $1 million Italian-made launches, a view restaurant worthy of the claim (it's called Inn on the Cliffs), and a heroic beachside bar, Duke's Canoe Club, which venerates Hawaii's only Olympian beach boy, the late, great Duke Kahanamoku. If only for Duke's, this fantasy resort is worth calling upon. Who ever said Hearst Castle was tasteful?

Guests are met at Kauai's new Lihue Airport by sleek black stretch limos or a Clydesdale-drawn hansom carriage, but you may drive up to the Westin Kauai hotel on Kalapaki Beach, only a 20–minute drive from Lihue Airport.

From Lihue Airport, take Ahukini Road (State Highway 570) to the first left which is Kapule Highway (State Highway 51). Turn left and stay on it to Nawiliwili Harbor, where the American Hawaii cruise ships *S.S. Constitution* and *S.S. Independence* dock every week. Just before the harbor, look for the signed entrance to Kauai Westin Lagoons, drive up to the porte cochere, say "'owzit" to the uniformed doorman, valet park (or park free in the lot on the right) and ride Kauai's first and only escalator down to the Grand Lobby. Non-guests may ride the escalator, the Venetian launches, the limousines and even the horse-drawn carriages for a token fee. It's like going to Disneyland.

The Kona Village, The Big Island

Two miles across sun-scorched lava beds on a dusty road full of potholes sits a cluster of 100 thatch shacks without television, telephone or other high-tech amenities. There also is no golf course. This, according to *The New Yorker*, is "the Hawaii you only dreamed about..."

Welcome to The Kona Village, which clings to a vision begun by Johnno Jacko, a Texas oilman and blue water sailor who dropped anchor offshore of the abandoned Hawaiian village of Kaupulehu on Kahuwai Bay in 1959, and caused to be created one of the world's most enduring and wonderful resorts.

He built his Shipwreck Bar out of the hull of his 42-foot schooner and started making grass shacks according to various Pacific island traditions. Sure, it costs $450 a day but all meals are included and so, too, is the sense of place, the lulling, total seclusion, and the restorative powers of pure, simple isolation. That is the secret shared by Fred Duerr, a magician of a host at Kona Village for 28 years.

Look for flags flying from a thatched-roof hut on Queen Kaahumanu Highway about five miles north of the Keahole Airport. That's the sole clue to the existence of Kona Village. Drive two miles across the lava beds on a dusty two lane road until you arrive at what appears to be a lost Boy Scout camp by the sea. When you see smiling women in pareaus moving in what appears to be slow motion, you will have arrived at Kona Village.

Hyatt Regency, Kauai

Dolphin rides, marble stallions and shiny bullet trains in the lobby may be okay for Las Vegas but the future of Hawaii lies in its past. Nobody knows that better than the Hyatt Regency hotel chain, which five years ago went for Vegas-like glitz and now is returning to yesteryear and the old-style Hawaiian resort. Its newest creation on the Garden Island of Kauai, the Hyatt Regency Kauai, is the latest example of a renaissance in Hawaiiana expressed in architecture.

What may be the last major resort on the fourth largest and northwesternmost island in the Hawaiian chain, the 600-room, $250-million Hyatt utilizes the Hawaiian style of architecture created by C. W. Dickey in the mid-1920s to recapture the old Hawaii of the "blue blazer" steamship era.

There had been talk of creating a resort with a carnival-like atmosphere, something with a Japanese wing, a Polynesian wing, a South American wing and, of course, a super pool with slides and wedding chapels. Instead, the three-story oceanfront hotel reflects the the timeless style introduced by Dickey, the father of Hawaii's architecture who adapted the California Mission–style to Hawaii's tropical climate and designed such features as wide eaves, high open windows and double-pitched roofs.

The "natural" swimming pools, a five-acre network of fresh pools and saltwater lagoons by a white sandy beach, is the best in Hawaii. Three waterfalls splash into the upper pool which feeds a twisting, lava rock-lined river with private grottoes and three whirlpools perfect for lovers; at sea level the river pool empties into a larger "playground" pool with a twisty water slide and water volleyball court. Wait, there's more. A large saltwater lagoon beside the 5,000 square foot white sand beach is deep enough for SCUBA lessons. All water is heated by the hot water from the resort's air-conditioning system.

Of the three restaurants here, my favorite is Tidepools, a collection of open-air thatch huts on a lagoon that needs only monkeys to recall steamy tropical nights down in old Zamboanga.

From Lihue Airport, turn left on Ahukini Road (State Highway 570) and drive to the Kaumuali'i Highway (State Highway 50), turn left and drive through the town of Lihue, past a shopping center and through sugar cane fields about eight miles until you see Koloa Road (State Highway 530). Turn left and drive through old Koloa town, past a collection of shops and restaurants to the first left which is Poipu Road. Turn left, drive past Poipu Beach resorts to the end of the road. Look for the green tile roof on the right hand side of Poipu Road.

Best Water Features

✸

IT used to be a well-placed carp pond was enough to soothe the urban soul, but not anymore. They're fooling around with Mother Nature in Hawaii these days.

You turn a corner at the resort and, suddenly, there's a 30-foot waterfall, or a white-water river, or a tranquil lagoon—all wholly created by artists. Leave it to Hawaii, which already has such a great outdoors, to replicate it in handy places for the amusement and convenience of the leisure class.

Artifice became reality a few years ago after architect Donald Goo of Wimberly Allison Tong & Goo, the premier tropical resort designers, discovered that 90 percent of Hawaii's visitors prefer to sit by a pool by the ocean, instead of plunging into the real thing. Amazing, but true.

As a result, Hawaii's hyper-reality soon began to include what is now known in design circles as "water features": man-made lagoons and waterfalls created of PVC pipe and lava rock and utilizing state-of-the-art hydraulics with such great illusory skill that the edges of reality are forever blurred. Now, anyone can swim in a shark-free, salt water lagoon in Hawaii without fear.

The popularity of waterfalls is such that many people in Honolulu now have installed their own private backyard waterfalls and lava rock pools which they can "turn on" with a wall switch, like any other appliance.

The best of Hawaii's water artists is John Groak, a sculptor from Carmel, California, who has created some of Hawaii's best man-made waterfalls including one on Kauai that spills sixty feet down a cliff into the real Pacific.

Even if they aren't real, some of these *faux* water works look it, and they are worth seeing, I suppose, if only as sociological curiosities and examples of how far we, as a civilization, have advanced from the days of the old swimming hole.

Umberto Ecco, the Italian cultural critic who has examined the phenomenon, believes "the American imagination demands the real thing, and, to attain it, must fabricate the absolute fake." I think he may be too harsh, but if you lack the adventure to discover the real thing, here's where to find authentic replicas:

Fort Street Mall–Chinatown, Honolulu

Waterfalls appear on Fort Street Mall and in Chinatown in downtown Honolulu—it's part of a municipal beautification project. One is seen by thousands daily; it sits on its own traffic island surrounded by a sea of passing motorists and even features a Hawaiian net fishermen. You may get a good look at it only if you get the red light on South King Street where it veers Diamond Head on Kapiolani Boulevard. Only Honolulu would have a drive-by waterfall.

Hyatt Regency–Kauai

Not even William Randolph Hearst had a five-acre lava rock lagoon with three waterfalls, its own island, salt-water tide pools with thatched–roof *hales* (houses) and a water slide by a white sand beach. The Hyatt Regency Kauai has all that and a health and fitness spa with a 25-meter lap pool in an open courtyard with open–air lava rock showers, so you may stand privately naked and bathe under the sun in the tropical breeze.

Hyatt Regency–Maui

At the Hyatt Regency Maui, the 750,000 gallon, half-acre free-form pool gleams with 14 karat gold tiles and has a 154-foot lava tube-like water slide, a secret honeymooner's cave and swim-up bar. Pool goers get pampered with Sun Shades 2000 (a protective sun filter), Evian water misters, custom towels with corners (that serve as pockets), cellular phones (if you really must call home), sunglasses, magazines, board games and—there's no escaping it—Nintendo. The pool even has its very own radio station, HVOP (Hyatt's Voice of Paradise), featuring complimentary Sony Walkman headsets to pipe soft rock and Hawaiian music gently into sun soakers' ears.

Maui Prince Hotel–Maui

When Yoshiaki Tsutsumi, the world's richest man, wants a carp pond, he gets a carp pond that's really something to see. It begins with a 30-foot waterfall in the middle of his Maui Prince Hotel, that roars past a fern grotto (popular for weddings), trickles over a stony brook, flows past a Zen sand and rock garden to a tranquil black bottom pond whose mirrored surface is broken by what appears to be thousands of carp. They kiss the surface in a endless series of *O's* while you sit dreamily eating at the Kiowai Terrace Restaurant, reflecting on the meaning of toast.

Hyatt Wailea–Maui

The grand Hyatt Wailea has what may be the ultimate. Maui's newest resort features a river with wild rapids anyone can ride. Waterfalls spill into a gorge that becomes a water slide with white water action. It's the best man-made river I've ever seen.

The Best Places to See Hula

NOTHING says Hawaii like hula and nothing says it better than the Merrie Monarch Festival—it's the Super Bowl and World Series of the dance of the islands.

Each year in Hilo, Hawaii, hundreds of hula dancers compete in a three-night contest named for King David Kalakaua, the Merrie Monarch and patron of hula, who in the late 1800s lifted the missionary ban on the sensuous dance to preserve the Hawaiian culture which lives on in song and dance.

This is not the *faux hula* danced in hotels or at commercial luaus, which often feature Filipino girls dancing the Tahitian *tamure* while some loud-mouth keeps shouting, "Alooooo-haaa!" Try to avoid such cultural denigrations and seek out the real thing; otherwise you will miss the essence of Hawaii.

If you can't go to the Merrie Monarch Festival, you can see it on television, usually telecast "live" on Honolulu's KITV Channel Four (which also has the most professional news shows).

The Merrie Monarch, as everyone calls it, features male and female dancers from 28 groups, known as *halau*, from Hawaii and California. They dance *Kahiko* (ancient) and *'Auana* (modern).

The ancient style is historically accurate not only to step but costume and flowers. Women dancers, with long, dark hair, knee-length ti leaf skirts, *hapu* crown leis on their head and fern ringlets at their ankles, look as if they stepped out of an 18th century James Webber print. The men wear the traditional *malo*, or loin cloth, and fern leis at head and feet.

Each dance opens with a Hawaiian chant, a dedication to Kalakaua or Pele, and is accompanied by such Hawaiian instruments as *'ili'ili* (smooth rocks used like castanets), the *pahu* (a carved wooded drum with a sharkskin head), the *pu'ili* (split bamboo), *ipu heke* (a gourd drum) and the *'uli'uli* (a gourd rattle filled with seeds and often decorated with feathers).

The chants, according to Pi'ilani Smith, a former Miss Aloha Hula and member of two-time defending champion Halau 'o na Mauoli Pua, reveal the character of the Hawaiian people, their humor, playfulness, sensuality, poetry and lyricism.

Hula chants also celebrate and preserve Hawaiian history, culture, tradition, genealogy, religion, legend and myth and serve as the flame that keeps the Hawaiian cultural renaissance burning brightly in the islands. And you thought hula was just a dance.

The **Merrie Monarch Festival**, now in its 29th year, is usually sold out a year in advance. The best way to see it is to go to the Kanak'ole Stadium, the huge covered pavilion where everyone gathers, usually in April, and ask around if anyone has an extra ticket. Or you can try writing Merrie Monarch Festival Headquarters, 400 Hualani Street, Hilo, Hawaii 96721 or call (808) 935-9168 and plead.

If you are unsuccessful, other great hula performances may be seen throughout the islands—at the **King Kamehameha Hula and Chant Competition** in Honolulu, in June; at the **Prince Lot Festival** at Honolulu's Moanalua Gardens, usually in July; and the **Na Mele o Hawaii Festival** at Kaanapali, Maui, in November. Or at various *hula halau* fundraisers held throughout the year. My favorite is **Halau Mohala Ilima** from Oahu. Since these are held at different times on different islands, you must check local papers for dates and times.

Three Great Hollywood Adventures in Hawaii

IF Hawaii looks familiar to you and you've never been here before, it's not *deja vu*, all over again—as Yogi Berra said—it's Hollywood.

Over the years Hollywood has made 130 films in Hawaii, chiefly on Kauai, which has appeared in *King Kong*, *Raiders of the Lost Ark*, *Uncommon Valor*, and soon will appear in *Hook*, the Steven Spielberg remake of *Peter Pan*. To visit Hawaii is to bump into the ghosts of films past.

Wash That Man Right Outa My Hair Beach–Kauai

It's been called "the world's most beautiful beach." It's certainly Kauai's best known, thanks to Mitzi Gaynor and Rosanno Brazzi who starred in *South Pacific*. It's hard to find (on the right, a half mile past the third bridge from Hanalei) and hard to get to (drive past it, park in the lot, walk back a mile across hot sand), and it's just as well. The beach on **Waikoko Bay** is pretty to look at, but big surf and strong currents make swimming dangerous.

Where Elvis Got Married in Blue Hawaii–Kauai

Elvis got married in *Blue Hawaii* on the fish pond in front of the Coco Palms dining room. More than 30 years later couples from all over the world still request *Blue Hawaii* weddings.

They float down the fish pond on an outrigger canoe just like Elvis did and walk to the Palm Chapel, which was built by Universal Studios for Rita Hayworth's movie wedding in *Sadie Thompson.*

The River of Raiders of the Lost Ark–Kauai

Harrison Ford ran for his life up the Huleia River on Kauai in the opening scenes of *Raiders of The Lost Ark.* The otherwise peaceful river is now popular with kayakers.

Five Things Kama'ainas Never Do
(but you may want to, anyway)

✻

"We are skating on the thin edge of kitsch here."
Jeremy Railton on Waikiki's Aloha Showroom

ONE night at the Ritz-Carlton, over dinner with Hawaii's veteran travel writers (Rita Ariyoshi, Robert W. Bone, Jocelyn K. Fujii, John & Bobbye McDermott), who have seen and done it all, I wondered what, if anything, they had never seen or done in Hawaii because it's touristy, kitschy or just plain dumb.

My random survey resulted in an odd collection of adventures which, in the interest of fair and impartial reporting, is presented here only so you may be properly forewarned and, a.) avoid them, or b.) experience what the "experts" missed. They are listed in no particular order; each having equal rank.

Fern Grotto–Kauai

On a visit to Kauai's Fern Grotto, you climb on a barge with 100 other people you'd never invite to dinner and motor up the Waimea River a mile to a cave full of ferns and come back. Thaaaat's all folks.

It used to be an experience you encouraged visitors to share, says author John McDermott, but the mobs of people have reduced this to the just another roadside attraction category. Some couples even get married there but a day at the beach with Michener's book, *Hawaii*, is more rewarding.

Don Ho Show–Waikiki

After 25 years with only two hit songs, the incredible Don "Tiny Bubbles" Ho, now in his 60s, is still going strong at the Hilton Hawaiian Village with the Don Ho Show. He packs them in nightly inside The Dome, plinks on a ukulele, then mumble-sings all two of his hits (the other one, I think, was "Pearly Shells"). He also hosts an otherwise lively Polynesian show of singers and dancers, kisses the blue-haired women in the front row, then invites adoring fans backstage to have their pictures taken with him for only $25. It is the longest running cabaret show in Waikiki, second only to Bobby Short at the Carlyle Hotel in New York City, but at least he can play the piano, too. My mother-in-law who lives in Florida loves this show, and so will yours.

Paradise Cove Luau–Waikiki

The Paradise Cove Luau is billed as "the most popular commercial luau" in Hawaii and that may be its only redeeming factor: it keeps thousands of people off the streets. If you like to pay $50 to eat overcooked pork on paper plates and drink sweet Hawaiian punch, while young Filipino girls dance the Tahitian *tamure* as an announcer makes lewd sexist remarks and keeps shouting "Ahh-loooo-HAAAAA!", then this culturally insensitive luau is for you. This is the hula show the missionaries should have banned.

Kenny Rogers Photo Opportunity–Honolulu

Of all the things to do in Hawaii, the Kenny Rogers Photo Opportunity may be the dumbest. Yet, everyday at Dole Cannery Square in Honolulu, thousands of tourists, usually in matching aloha shirts, pay $5 to have their picture taken standing next to a life-size cardboard cutout of singer Kenny Rogers, whose link to Hawaii is tenuous (he's the spokesman for Dole pineapple juice). What makes this photo opportunity even more bizarre is that it's taken in front of a wall-size mural of Lanai's soon-to-be extinct pineapple fields. P.T. Barnum would approve, but this tacky exploitation gives Hawaii and pineapples a bad name.

Request the "Hawaiian Wedding Song"

The tourist from Texas wanted to hear it, but the Makaha Sons of Niihau, one of Hawaii's best groups, refused to sing "The Hawaiian Wedding Song" because it's not the real Hawaiian wedding song.

The truth is there are two real Hawaiian wedding songs, both written by composer Charles Edward King (1874-1950), the dean of Hawaiian music. The one made popular by singer Andy Williams isn't the same eternal love song composed by King in 1926, for his operetta "Prince of Hawaii."

That song, a duet for baritone and soprano, "Ke Kali Nei Au," which means "waiting for thee" is known in Hawaii as the Hawaiian wedding song, because it is often sung at weddings.

Many Hawaiians call his "Lei Aloha Lei Makamae," written in 1934, *their* wedding song, although it is not widely known in the islands or the mainland, today.

If you want to make a request, ask for "Ke Kali Nei Au," and the Makaha Sons of Niihau may oblige; that's what they sang for the Texas tourist that night.

◎ *Akamai Alert:* If you have a suitable candidate for this category, please send your nomination on the worst Hawaii postcard you have ever seen to: Great Outdoor Adventures of Hawaii Kitsch List, P.O. Box 777 Kapiolani Blvd., Suite 2315, Honolulu, Hawaii 96813. *Mahalo for your kokua.* (Thanks for your help.)

Weddings in Hawaii

JIM and Jeanne Houston got married on Waikiki Beach, and Ken and Peggy Wills got married in The Valley of the Temples. Annie and Danny got married on a desert island.

You can get married by a waterfall, on the beach, under a rainbow, on a sailboat, or even underwater, like my Kauai diving pal George "Captain Nemo" Thompson.

A Hawaiian wedding is one of life's greatest adventures in one of the world's greatest places. And you don't have far to go for a Hawaiian honeymoon.

Nearly 20,000 marriages a year are performed in Hawaii, mostly on Oahu, and 44.6 percent of the couples are non-residents. The groom is usually 31, and the bride 28, and 40 percent of the couples have been married before.

Get a Hawaii marriage license in person at the State Health Department, 1250 Punchbowl St., Honolulu, Hawaii 96813, (808) 548-5862, or a state-approved Marriage License Agency. On Kauai, it's the bait and tackle shop in Kapaa.

A marriage license costs $16 cash, is good for 30 days and is good on all islands.

Brides must get a rubella screening test certificate from a physician and bring it to the health department or license agent when applying for a marriage license.

No residence or citizenship requirement and no documents are necessary if you are 20 or older.

For a free copy of *Weddings in Hawaii*, a comprehensive list of wedding service info, write the Hawaii Visitors Bureau at 2270 Kalakaua Ave., Suite 801, Honolulu, Hawaii 96815, or call (808) 923-1811.

APPENDIX

※

276
WHO's WHO
GREAT ADVENTURERS OF HAWAII

295
BEST BOOKS
AN ADVENTURER'S BIBLIOGRAPHY

299
BEST NUMBERS
A DIRECTORY OF IMPORTANT NUMBERS

WHO's WHO
GREAT ADVENTURERS OF HAWAII

Since prehistoric times, the Hawaiian Islands have been the home, destination and stopover for a remarkable collection of adventurers. That is no less the case today, as you will see from this compendium of who's who of the great Hawaii adventurers:

The Polynesians

The first great adventurers were the Polynesians in 300–500 A.D., who crossed the wide open expanses of the Pacific in double-hulled voyaging canoes. They followed the stars, probably from Marquesas, northeast of Tahiti. The name of the first Polynesian navigator is lost but the epic voyages of Mo'ikeha, Pa'ao, and La'a-mai-Kahiki are recalled in the oral traditions and genealogical records of the Hawaiians. By 850 A.D., all main Hawaiian islands were occupied.

Captain James Cook

The English explorer, commander of *H.M.S. Resolution* and *Discovery*, sighted Oahu, Kauai and Niihau on January 18, 1778. He claimed the islands known as Owhyhee for Great Britain, then re-named them the Sandwich Islands in honor of John Montagu, the fourth Earl of Sandwich, First Lord of the Admiralty, and Cook's main man. Named "discoverer" of Hawaii, his sailors introduced venereal disease and small pox. His ambition was "not only to go further than anyone had done before, but as far as it was possible for man to go." He was killed "without mercy" by natives at Kealakekua Bay on 1779, under the watchful eye of Chief Kalaniopu'u.

"His entrails were used to rope off the arena and the palms of his hands used for fly swatters at a cockfight," according to Kamakau, the historian. A young man who witnessed the murder became Hawaii's first king.

King Kamehameha The Great

The conquerer of Hawaii, Lanai, Molokai and Oahu, he was born in 1758, on the Kohala Coast of the Big Island of Hawaii. He was the first to unify all Hawaiian islands under his rule. His 1796 attempt to conquer Kauai failed but he won the island by diplomacy in 1810. Hawaiian astronomers noted that a bright star appeared in the heavens in the year of his birth; the star was probably the 1758 orbit of Halley's Comet. He died in Kona in 1819, 40 years after Captain Cook arrived, and is buried in a cave near the seashore at an unknown site called the Morning Star. The site remains undiscovered to this day.

Captain Nathaniel Portlock

In 1786, Captain Nathaniel Portlock, who had sailed with Cook, commanded his own expedition aboard the *King George*, to seek the profits the fur trade promised en route to China. The Hawaiian Islands were ideally located as the place to rest and re–provision, although after the death of Cook, Hawaii gained a reputation as the "cannibal islands." In 1789, Portlock wrote *A Voyage Around the World in 1785-1788.*

Captain George Vancouver

Vancouver sailed with Cook as midshipman on his second and third voyages in the Pacific. He arrived in the islands in 1792 in command of his own expedition aboard the *Discovery* to complete the charting of Hawaii begun by Cook. Vancouver was the first to sail around the north shore of Kauai, completing the first mapping of the major Hawaiian islands. A lifelong bachelor, he returned to England in 1794, where he died before editing the journals of his last voyage.

William Brown

Brown was a British sea captain who sailed in the fur trade between the Northwest of America and Canton. He dropped anchor in Hawaii in the winter of 1792; he was the first white man to take a ship inside the reef where he discovered "a small but commodious basin with regular soundings from 7 to 3 fathoms, clear and good bottom, where a few vessels may ride with the greatest safety." He christened the harbor Fair Haven, although it was already known as Honolulu to the natives. He was killed on New Year's Day, 1795, by Hawaiians who stole his ships.

Urey Lisiansky

Lisiansky was a Russian sea captain who commanded the Russian expeditionary vessel *Neva* and in June of 1804, anchored his ship for a few days at Kealakekua Bay on the Big Island. He observed sugar cane growing in scattered patches, envisioned the Hawaiians would profit from their agriculture and sailed on. The tiny 432-acre uninhabited island of Lisanski, which he discovered in 1805, in the northwest Hawaiian chain, bears his name today. It is home for the Hawaiian monk seal.

Don Francisco de Paula Marin

Don Francisco sailed from Spanish California with the fur trader Captain John Kendrick in the mid 1790s to prospect sandalwood and stayed to become the first horticulturist in the islands. He began producing small quantities of sugar in Honolulu in 1819. A self-made individual, he imported doves from Mexico and dozens of new plants, including the mango. He experimented with rice half a century before it became a significant Hawaiian crop, founded Honolulu's first winery and produced vintage wine in 1815. His vineyard is now buried under tons of asphalt known as Vineyard Boulevard.

John Palmer Parker

Parker went to sea on a New England merchant ship, jumped ship in Hawaii in 1809, made friends with King Kamehameha I, managed the royal fish ponds at Honaunau, was the first white man allowed to shoot the king's cattle, and introduced irrigation. He won the hand of Chiefess Keliikipikaneokaolohaka, granddaughter of Kamehameha I and Kaneikapolei. They were married in 1816 on the Big Island. He served as the king's *konohiki* (agent) in the cattle trade, was granted a deed to two acres at the base of Mauna Kea for $10 from King Kamehameha III, and on January 14, 1847, founded the Parker Ranch.

New England Whalers

Out of New Bedford, Connecticut, the first whalers arrived in Hawaiian waters on September 29, 1819, aboard the *Balena* (Spanish for whale) and the *Equator*, an equally splendid name for a whaling ship. That year, 596 other whaling ships arrived, 429 anchored off Lahaina, the rest off Honolulu. Mosquitoes were introduced to Hawaii by a whaling vessel during a visit to Lahaina, Maui, in 1826. They are on every island today.

Reverend Hiram Bingham

After a perilous seven-month voyage around the Cape of Good Horn, the Reverend Hiram Bingham arrived at Kailua on the Big Island of Hawaii from Boston, Massachusetts, aboard the brig *Thaddeus*, on April 4, 1820, to convert the naked heathens to Christianity, and introduce the alphabet, the printing press and the white man's way of life.

James Robinson and Robert Lawrence

Robinson and Lawrence arrived in 1822, on a schooner rebuilt from wreckage after their ship went aground on Pearl and Hermes Reef, 1,050 nautical miles leeward of Honolulu. It took four months to rebuild the schooner and ten weeks to make Oahu with only a battered quadrant and three gallons of water.

They built the first wharves in Honolulu, started a shipyard at Pakaka Point and made a fortune as Robinson & Company. "The harbor made the town and the town made the islands," historian Gavan Daws wrote in *The Hawaiians*. At the height of whale season a man could walk across 150 ships to the harbor.

Francis & James Sinclair

The Sinclairs arrived in Honolulu on September 17, 1863, from New Zealand, aboard the 300-ton barque *Bessie,* in search of land to settle. Offered large tracts in Waikiki and Ford Island in Pearl Harbor, they decided to sail for California when King Kamehameha IV offered them the island of Niihau for $10,000 gold. Keith and Bruce Robinson, direct descendants of the Sinclairs, operate a cattle ranch on Niihau today.

George N. Wilcox

Wilcox was the first *haole* to scale Mount Waialeale. He chose the dangerous Wailua side of the mountain.

Valdemar Knudsen

Knudsen, an adventurous Norwegian, came to Kauai after striking it rich as a merchant during the California gold rush. He served as delegate to the constitutional convention which led to California statehood, then returned to Norway for a visit. In 1852, on the way back to California, he contracted malaria as he crossed the Isthmus of Panama, and was left for dead in a small village. He regained health, however, and boarded a ship for Mexico, but left before it sailed when he found a ship sailing for Hilo. The ship ended at Koloa on Kauai, where Knudsen managed Grove Farm and built the road to Kokee.

William Brigham

Brigham came to Hawaii in 1865 with Horace Mann, the botanist son of Horace Mann the educator; Mann returned to Harvard in 1865, published some of his findings, and died of tuberculosis at 24. Brigham published Mann's findings, and later became first director of the Bishop Museum (1889-1919). He rescued the last Hawaiian grass shack from Kalalau Valley on Kauai, which now reposes in Hawaiian Hall at the museum.

Father Damien de Veuster

A Belgian priest, Father Damien came to Molokai to aid leprosy victims. He died on April 15, 1889, of leprosy. He was buried under the tree where he spent the first night in Kalaupapa. In 1936, his body was returned to Tremeloo, Belgium, where he was born.

A life-size statue of Father Damien by sculptor Marisol Escobar stands on the mauka side of the state Capitol building.

King David Kalakaua

Called the Merrie Monarch, King David Kalakaua envisioned himself as a Polynesian emperor. He traveled to Europe and the United States, revived the hula and dreamed of expanding his Pacific empire.

Born in 1836, he died at the Sheraton Palace Hotel in San Francisco on the 20th of January 1891, after a 17-year reign. His body was returned to Hawaii aboard the black crepe-draped *U.S.S. Charleston.*

Jack London

"See Hawaii and live!" author Jack London exclaimed after he sailed his 43-foot ketch, *Snark,* into Pearl Harbor on May 21, 1907. He spent five months in the islands, became known as "Keaka Lakana," and wrote 1,000 words a day that added up to two volumes of short stories about Hawaii.

His most popular short story, "To Build a Fire," about a man in Alaska freezing to death, was written in Hawaii, and his finest novel, *Martin Eden*, was penned on his two year South Seas sailing adventure. The voyage was chronicled by his wife, Charmian, in *The Log of the 'Snark.'*

London died on November 22, 1916, in the Valley of the Moon in California while writing a Hawaii novel, *Eyes of Asia*, finished by his wife and published in 1924.

Commander John Rodgers

Commander Rodgers was the first pilot to almost fly to Hawaii. John Rodgers was the son of a rear admiral and great-grandson of Commodore Matthew Perry. He graduated from the Naval Academy in 1903, and learned to fly in 1911 from Orville and Wilbur Wright.

On Monday, August 31, 1925, Captain Rodgers, 44, lifted off from San Francisco in a Boeing PN9-1 seaplane named the *Flying Dreadnought* with 40 ham sandwiches and a crew of four that included Lt. Byron J. Connell, 31, co-pilot; Kiles R. Pope, 30, chief aviation pilot; William H. Bowlin, 26, mechanic; and Otis Stanz, 26, chief radioman.

The seaplane's twin Packard V-8 engines ran out of gas 25 hours and 23 minutes after take off and Rodgers ditched at sea about 300 miles off Maui. When no rescuers arrived, they rigged a sail and made 50 miles a day "like a mutant square rigger"—as historian MacKinnon Simpson wrote—until they spotted Oahu's jagged Koolau peaks. Wind and sea sent them sailing on to Kauai where they arrived on September 10, after a nine day sea leg. Total voyage: 1,870 miles by air and 450 by sea. Rodger's feat is memorialized in a bronze plaque at Honolulu International's terminal which is named for him.

Lt. Lester J. Maitland and Albert F. Hegenberger

At 7:08 a.m., June 28, 1927, Maitland and Hegenberger lifted off from Bay Farm Island beyond Alameda, California, in a Fokker-built, three-engined Fokker C2-3 Wright 220 Army transport plane and landed the next day at 6:30 a.m. at Wheeler Field, Oahu, on the first successful 2,425 mile flight across the Pacific. The *New York Herald Tribune* called it "a triumph of navigation" by "valiant trailblazers."

Their plane was the first to land in the islands after a non-stop flight from the West Coast. Total flight time: 25 hours and 49 minutes.

Both men received the Distinguished Flying Cross and played major roles in World War II. Hegenberger became a major general, served in China and became Commander of the 10th Air Force in China after the war. Maitland, in command of Clark Field in the Philippines where the Japanese attacked on December 8, 1941, escaped to Australia. He became an Episcopal minister and returned to Hawaii.

Ernie Smith and Emory Bronte

The first civilians to fly to Hawaii, Smith and Bronte took off in a Travelair monoplane named *City of Oakland* at 10:40 a.m., July 14, 1927, from Oakland airport (then known as Bay Farm Island) and set a course for Maui, flying 120 miles an hour at 6,000 feet aiming for a record flight.

"We ran out of gas and sighted Hawaii about the same time," Smith recalled. "And had time to figure out a safe landing. As we went down we could see a patch of thick brush beyond two trees at just the right distance apart to take off the wings and land the rest of the plane safely."

The Travelair crash–landed on Norman Maguire's Molokai ranch. Pilot Smith and navigator Bronte emerged shaken but unhurt. The pair had flown 25 hours and 2 minutes across the Pacific to land in aviation history.

Captain Edwin C. Musick

On April 16, 1935, Captain Musick and a four-man crew, Capt. R.O.D. Sullivan, Frederick Noonan, William Jarboe and Victor Wright took off from from Alameda, California aboard the *China Clipper*, a Martin M-130, on the first airmail flight across the Pacific to the Philippines by way of Hawaii.

The silver plane, which carried two tons of mail and 12 crates of turkeys for the first Thanksgiving on Midway and Wake, touched down in Manila Harbor at 3:31 p.m. (Manila time). Total flight time: 59 hours and 48 minutes. The Pacific had been spanned by aviators. On October 21, 1936, Pan American initiated regular six-day weekly passenger service between San Francisco and Manila via Honolulu.

Capt. Musick was lost at sea on January 11, 1939, after taking off from Pago Pago, American Samoa, while attempting the first air link between the U.S. and New Zealand.

Kenneth Pike Emory

A pioneer anthropologist, Emory sailed with Jack London, worked with Margaret Mead, encouraged Jacques Cousteau, spoke three Polynesian dialects, found "lost" temples, and began the first archaeological survey of the Hawaiian islands on August 20, 1920, inside Haleakala Crater on Maui. He was born November 23, 1897, in Fitchburg, Massachusetts and arrived in Hawaii in 1900, when he was three years old with his adventurous father, Walter, an architect. Kenneth studied biology at Dartmouth, returned to Hawaii as a $75-a-month Bishop Museum ethnologist, then returned to Harvard for his master's degree in anthropology and a doctorate at Yale.

Amelia Earhart

Earhart was the first woman to fly solo from Hawaii to the U.S. Mainland. Her flight in 1935 took 12 hours and 50 minutes from Honolulu to Oakland. Three years later on a round-the-world flight with navigator Fred Noonan, Earhart went down in the Pacific on July 2, 1937, aboard a twin-engine Lockheed 10-E Electra after taking off from New Guinea on a flight to Howland Island. Her disappearance remains a mystery to this day. A bronze plaque on Diamond Head Road memorializes her solo flight from Hawaii.

Captain Mitsuo Fuchida

At 7:30 a.m., Dec. 7, 1941, Captain Mitsuo Fuchida uttered "Tora! Tora! Tora!" ("Tiger! Tiger! Tiger!"), the code words that told the Japanese Navy they had caught the Pacific fleet unaware. The daring raid brought the United States into World War II. In 1945, on VJ Day, he watched as Emperor Hirohito surrendered aboard the *U.S. Missouri* in Tokyo Bay.

Admiral Isoroku Yamamoto

Commander in chief of Japan's Combined Fleet, Yamamoto was the "father" of the daring air raid, which resulted in the sinking of the *U.S.S. Arizona* with 1,100 sailors. President Franklin Delano Roosevelt called it a "day of infamy," declared war against Japan, and the U.S. entered World War II. The white, concave Arizona Memorial, designed by Vienna-born architect Alfred Preis, was built after Elvis Presley staged a benefit concert on March 25, 1961, which raised $62,000 for the building fund. The memorial attracts more than 2 million visitors a year.

Airman First Class Shigenori Nishikaichi

Shigenori Nishikaichi, 21, of Hashihama, Imabari, was a Japanese Zero fighter pilot, one of nine launched in the second wave from the aircraft carrier *Hiryu* on Dec. 7, 1941. His squadron attacked the U.S. Naval Station at Kaneohe Bay, killing 17, wounding 67 and destroying 32 Navy PBY Catalina sea planes and the main hangar; and then attacked Bellows Field, wounding four men on the ground and destroying three P-40 fighters, an observation plane and a gasoline truck. On his way back to the Kahuku Point rendezvous, he shot down a U.S. Navy P36 fighter, took six bullets to his own plane; one that pierced the gas tank. He crash-landed on Niihau, was knocked unconscious and taken prisoner. He died at the hands of **Ben Kanahele**, 49, who although shot three times by the Japanese, picked up Nishikaichi, dashed him against a stone wall, then slit his throat. The incident, retold in a December 1942 Reader's Digest article, "Never Shoot an Hawaiian More than Twice," inspired composer Alexander Anderson to write the popular World War II song, "They Couldn't Take Niihau Nohow." Kanahele received the Purple Heart, Medal of Merit and citations signed by President Franklin D. Roosevelt. A cenotaph honors the slain Japanese pilot in his hometown of Hashihama, Imaburi, Ehime Prefecture, Japan.

Yosihiko Sinoto

Explorer and archaeologist Yosihiko Sinoto is the last in a line of distinguished Pacific scientists who served the Bernice Pauahi Bishop Museum in Honolulu. As a boy in Japan, Sinoto uncovered Jomon pottery now in Kyoto museums and decided to become an archaeologist. He arrived in Hawaii in 1954, assisted Dr. Kenneth Emory on the first dig at South Point, Big Island of Hawaii, where Sinoto made the first comprehensive study of more than 6,000 prehistoric Oceania fishhooks. In the 1960s, he restored ancient Polynesian temples on Bora Bora, Raiatea, Moorea and Huahine. In 1972, Sinoto discovered the "Pompeii of Polynesia" when he unearthed an entire prehistoric Tahitian village on the island of Huahine. He is now attempting to restore Easter Island's statues.

Commander Buzz Aldrin

The first man on the moon, Commander Aldrin splashed down aboard the Apollo 11 space ship, *Columbia 3*, off the coast of Hawaii, was taken aboard the *U.S.S. Hornet*, and brought ashore to Pearl Harbor. A bronze plaque at Hickam Air Force Base marks the spot where the moon men first touched Earth.

Bill Lee

Sailor, boat designer, and skipper of the fastest single-hulled sailboat across the Pacific, Bill Lee is a three-time winner of the biennial TransPac race from Long Beach to Honolulu.

His elapsed time of eight days, 11 hours, one minute and 45 seconds is the record, set in 1977 aboard the 67-foot sloop *Merlin* of Santa Cruz, California. The distance is 2,216 nautical miles from Point Fermin in San Pedro Harbor to the R-2 bell buoy off Oahu's Diamond Head. Bill Lee's sloop, *Merlin*, has won the race three times.

The oldest race across the Pacific, instituted by King Kalakaua, it was first held June 11, 1906, with three yachts competing—the 86-foot schooner *Lurline* of Los Angeles; a 48-foot schooner, *La Paloma* of San Francisco; and the 112-foot yawl, *Anemone* from the New York Yacht Club. The first race was won by Harry Sinclair, commodore of the South Coast Yacht Club (now the Los Angeles Yacht Club) aboard the *Lurline* with an elapsed time of 12 days, 10 hours.

Nainoa Thompson

Thompson was the navigator for *Hoku'lea*, (Star of Gladness), a 62-foot double-hulled voyaging canoe, which he guided under sail from Honolulu to Tahiti in 1976 to recreate the Polynesian voyages of discovery. Departing from Honolulu on May 1 and reaching Tahiti on June 4, he followed stars and waves to chart a course across the Pacific like his Polynesian ancestors.

Duke Kahanamoku

One of Hawaii's all-time surfing greats, Duke Kahanamoku won a Gold Medal in the 100-meter free style swim at the Olympic Games in Stockholm, Sweden in 1912. The father of modern surfing, he won thousands of converts in his travels to Australia, California and the Atlantic Coast. A statue of Duke stands in Waikiki. Each year, the world's top surfers compete in the Duke Kahanamoku Invitational Surfing Championship on Oahu's North Shore.

Fred Hemmings

World champion surfer, paddler, waterman, father of professional surfing in Hawaii, author of *Surfing: Hawaii's Gift to the World of Sports*, Fred Hemmings now serves as Hawaii state senator. Born in Hawaii, he began surfing as a boy, won the title of World Champion in 1968 at the World Championship in Puerto Rico, and traveled the world as goodwill ambassador with Duke Kahanamoku, the founder of International Professional Surfers.

Sylvia Earle

Aquanaut and marine biologist Dr. Sylvia Earle of Oakland, California, took a giant step for humankind underwater in Hawaii in 1979. One of the world's foremost divers, she made the deepest untethered dive in history—1,250 feet—off Oahu's Makapu'u Point. A single underwater camera, operated by Al Giddings, recorded the record-breaking dive as she descended to the ocean floor strapped to the front of a submarine to visit a part of Hawaii most will never see.

"When I got to the bottom, I stepped off and walked on the

ocean floor for two and a half hours ... about how long Buzz Aldrin and Neil Armstrong were on the moon."

She planted an American flag, then began exploring. "I had the fun of seeing all kinds of critters out there, like the seven large rays that came gliding by, and the big crabs stalking on the sea floor, or the spiral coral that flashed with blue fire, with luminescence, when I touched them. The place was so obviously alive with creatures."

Earle, 55, who has spent more than 5,000 hours under the sea, once logged a two-week stint in 1970. "It was like being able to sit and listen to a whole symphony instead of just catching snatches of a piece of music," she said.

She grew up in Clearwater, Florida ("which doesn't live up to its name anymore"), began diving in Florida river beds at 17, earned a degree in marine botany at Florida State University and was an early devotee of SCUBA, invented in 1943. She was one of the first three pilots to take a one-person sub to 3,000 feet. She serves as chief scientist at the National Oceanic and Atmospheric Administrations (NOAA). The sea urchin, *Diadema sylvie*, and the underwater plant, *Pilina erli*, are named for her.

Ellison Onizuka

An United States Air Force test pilot and astronaut, Ellison Onizuka was the son of a Big Island coffee grower. Onizuka was killed in the Challenger space shuttle explosion of 1986. He is buried at the National Cemetery of the Pacific beside World War II correspondent Ernie Pyle.

Oscar Chalupsky

South Africa's Oscar Chalupsky is the undisputed world champion of Hawaii's ocean kayak race across the treacherous Kaiwi channel between Molokai and Oahu. He has won the 32-mile race seven times in a row, from 1983 to 1989. He holds the record for fastest time of three hours, 27 minutes and 31 seconds. His record is being challenged by six-time victor Grant Kenny of Queensland, Australia.

Jim Wills

Hawaii's top hang glider pilot, in 1986 Wills set a world aerialist record for time aloft by riding thermals above Makapu'u for 34 hours—the time it took Charles Lindbergh to fly across the Atlantic Ocean 59 years earlier. Wills also flew all the islands of Hawaii in a motorized hang glider.

Buzzy Kerbox

Kerbox is a windsurfer, daredevil, swimsuit model and the first person from Hawaii to cross the English Channel on paddleboard with Laird Hamilton. He is now planning to windsurf the treacherous 70-mile Kauai Channel between Oahu and Kauai. King Kamehameha the Great tried twice to cross the channel in sailing canoes and failed both times.

Marty and Maggie McClendon

At 3 p.m. on May 28, 1989, Marty and Maggie McClendon entered in the state of matrimony in 70 feet of water off Kailua-Kona with two pufferfish as attendants. A giant Kahala fish nibbled her ti leaf bouquet and a 7-and-a-half foot barracuda came by to check out the action. The underwater wedding, witnessed by 46 people aboard a submarine, is listed in *The Guinness Book of Records*. After the ceremony, the newlyweds rode off on an underwater scooter.

BEST BOOKS
AN ADVENTURER'S BIBLIOGRAPHY

❋

If you want to read more about Hawaii before you go, these books are essential:

Shoal of Time: A History of the Hawaiian Islands, by Gavan Daws. Best island history.

Islands in a Far Sea: Nature and Man in Hawaii, by John L. Culliney. The delicate balance of paradise.

Hawaii: A Natural History, by Sherwin Carlquist. Hawaii's flora and fauna examined.

Volcanoes in the Sea: The Geology of Hawaii, by Gordon A. MacDonald, Agatin Abbott, Frank L. Peterson. Birth of the island chain.

Hawaii, by James Michener. All-time best-seller.

The Hawaiians, by Robert Goodman with Gavan Daws and Ed Sheehan. Island people by ex-National Geographic shooter.

The Journals of Captain James Cook, by Captain James Cook. First English guidebook to islands.

Mark Twain's Letters from Hawaii, by Mark Twain. Wry look at Hawaii of 1866.

Ronck's Hawaii Almanac, by Ronn Ronck. Hawaii's sole almanac, needs update.

Atlas of Hawaii, 1973, by the University of Hawaii.
  Indispensable but out-of-date.

Hawaiian Music And Musicians, edited by George S. Kanehele.
  Illustrated history of Hawaii's music.

Fax To Da Max: Everything You Didn't Know You Wanted to Know About Hawaii, by Jerry Hopkins with Doug "Peppo" Simonson, Pat Sasaki and Ken Sakata.
  Best-selling "pidgin" fact book.

Of all the Hawaii guidebooks, only six are by writers who live in the islands, know them inside and out and can write with some depth of knowledge. Other guidebooks, by "parachute" authors who visit once a year for two weeks, offer the usual information on known tourist attractions. The following books deliver authentic information for adventurous travelers who want more than a travelogue:

The Best of Hawaii, by Jocelyn Fujii. Local girl's
  favorite haunts.

The Penguin Guide to Hawaii 1990, edited by Alan Tucker.
  Six Hawaii writers offer real "inside" stuff.
  "Best Guide Book" 1990—Hawaii Visitors Bureau

The Maverick Guide to Hawaii, by Bob Bone.
  Ex-New Yorker in Aloha-land.

Essential Guides to Hawaii. Pretty pictures, nice graphics.

Our Hawaii, by John & Bobbye McDermott. Two kama'aina
  residents share island secrets.

Euell Gibbons Beachcomber's Handbook, by Euell Gibbons.
  First "how-to-live-free" in Hawaii guide.

Hawaii For Free, by Frances Carter. Best "free" guide.

Bicycling In Hawaii—Trips on All the Islands,
  by Robert Immler.

Hawaii's Best Hiking Trails, by Robert Smith.

Hawaiian Petroglyphs, by J. Halley Cox with Edward Stasack.

Paddling My Own Canoe, by Audrey Sutherland.

Incredible Hawaii, by Ray Lanterman and Terence Barrow.

My Time in Hawaii, by Victoria Nelson.

Stories of Hawaii, by Jack London.

Kauai the Separate Kingdom, by Edward Joesting.

Field Guide to The Birds of Hawaii and The Tropical Pacific, by H. Douglas Pratt, Phillip L. Bruner and Delwyn G. Berrett.

The Beaches of Oahu, by John R. K. Clark.

Chanting the Universe, by John Charlot.

Whale Song: The Story of Hawaii and the Whales, by MacKinnon Simpson and Robert Goodman.

The Whales of Hawaii, by Kenneth Bacomb III.

Whale Watching Guide to Hawaii's Marine Mammals, by Dane McSweeney.

Six Months in The Sandwich Islands, by Isabella L. Bird.

At Dawn We Slept: The Untold Story of Pearl Harbor, by Gordon W. Prange and Donald M. Goldstein.

Hawaii Under the Rising Sun, by John J. Stephan.

The Best Hawaiiana Book Store

Tusitala, the name Samoans gave Robert Louis Stevenson when he sailed the South Pacific in the late 1800s, also is the name of Hawaii's best bookshop, at least for rare, fine, used books about the Pacific.

The two-story bookshop in Kailua has more than one mile of bookshelves with entire walls devoted to such great Pacific titles as *Headhunting in the Solomon Islands,* by Caroline Mytinger, *Tales of Fishing Virgin Seas,* by Zane Gray; and other collectibles, including first editions, autographed copies and out-of-print books.

Tusitala Book Store
116 Hekili Street
Kailua, Oahu, Hawaii 96734
(808) 262-6343

BEST NUMBERS
A DIRECTORY OF IMPORTANT NUMBERS

———— ✺ ————

Emergency (Police, Ambulance, Fire)	911
Directory Assistance (Local)	1-411
Inter–Island Assistance	1-555-1212
Time of Day	983-3211
Hawaii Visitors Bureau	(808) 923-1811
Honolulu Department of Parks and Recreation	(808) 523-4525
Department of Land, Natural Resources and Conservation	(808) 548-6957
TheBus (Oahu)	(808) 848-5555
Whale Hotline (Maui)	(808) 879-4253
Volcano Hotline (Hawaii) (24 hour recorded updates)	(808) 967-7977
Weather at Haleakala Crater	(808) 572-7749
Plant Protection & Quarantine	(808) 541-2951

Weather Forecasts:
  Honolulu 833-2849
  Oahu 836-0121
  Hawaiian Waters 836-3921
  Pilot Weather-FAA 734-6677

National Weather Service (recorded messages):
  Marine 836-0121
  Surf 836-3921

Pacific Tsunami Warning Center 689-8207

Coast Guard Rescue:
  Oahu 536-4336
  Maui 244-5246
  Kauai 245-4521
  Hawaii 935-6370

Lifeguard Service 922-3888

Hyparbaric Center Oahu 523-9155
  (bends treatment)

Always dial 1 before calling neighbor islands.

INDEX

A

A Pacific Cafe 181
A'a..120
Aaron's Dive Shop 208
Abbott, Agatin....................................120
Achoy, Bobby...39
Adams, Ansel......................................160
Adams, Mike 47
Adventures on Horseback 237
airplanes 20
Akaka Falls 249
Aki, Charley...94
Akiona, Sid..107
Ala Moana Beach Park........................67
Ala Moana Shopping Center........34, 67
Ala Wai Canal 45
Alakai Swamp.............................161,172
Aldrin, Commander Buzz 289, 291
Alexander & Baldwin
Sugar Museum....................................98
Allerton, Robert 168
Aloha Cottages 101
Aloha Flea Market.........................67, 70
Aloha Parasail.......................................65
Aloha Showroom 71
Aloha Stadium 67
aloha shirts 69
Ambassador Hotel
Coconut Grove..................................131
American Association for
Advancement of Science...................102
American Canoe Association 41

American Hawaii
Cruises 124, 250, 256
An Inconvenient Woman...................228
Anderson, Alexander 288
Anderson, R. Alex 194
Anini Beach 241
Apua Point............................118, 121-22
Araki, Hotel 144
architecture....................................54-56
Ariyoshi, Rita 269
Armstrong, Captain Tom..................127
Armstrong, Neil 291
Atlantis Submarines 130-31
Awaawapuhi Trail.....................162, 231

B

Bailey's Antique Clothing Shop 70
Banyan Tree Terrace..........................192
Barefoot One..65
Beach Bus 32
Beach, Donn.......................................180
Becket, Ellerbe 56-57
Bed & Breakfast Honolulu 83
bed & breakfast.....................80-84, 124
Bennett, Captain Donald D..............123
Benson, Mike 47
Bergerson, Vic 178-79
Bernice Pauahi Bishop Museum........61
bicycling............................96-98, 140
Big Beach 239
Big Island 239, 249, 257

301

Big Wind Kite Factory..................195-96
bike rentals 97
Bill Collector..127
Bingham, Reverend Hiram 281
Bird, Isabella..141
*Birds of Hawaii and the
Tropical Pacific, The* 92,172
birdwatching......................170-173, 191
Bishop Museum 54, 546, 172
Black Bart..127
Blakey, Scott..241
Blue Hawaii 177, 268
Blue Hawaii Wedding........................177
boating (zodiac) 162-63
boats (fishing) 127
boats (glass bottom) 65
Bob Twogood Kayaks Hawaii 254
Bode, Lorey 42
Bone, Robert W. 269
book list 295-97
booze cruise....................................66, 251
Brazzi, Rosanno 267
Brigham, William T. 56, 282
Bronte, Emory.....................................285
Brown, William 279
Bryan, Di Salvatore 37
Budlong, Gary.....................................254

C

Cadiz, Ala 109
Cafe Asia by Keo 75
camping 91-93, 95, 191
Cannery Square...................................271
canoeing (outrigger)..............................43
canoeing 45
Canoes (store) 38
Cappuccinos..83
Captain Zodiac Expeditions..............163
Captain's Room, The...........................72
Carter, Paxton 60
Casanova Italian Restaurant & Deli...99
Casey, Captain Bill Casey 128
catamarans 107
Catchem!..127
Cebu Pool Hall......................................58

Chain of Craters Road.................120-22
Chalupsky, Oscar 42, 293
Charley's Trail Rides & Pack Trips 94
Chiang Mai Northern Thai Cuisine...74
children............................……33, 34, 52
China Sea Tattoo Parlor 57
Chinatown ....57-58 , 261
Chun, Ellery 69
Clark, David 234
Cliff, Montgomery 70
Club Hubba Hubba 58
Club Rock-Za.......................................72
Coasters..64
Coco Palms, The 176, 268
Coffee Cultural Festival 126
Coffee Works, The..............................31
coffee shops...................................30, 31
Cogswell, Bill.....................................131
Colony's Kaluakoi Hotel
& Golf Club..41
Cook, Captain James 126, 165, 277,
....278, 279
Courts of the Missing 59
Cousteau, Jacques..............................286
Crater Rim Road...............................121
Croissanterie 30
Cruiser Bob's Original Haleakala
Downhill...97-98
cruises...250-52
cruising (car) 243-247

D

Dalke, Michael 68
Dall, Captain Bob................................65
dawn patrol.....................................29-30
Daws, Gavin 281
de Veuster, Father Damien...............283
Decker, Robert & Barbara 120
DePamphillis, Danny........................180
Desert Isle..226
Devastation Trail 245
Diamond Head...............33-34, 44, 226
Diamond Head Wahine Classic.........44
Dickey, C.W. 55, 258
Discovery..251

diving 207-208
Division of Aquatic Resources 49
Dollar Rent-a-Car 97
Dome, The 270
Don Ho Show 270
Duerr, Fred 257
Duke Kahanamoku Beach 45
Duke's Canoe Club 256
Dunne, Dominick 228
Dupont Trail 36
Dye, Perry O. 49

E

Earhart, Amelia 172, 287
East-West Center 56
Ecco, Umberto 261
Edward, Webley 63
emergency numbers 301-302
Emory, Kenneth Pike 286, 289
England, Hugh 109
Escobar, Marisol 283

F

Falls of Clyde 64
Fantasy Island 177, 249
Fern Grotto 269
Finlayson, Captain Charley 127
fishing (catfish) 48-49
fishing (marlin) 129-130, 227
fishing (rainbow trout) 164
flea markets 67
Ford, Harrison 268
Forestry & Wildlife Division 166
Fort Street Mall 261
four-wheeling 207
Francisco de Paula Marin, Don 280
Freshwater Game Fishing & Entry
Fishing Card 49
Friends of Little Beach 239
From Here to Eternity 58, 70
Fuchida, Captain Mitsou 287
Fujii, Jocelyn K. 269
Fun Bike Rentals 97

G

Galileo 103
garage sales 68
Garden Cafe 153
Garden Island Ranch 169-70
Garden of the Gods 204, 207
Gaynor, Mitzi 267
Gibbons, Euell 206
Giddings, Al 291
Gilbeys gin 119
Go Bananas 254
Go Go Bikes 97
Goat Island 32
golf 49-50
Gordon, Brent 102
Government House 111
Grander's Wall 128
Grass Shack, The 56
grass shacks 54
Graves, Morrie 182
Gray, Francine du Plessix 67
Green Garden Restaurant 234
Green Wall 47
Greff, Clancy 162
Grimm, Tom 234
Groak, John 261
*Guinness Book of World
Records, The* 132, 254
Guslander, Grace Buscher 176

H

Haena 163
Haiku 108
Halau Mohala Ilima 266
Halawa Bay 254
Halawa Stream 194
Halawa Valley Falls 193-94
Hale Pa'i 111
Haleakala 90-91, 95-98, 226
Haleakala National Park 91, 93
Haleiwa 38
Halekulani 82
Halemaumau 124
Halemaumau crater 118

Index 303

Halemauu Trail...................................94
Hamakua coast.............................141-42
Hamakua Sugar Company 145
Hana...........................98-100, 110, 237
Hana Bay Vacation Rentals................101
Hana Coast 226, 237
Hana Road..98
Hanakapiai 238
Hanalei 177, 267
Hanalei Bay 184
Hanapepe 234
Hanauma Bay................................32, 40
hang gliding................................47, 227
hang gliding simulator........................47
Harrison, Tommy..............................131
Hasegawa's General Store.................100
Hau Tree Lanai 76, 84
Hawaii................113-154, 226, 229, 264
"Hawaii Calls".....................................63
Hawaii Five-O....................................37
Hawaii Heritage Center................58, 59
Hawaii Kai............................42, 73, 81
Hawaii Nature Guides 161
Hawaii Prince Hotel..........56, 57, 72, 80
Hawaii Prince Waikiki, The 83
Hawaii State Capitol 56
Hawaii State Parks 121
Hawaii Tropical Botanical
Gardens............................141-42, 245
Hawaii Visitors Bureau 274
Hawaii Volcanoes
National Park 118, 121
Hawaiian Dream Bed & Breakfast 82
Hawaiian International Ocean
Challenge..43
Hawaiian Ocean Fest 42, 46
Hawaiian Roughwater 46
Hawaiian Shirt, The............................70
"Hawaiian Wedding Song, The".......271
Hawi 245
Hayworth, Rita.................................268
Hegenberger, Albert F. 285
helicopter rides 123, 225, 233-35
Hemmeter, Christopher 256
Hemmings, Fred 39, 292

Highway 11..144
Hiilawe Falls 143
hiking 30-33, 36, 91-94, 101, 132-34,
141-43, 147-48, 160-63, 190-92, 193-94,
....227
Hildebrant, Kevin 237
Hill of Sacrifice..................................59
Hilo 149, 245, 264
Hilton Hawaiian Village.......54, 56, 270
Hodson, Glenn.................................246
Hogan, Carol & Bob 252
Holoholokai Beach Park...................148
Holua...92
Holua cabin 92
Hongwanji Mission 111
Honokaa 144
Honokohau Harbor..........................130
Honolulu.35, 36, 48, 54-56, 67, 75, 177,
79-84, 226, 261, 266, 271, 273
Honolulu Book Shops 62
Honolulu Books................................121
Honolulu Harbor..............................252
Honomuni House.............................196
Honomuni Valley 196
Hook..267
Hookena Beach Park 147
Hookipa Beach 108-110, 242
horseback riding 91-92, 94,137-39, 144,
....
169-70, 226, 236-37
Hosmer Grove Campground 95
Hosmer Grove Campground and
Nature Trail 91-92
Hotel Bora Bora 55
Hotel Hana Maui 101
Hotel King Kamehameha .131, 140, 150
Hotel Lanai, The 209
House of Blue Ginger 83
House of the Sun, The
..............................90-91, 93-94, 226
Huevos Restaurant.............................75
Huggo's 149
Hula..264-266
Huleia 167-68
Huleia National Wildlife Refuge 167-68

Huleia River 268
Hulopoe Bay 207-08, 230
Humuhumunukunukapua'a 131-32
Hunting Adventures of Maui..........109
hunting....108-109, 165-66, 191-92, 206
Hyatt Regency Kauai..56, 175, 181, 215, ... 217, 258-59, 262
Hyatt Regency Maui 102-103, 262-63
Hyatt Regency Poipu 218
Hyatt Regency Waikoloa 134-35, 136-37, 151
Hyatt Wailea......................................263
Hyatt's Voice of Paradise..................262

I
Ihu Nui 128, 150
Immler, Robert 96
Inter-Island Helicopters 234
International Billfish Tournament ..128
Interpretive Display.........................123
Island Adventure..............................168
Island Biker, The 97
Islands of the Pacific, The 160

J
Jacko, John 257
Java Java...67
Jeyte, Albert 125
Jimmy's Grill 181
Jones, James......................................58
Jossellin, Jean-Marie 181

K
Kaala Peak 26
Kaanapali...266
Kaanapali Beach Resort 89
Kaanapali Coast 102
Kahala..68
Kahala Hilton 84
Kahanamoku, Duke 292
Kahoolawe 219-22

Kahuku 75
Kahului Bay 108, 110
Kahuna Falls....................................249
Kai Nani 107
Kailua & Cream 31
Kailua.....33, 48, 78, 81, 82, 83, 208, 298
Kailua Bay.......................................253
Kailua Pier.......................................129
Kailua-Kona.........149-50, 153, 244, 252
Kaiwa Ridge................................33, 34
Kaiwi Channel...................................41
Kalakaua Avenue........................246-47
Kalalau Lookout...............................245
Kalalau Trail....................................227
Kalalau Valley.................................234
Kalalua Point.....................................37
Kalalua Valley...................................54
Kalapaki Beach................................256
Kalapana...233
Kalaupapa 192-93
Kalihili..81
Kaloko-Honokohau 239-40
Kaluanua stream........................50, 248
Kamakou Preserve.............170, 190-92
Kamoamoa.......................................119
Kanahele, Ben..................................288
Kanak I'Kaika 41
Kanak'ole Stadium...........................265
Kaneohe...............................47, 82, 83
Kaneohe Bay.....................................65
Kapaa 175-76, 181, 273
Kapalaoa cabin 92
Kapiolani Boulevard 261
Kauai ...155-84, 225, 227, 231, 233, 236, ... 238, 241, 245-49, 253, 256, 258, 262, ... 267-69
Kauai by Design 183, 217
Kauai by Kayak 254
Kauai Vacation Rentals....................184
Kauai Westin Lagoons 256-57
Kauapea Beach...........................238-39
Kaunakakai................................192,196-97
Kaupo Gap 94
Kaupo Store......................................94

Index 305

kayaking............41-44, 164, 167-68, 226,
.... 253-54
Ke'e Beach 105
Keahole Airport 233, 257
Kealakekua Bay............................131-32
Keamanu Bay 216, 217
Keanae 101
Keanahaki Bay..............................216
Keau Sr., Ben..................................98
Keau, Keith....................................100
Kendrick, John 280
Kenny Rogers Photo Opportunity...271
Kenny, Grant.................................293
Keo..74
Keo's Thai Cuisine..........................74
Keomuku......................................207
Kerbox, Buzzy 293
Kewalo Basin..................................79
Kilauea 118-21
Kilauea crater 124
Kilauea Lighthouse..................172-73
Kilauea Lodge & Restaurant.............125
Kilauea Lodge..............................245
Kilauea Point 171-73
Kilauea Visitor Center 120
Kilauea Volcano............................233
King David Kalakaua...........264-65, 283
King Kamehameha 122, 278, 293
King Kamehameha Hula and Chant
Competition..................................266
King Kamehameha I 137
King Kamehameha II.....................137
King Kong 267
King, Charles Edward 271
Kiowani Terrace Restaurant..............263
kitsch......................................269-72
KITV, Channel Four......................264
Kohala Coast 145, 147-48, 150-53
Koke'e 160-62, 164
Koke'e Lodge 161-62, 245
Koke'e Museum 161, 164
Koke'e Park 165
Koke'e Park Headquarters............165
Koke'e Public Fishing Area 165
Koke'e State Park 171, 245

Koke'e Trails, The 161
Koke'e wilderness forest 170
Koko Head 30
Koko Head Crater...........................31
Koko Isle...42
Koko Marina Shopping Center....42, 81
Kolekole stream 249
Koloa 181
Kona 126,130
Kona Coast 127, 227, 239
Kona Marlin Center 129-30
Kona Village..................................150
Kona Village Resort.................153-54
Kona Village, The 257-58
Kramer, Gil...................................128
Kualoa Ranch & Activity Club...........47
Kuhio Beach 30, 38, 39
Kula Lodge 98

L
L'Auberge Swiss 78
Laguna Niguel Billfish Club 150
Lahaina....................103, 110-11
Lahaina Prison 111
Lahaina Restoration
Foundation 110-11
Lahaina-Kaanapali &
Pacific Railroad......................110-11
Laiwi......................................168-69
Laka's Hula Platform 106
LaMariana Restaurant & Bar........77, 78
Lanai..............................199-210, 230
Lanai City 204, 206, 209
Lanai City Service & Rentals 207
Lanaihale 203, 205
Langan, Chris 136
Lanikai Beach 32, 33, 226, 241
Lanikai Bed & Breakfast 82
Law, Jack..72
Lawrence, Robert.........................281
lawyers...303
Layton, Joe....................................71
Leahi..66
Lee, Bill...290
Lehua..217

Leighty, William 102
leis 10, 11, 218
Levinson, Frank 237
Li'l Hooker 127
Lihue 184
Lihue Airport 256
Liljestrand, Bob 254
limousines 17
Linda's Vintage Isle 70
Lindbergh's grave 100
Lindbergh, Charles 99, 293
Lions Coffee Roasters 31
Lisiansky, Urey 279
Little Beach 239
Lodge at Koele, The 206, 209
London, Jack 283, 286
Los Arcos 76
Lunai 122
Lutkenshouse, Dan 141

M

Ma'alea Bay 108
MacDonald, Gordon 120
Magana, Hank & Mary 76
Magnum P.I. 125
Mahoney, Eddie 134
Maitland, Lester J. 285
Makaha Sons 271
Makai Market Food Court 67
Makapu'u Beach 43, 46
Makapu'u Ridge 47, 227
Makawao 92, 98-99
Makaweli 235
Makena Beach 105-06
Malaekahana Bay 32
Malaekahana Beach 32
mai tai 15, 177-180
Mamala Bay 226
Manele Bay Hotel 210
Mann, Horace 282
maps 14, 24, 25, 86-87, 114-115, 156-
.......................57, 186-87, 200-01, 212-13
Marchant, David 42
Marriage License Agency 273

Marshall, Kim 135
Marston, Christian 174, 177, 180
Marston, Louise 174
Maunakea Marketplace 58
Mauanalei Gulch 205
Maugham, W. Somerset 61
Maui 85-112, 226, 237, 242,
....262-63, 266
Maui Air Force 109, 242
Maui District Forester 191
Maui Prince Hotel 107, 239
Maui Windsurfing Company, The ..109
Mauna Kea 132-36, 237
Mauna Kea Beach Hotel 152
Mauna Kea Stables 138-39
Mauna Lani 245
Mauna Lani Bay Hotel 233
Mauna Lani Bay Hotel
and Bungalows 152
Mauna Loa 118, 195
Maunawili Valley 50
May, Morton "Buster" 149
McClendon, Marty & Maggie 293
McDermott, John & Bobbye 269
McGregor, Davianna 221
Mead, Margaret 286
memorials 59-61
Men's Fitness 43
Mera, Ernesto 83
Merrie Monarch Festival 264
Merrie Monarch Festival
Headquarters 265
Mid-Nite Inn 196
Miller, Bart 127
Milnes, Les 169, 236
Mishler, Captain Tom 106, 229, 235
Miss Kona Coffee Queen 126
Mission Houses Museum, The 55
Mitchell, Paul 56
Mo'okini Heiau 145
Mo'okini Luakini 145-46
Moana Hotel 56, 62-63, 82
Moanalua Gardens 266
Moaula Falls 194
Mokulua 35, 226

Molokai 41, 185-198, 253
Molokai Express....................................40
Molokai Ranch Ltd. 191
Molokai Ranch Wildlife
Safari Park 195
Molokai Solo 254
Molokini 106-07
Montalban, Ricardo...........................177
Moon, Bob 208
Morgan, John 47
Mount Kaala 35-36
Mt. Waialeale 173, 234, 245
Mueller, Freddie...................................78
mule riding 192-93
Munro Trail...............................205, 207
Munro, George C...............................205
Musick, Captain Edwin C. 286
"My Time in Hawaii" 122

N

Na Mele o Hawaii Festival................266
Na Pali coast 162-63
Naapala Trail Rides............................144
National Historical Park...................239
National Park Service 60, 92, 230
National Tropical Botanical
Garden 168-69
Natural History Museum, The 245
Nature Conservancy of
Hawaii, The 191
Nawiliwili Harbor..............................168
Nelson, Victoria..................................122
Nene goose 92, 93
New England Whalers 281
New Otani Kaimana Beach 84
newspapers...62
Newton, Sir Isaac..................................53
Nicholas...46
nightclubs 71-72
Niihau shell leis 218
Niihau 211-218, 225, 228, 235, 271
Niihau Helicopters............216, 229, 235
Nishikaichi, Shigenori 288
North Shore..37
Nualolo Cliff Trail.....................162, 231

Nualolo Kai 163
nude beaches.................................238-40
Nuuanu Freshwater Fish Refuge 48
Nuuanu Reservoir................................48
Nuuanu Valley 54

O

O'Connell, Brian 101-103
Oahu 23-84, 226-227, 241,
....246-48, 266, 298
Oahu Market..58
Ola'a Rainforest 170, 229
Onizuka Center for International
Astronomy...134
Onizuka, Ellison..................59, 134, 292
Only Show in Town, The............175-76
Onomea Valley...................................141
Ossipoff, Vladimir3 56-57
Outfitters Kauai 164, 254
Outrigger Canoe Club..................56-57

P

Pacheco, Maria.....................................75
Pacific Blue..128
Pacific Broiler.......................................80
Pacific Hawaiian Bed & Breakfast......83
Pacific Whale Foundation 104
paddle boarding 44, 45
Paddling My Own Canoe............253-54
Padovani, Philippe.............................152
Pahoehoe...120
Pahulehua, Momi 217
Paia 110
Pali Highway..51
Pali Lookout...54
Paliku..92
Paliku cabin..92
Palm Chapel.......................................268
paniolos...138-39
Papillon 123, 233
Paradise Cove Luau 270
Paradise Found.....................................69
Paradise Pedaling Inc...........................97
parasailing.......................................64-65

Parker Ranch 138-39, 236-37
Parker Ranch Round-up 139
Parker Ranch Shopping Center 136
Parker, John Palmer 280
Pau Hana Inn 192, 197
Pau Hina Hina Lookout 246
Pau, Halau'o na Mauoli 265
Pearl Harbor 59-61
Pei, I.M. 56
Pele 13, 119, 265
Perry, Commodore Matthew 284
Peterson, Frank 120
Petroglyph Bar 153
Picasso, Pablo 232
pidgin 12, 13
Pipeline 37
Poipu 175
Poipu Beach 181, 182, 215, 254, 259
Polynesians 277
Portlack, Captain Nathaniel 278
Preis, Alfred 56, 60, 288
Preserve Manager 191-92
Presley, Elvis 177, 268, 288
Press, Harry 65
Prince Court 80
Prince Lot Festival 266
"Prince of Hawaii" 271
Protect Kaho'olawe Aloha 'Aina 221
Pu'uhonua O Honaunau 147
Puako Petroglyph Archaeological
District 148
Puako Petroglyph Park 148
Puako Trail 147-48
Public Information Office 166
Punchbowl, National Cemetery of the
Pacific 59-60
Puu Olai Cinder Cone 105
Puu Ulaula Observatory 93
Puu Ulaula Overlook 95
Puuwai 215-16
Pyle, Ernie 59

Q

Quarnstrom, Lee 70
Queen Emma 168

Queen Emma Garden Apartments 56

R

Raiders of the Lost Ark 267-68
Railton, Jeremy 269
rainbows 53-54
Ramsay Chinatown Gallery 58
Ranger, Melissa 91
Rella Mae 251
rental cars 18
Restaurant Row 75
restaurants .. 58, 64, 79-81, 180-182, 196
Rice, Freddy 128
Ritz-Carlton 55, 245
Ritz-Carlton Mauna Lani 152
Road Guide to Hawaii National Park 120
Robinson, Bruce 282
Robinson, James 281
Robinson, Keith 282
Rodgers, Commander John 284
Roosevelt, Franklin Delano 288, 289
Roussel's 149, 245
Roy's 73
Royal Hawaiian 83
Royal Hawaiian Country Club 49
Royal Hawaiian Hotel 38, 55
Royal Kona Coffee Mill
& Museum 126
Royal Waikoloan 153

S

S.S. *Constitution* 123-24, 250, 256
S.S. *Independence* 124, 250, 256
Sacred Falls 248-49
Sacred Falls State Park 249
Saddle Road 134
Sadie Thompson 177, 268
sailing 226
Scott, Elaine 139
Secret Beach 238-39
Shark's Cove 216, 228
Sharkbait Productions 121
sharks 130-31, 228
Sheehan, Ed 125

Sheraton Moana Surfrider Hotel .30, 39
Shipwreck Bar 257
Shipwreck Beach 204, 207
Shop Pacifica 62
shuttle service 18
Simpson, MacKinnin 284
Sinclair, Francis 282
Sinclair, James 282
Sinoto, Yosihiko 289
Ski Guides Hawaii 137
Skidmore, Owing & Merrill 56
skiing (snow) 136-37
Skin Deep Tattooing 99
Sliding Sands Trailhead 93
Smith, Ernie 285
Smith, Pi'ilani 265
Smoot, Carey M. 56
snorkeling 40-41,106-107,
....131-132, 217, 225
South King Street 261
South Pacific 267
Space City 136
Spartan Reef 110
Spectre of Haleakala 96
Spielberg, Steven 267
stargazing 101-103
"Starwatch" 134
starwatching 134-35
State Department of Fish
and Game 206
State Department of Land and Natural
Resources 166
State Division of Aquatic Resources 165
State Division of Forestry 36
State Health Department 273
State Historical & Underwater Park &
Marine Life Conservation District ...132
Stevenson's Library 175
Stevenson, Robert Louis 175
Strehl, Gary 80, 83
Summit Tours 136
sunrises 226
Sunset Beach Ride 170, 236
sunsets 94-95, 169-70
surfing 29, 37-39

surfing tips 39
Sutherland, Audrey 253-54
swimming 32, 100, 140

T
Tahiti Nui 174, 177-80, 218
Tak Wah Tong Chinese Herb Shop ...57
Tamashiro Market 81
taxis 17
Ted Fio Rito 131
"The Cock-eyed Mayor
of Kaunakakai" 194
TheBus 19
Thompson, Nainoa 290
Thomson, George 273
Thurston Lava Tube 122-23
Tidepools (restaurant) 181, 183, 259
tidepools 33
Tobin, Peter 144
Tong & Goo 56, 261
Tower Records 62
Trader Vic's Original Mai Tai 178
trains 110-11
Traphagen, Oliver 56, 62
Tropical Fishing Foray 170
Tropical Vision Video 121
Tunnels Beach 163
Tusitala Book Store 298
Twain, Mark 38
Twin Falls 101
Tyler III, Curtis 140

U
U.S. Immigration Center 55
U.S. Seamen's Hospital 111
U.S.S. Arizona 60
U.S.S. Arizona Memorial 56, 60-61
Uncle George's Lounge 124
Uncommon Valor 267
United States Navy 60
Universal Studios 268
University of Hawaii's Institute for
Astronomy 134-35
Utraman 139-40

V

Valley of the Lost Tribe 227
Valley of the Temples 273
Vancouver, Captain George 137, 279
Victorian Hotel 63
Victorian Moana Hotel 56
Visitor Center 123
Visitor Information Center 134
Visitors Center Theater 60
Vog 120
Volcano (village) 125
Volcano Art Center 245
Volcano Bed & Breakfast 124
Volcano House 124
Volcano Lodge 245
Volcano Watching 120
Volcanoes in the Sea 120
Volcanoes National Park 229
Volcanoes Park Headquarters 122-23
volcanoes 118-25
VolcanoScapes I 121
VolcanoScapes II 121

W

W.H. Keck Telescope 136
Waialua Sugar Company 36
Waianea Range 35
Waikamoi Ridge 101
Waikiki .. 29, 32, 37, 38-39, 246, 251, 270
Waikiki Beach 29, 273
Waikiki Joy 83
Waikiki Trolley 20
Waikiki's Aloha Showroom 269
Waikoko Bay 267
Waikolu Lookout 191
Waikolu Lookout Campground 191
Wailua Bay 176
Waimea 183, 236-37
Waimea Bay 169
Waimea Canyon 160, 165
Waimea Canyon Road 245-46
Waimea Plantation Cottages ... 170, 183, ... 236
Waimea River 269

Waine'e Church 111
Waioli Mission House Museum 174
Waipi'o 142-44
Waipi'o Valley Shuttle 144
Waipi'o Valley Treehouse 144
Waipi'o Valley Wagon 144
Waipi'o Wayside Inn 144
Waldenbooks 62
Walsh, Christiane 124
Wao Kele O Puna 170, 229-30
Ward Warehouse, The 31, 62
Warnecke, John Carl 56
waterfalls 248-49
Waterfront Row 128
Weddings in Hawaii 274
weddings 273-74
Westin Kauai Hotel 256
Whale I 104
Whale II 104
whale watching 31, 104-106
Wilcox, Abner & Lucy 174
Wilcox, George N. 282
Willows, The 77
Wills, Jim 293
Wimberly, George "Pete" 55
Winchester, Simon 173
Windjammer Cruises 251
Windsurfing Tours Maui 109
windsurfing 108-09, 241-42
Windward Bed & Breakfast 82
Witch's Brew 40
Wo Fat's 58
Wo Hing Temple 111
Wright Brothers 284

Y

Yamamoto, Admiral Isoroku 288
Yamasaki, Minoru 56

About Rick Carroll

Rick Carroll is one of the most gifted and adventurous journalists in Hawaii and the Pacific today. As United Press International's special features correspondent in Hawaii and the Pacific, his reports from such datelines as Nuku'Alofa, Huahine and Easter Island appear in newspapers around the world.

He's hiked Easter Island to photograph the mysterious statues, explored French Polynesia by tramp freighter and set foot on all main Hawaiian islands, including Lanai, Niihau and Kahoolawe. He's met and interviewed the King of Tonga, the Sultan of Sulu, the former Premier of China, the Governor of Hawaii and deposed Philippines First Lady Imelda Marcos.

Son of a World War II pilot, Carroll grew up in Japan and returned to California to study journalism and advertising at San Jose State University in the 1960s.

An award-winning San Francisco Chronicle writer, he covered daily news for 20 years in California before heading back to Asia and the Pacific on a real life adventure. In 1984, he sailed the pirate-infested Sulu Sea from Zamboanga to Tawi Tawi with medical missionaries in the final days of the Marcos era, and tracked down New Peoples Army guerillas on Negros Island during the historic 1986 ceasefire in the Philippines.

He won a National Headliners Award from The Press Club of Atlantic City, New Jersey, and a Certificate of Excellence from the Hawaii Publishers Association for his first-person accounts of adventures in the Philippines.

A resident of the tropics since boyhood, he first sailed across the Pacific when he was 14, and worked for newspapers and magazines in Hawaii and Japan.

Author of three guidebooks, he is chief contributor to The Penguin Guide to Hawaii, named "Best Guide Book" by the Hawaii Visitors Bureau in 1990.

A Lowell Thomas Award-winner of the Society of American Travel Writers of Washington D.C., he is the recipient of the 1991 Gold Award of the Pacific Asia Travel Association.

He is a member of The Nuku'Alofa Club in the Kingdom of Tonga, the oldest adventurers' club in the South Pacific; and the Adventurers Club of Honolulu.

His wife, Marcie, a former San Francisco Chronicle editor and Hawaii Visitors Bureau director, is a Honolulu travel marketing consultant.

They live in an old Hawaii-style beach house on Oahu's windward side that serves as a bed and breakfast for other Pacific adventurers.

Mahalo

This book would be impossible without the enormous assistance of many whom I am delighted now to thank in print.

For more than a decade, editors in New York, San Francisco, Los Angeles and Honolulu have sent me on great adventures in Asia, Hawaii and the Pacific and this book is the result of the genius and wisdom of:

Alan Tucker of Berlitz Travellers Guides (Hawaii and the South Pacific); Michael Middlesworth (Sulu Sea); George Fuller (Kingdom of Tonga); the late Buck Buchwach (Easter Island); Cheryl Chee Tsutsumi (Hawaii and the Pacific); Sue Yim, (Society Islands); and especially Robert A. Martin of Los Angeles who dispatched my Hawaii/Pacific stories around the world on the wires of United Press International.

Michelle Corbin and Christiane Walsh of American Hawaii Cruises, who were there at the beginning of the book one night at sea between Kahului and Nawiliwili on the *S.S. Constitution.*

I have also to thank my constant colleagues in adventure: Dr. Yosihiko Sinoto of Honolulu's Bishop Museum (Hawaii, Easter Island, Huahine, Marquesas); architect/surfer/friend Carey M. Smoot (Hawaii & Bali); artist/friend Michael Dalke (Indonesia); and Dr. Ernesto Espaldon, the "Schweitzer of the Pacific," who took me on real life-and-death adventures during the darkest hours of the Philippines.

And those whose whole life is an adventure: my parents, Virgil and Daralene, who instilled in me a keen sense of adventure and suffered all the stories; angler Jerry Klink of La Paz, who taught me well about marlin and men; my pilot/pal Ron

Van Kregten; my down-to-earth agent and friend, Donald Mastriano, the great reality check of Honolulu.

Many others have always been there for me, especially Christian Marsten and Nani Ah Sing of Hanalei; George (Capt. Nemo) Thompson; Clancy Greff, Phyllis Segawa, Patrick Ching; my friends on Niihau, Momi Pahulehua and Jen Kaohelaulii; helicopter pilots Tom Mishler and Richard Finke; my Hawaiian blalah Keoni Nakanelehua; *Discovery* sailors Carol and Bob Hogan; photographers Tom and Michelle Grimm of Laguna Beach; Sandy Nisley-Leader of Monterey; Michael Adams, the oldest, boldest, living hang-glider pilot I know; Gene Cotter and other friends at the Hawaii Visitors Bureau: Stanley Hong, Tom Sakata, Manu Boyd, Ray Milici, Lindy Boyes and George Applegate.

Many in Hawaii's tourism industry but particularly Noelani Whittington of the Kohala Coast Resort Association; Ruth Limitiaco of The Limitiaco Company; Summer Harrison, Lisa Buterakos and Joanna Robles of Hyatt Hawaii; Stephanie Ackerman of Aloha Airlines; Cynthia Ureno of Atlantis Submarines; and Laura Heidt at Kona Village.

Hawaii's public relations professionals: Ruth Ann Becker, Cheryl Gregorio, Margy Parker, Donna Jung, Patti Cook, Kaui Goring, Lei-Ann Stender, Connie Wright.

My good friends at the Sierra Club, Audubon Society, The Nature Conservancy, RainForest Action Network, Pele Defense Fund and the National Park Service, especially Daniel Taylor, who keeps the Ola'a Rain Forest safe and Dr. Noa Emmett Aluli, who fights the good fight to keep Hawaii Hawaiian.

I am especially grateful to my former colleague Alan Temko, the San Francisco Chronicle's Pulitzer Prize-winning architectural critic, who, one night in 1982 in Hanno's, opened the door to Hawaii for me; and George Chaplin who convinced me to stay on in the islands.

And my best friends: Jim Wilson and Berit Keeble of Carmel Valley, California, who urged me to write about "my" Hawaii, and Jerry and Debbie Kermode, who sailed with me on *M'Lady* through heavy seas out of Santa Cruz and now share the good life in the islands.

My greatest thanks goes to Marcie, critic/editor/wife and undaunted companion on life's greatest adventure.

Thank you one and all. *Aloha nui loa.*

Rick Carroll

RECREATION TITLES AVAILABLE FROM FOGHORN PRESS

■ The Complete Guide, Camping Series

California Camping by Tom Stienstra describing 1500 campgrounds. $16.95

Pacific Northwest Camping by Tom Stienstra describing 1400 campgrounds in Washington and Oregon. $16.95

Rocky Mountain Camping by Tom Stienstra describing 1200 campgrounds in Colorado, Wyoming and Montana. $14.95

PLUS *The Camper's Companion* by Hal Kahn & Rick Greenspan, a pack-along guide to better outdoor trips for hikers, campers, cyclists, canoeists. $12.95

■ Outdoor Adventure and Getaways Guides

Great Outdoor Getaways to the Bay Area and Beyond by Tom Stienstra describing secret and little known camping, hiking and fishing spots. $16.95

Great Outdoor Adventures of Hawaii by Rick Carroll describing more than 120 unusual outdoor adventures. $14.95

■ The Complete Guide, Golf Series

California Golf by Ray March describing over 700 golf courses. $16.95

Hawaii Golf by George Fuller describing every golf course in the golfer's paradise of Hawaii. $16.95

Golf Vacations of California by Eliane Pepper describes preplanned 7 and 10-day golf vacations, gives info on resorts. $16.95

ORDER INFORMATION

To order by phone, call toll free (800)842-7477 or (415)241-9550. We accept visa or mastercard. To order by mail, enclose your name, street address and phone number along with a check or money order or visa/mastercard number (include exp. date) for the total book amount plus $3.50 shipping.

Mail to: **Foghorn Press**
555 De Haro Street, The Boiler Room, #220
San Francisco, CA 94107

*Books are shipped via UPS within 48 hours of receipt of your order

Courtesy Discount: If you currently own an old edition of a Foghorn Press title, you may mail in the copyright page from that edition with an order for a new edition of the same book and take a $3 courtesy discount off the price. Call or write for more information. Only redeemable through Foghorn Press.

■ TRADE DISTRIBUTION

Book trade: Distributor: Publishers Group West, 4065 Hollis Street, Emeryville, CA 94608. (415)658-3453. Wholesalers: Ingram Book Co., Baker & Taylor, Gordons Books, Pacific Pipeline, Bookpeople, L-S Distributors and Inland Book Company.

Libraries: Quality Books, Unique Books or Foghorn direct.

Outdoor wholesalers: Sunbelt, Alpenbooks, Mountain 'N Air, Universal Telescopic, Maverick Distributors, Falcon Press and Menasha Ridge.

Canada: Raincoast Books. **UK and Europe:** World Leisure Marketing